# The Value of English in Global Mobility and Higher Education

**Critical Perspectives on Language, Mobility and International Education**

Series Editors:
Kumari Beck (Simon Fraser University, Canada)
Angel M. Y. Lin (Simon Fraser University, Canada)
Yang Song (Fudan University, China)
Michelle Mingyue Gu (The Education University of Hong Kong, Hong Kong)

This book series aims to provide a trans-disciplinary space for scholars to publish critical studies revolving on the intertwined relations between language, mobility and international education in different geopolitical, cultural and societal contexts. It welcomes submissions from both established scholars and dynamic, emergent scholars.

# The Value of English in Global Mobility and Higher Education

*An Investigation of Higher Education in Cyprus*

Manuela Vida-Mannl

BLOOMSBURY ACADEMIC
LONDON • NEW YORK • OXFORD • NEW DELHI • SYDNEY

BLOOMSBURY ACADEMIC
Bloomsbury Publishing Plc
50 Bedford Square, London, WC1B 3DP, UK
1385 Broadway, New York, NY 10018, USA
29 Earlsfort Terrace, Dublin 2, Ireland

BLOOMSBURY, BLOOMSBURY ACADEMIC, and the Diana logo are
trademarks of Bloomsbury Publishing Plc

First published in Great Britain 2022
Paperback edition published 2023

Copyright © Manuela Vida-Mannl, 2022

Manuela Vida-Mannl has asserted her right under the Copyright, Designs and
Patents Act, 1988, to be identified as Author of this work.

For legal purposes the Acknowledgments on p. vii constitute an
extension of this copyright page.

Series design by Charlotte James
Cover image © filo/iStock

All rights reserved. No part of this publication may be reproduced or transmitted in
any form or by any means, electronic or mechanical, including photocopying,
recording, or any information storage or retrieval system, without prior
permission in writing from the publishers.

Bloomsbury Publishing Plc does not have any control over, or responsibility for, any
third-party websites referred to or in this book. All internet addresses given in this
book were correct at the time of going to press. The author and publisher regret any
inconvenience caused if addresses have changed or sites have ceased to exist, but
can accept no responsibility for any such changes.

A catalogue record for this book is available from the British Library.

Library of Congress Cataloging-in-Publication Data

Names: Vida-Mannl, Manuela, author.
Title: The value of English in global mobility and higher education: an
investigation of higher education in Cyprus / Manuela Vida-Mannl.
Description: London; New York, NY: Bloomsbury Academic, 2022. |
Series: Critical perspectives on language, mobility and international education |
Includes bibliographical references and index.
Identifiers: LCCN 2021029033 (print) | LCCN 2021029034 (ebook) |
ISBN 9781350230958 (hardback) | ISBN 9781350230965 (pdf) |
ISBN 9781350230972 (ebook)
Subjects: LCSH: English language–Globalization. | English language–Study
and teaching (Higher)–Cyprus. | Language and education–Cyprus.
Classification: LCC PE1072.V53 2022 (print) |
LCC PE1072 (ebook) | DDC 428.0071/15693–dc23/eng/20211018
LC record available at https://lccn.loc.gov/2021029033
LC ebook record available at https://lccn.loc.gov/2021029034

ISBN: HB: 978-1-3502-3095-8
PB: 978-1-3502-3115-3
ePDF: 978-1-3502-3096-5
eBook: 978-1-3502-3097-2

Series: Critical Perspectives on Language, Mobility and International Education

Typeset by Newgen KnowledgeWorks Pvt. Ltd., Chennai, India

To find out more about our authors and books visit www.bloomsbury.com
and sign up for our newsletters.

# Contents

| | |
|---|---|
| List of Illustrations | vi |
| Acknowledgments | vii |
| List of Abbreviations | viii |
| Introduction | 1 |
| 1. The Value of English and Its Three Layers | 9 |
| 2. Assessing the Value of Language | 41 |
| 3. Cyprus: A Case Study | 67 |
| 4. The Value of English in Cyprus's Higher Education | 117 |
| 5. English in a Globalized World | 171 |
| Conclusion | 195 |
| Appendix 1: Study Design | 203 |
| Appendix 2: Relevant Questionnaire Data | 207 |
| References | 213 |
| Index | 235 |

# Illustrations

**Figures**

| | | |
|---|---|---:|
| 2.1 | The value of English (ENL speaker) | 62 |
| 2.2 | The value of English (EFL speaker) | 63 |
| 2.3 | The value of English (ESL speaker) | 63 |

**Tables**

| | | |
|---|---|---:|
| 3.1 | Languages in the RoC and Their Prestige | 82 |
| 3.2 | Languages in the TRNC and Their Prestige | 82 |
| 3.3 | Participants | 91 |
| 3.4 | Language Attitudes of All Participants | 108 |
| 3.5 | Language Attitudes UCLan Cyprus | 109 |
| 3.6 | Language Attitudes EMU | 110 |
| 3.7 | Language Attitudes UCy | 112 |

# Acknowledgments

This study is the result of a four-year journey that I was only able to undertake because of the guidance and support of my supervisor, Christiane M. Bongartz. She introduced me to the beautiful island of Cyprus and encouraged my research thereby, among other things, giving the initial idea for the project and offering constant guidance, ideas, and stimuli during our countless conversations. I am grateful for her support and advice as well as her encouragement to always "dig a little deeper."

At the heart of this project are my participants. Their willingness and openness in sharing their individual opinions, journeys, and experiences can only be described as exceptional and bountiful. Academically, I highly appreciate the insights offered during our conversations, while, personally, I am thankful for my participants' generosity and trust. In addition, I would like to express my appreciation to local teachers, scholars, and contact people for establishing my contact with students in university and private settings and/or supporting me during various application processes. They provided me with a deeper understanding of the Cypriot perspective of the embeddedness of this research.

Furthermore, I am grateful to David Block, Sviatlana Karpava, Rajend Mesthrie, Bettina Migge, Elizabeth R. Miller, John O'Regan, Phoevos Panagiotidis, Andreas Rohde, Edgar Schneider, Anne Storch, and Stavroula Tsiplakou for offering their expert opinions on my research project and various parts of my conceptual framework. Their feedback provided me with additional perspectives and considerations, and I am thankful to each of them for investing their time and expertise.

On a personal note, I would like to express my deepest gratitude to my family and friends. I am especially thankful to my parents, Andrea and Günter Vida, for their endless encouragement and support. Their permanent confidence in me and my choices is reassuring as well as inspirational. Finally, I could not have completed this study without my husband Bastian Mannl. His understanding and support give me the opportunity to pursue my goals while keeping me firmly rooted. Most importantly, however, he makes me take a break once in a while.

# Abbreviations

| | |
|---|---|
| Ct | Cyprus-tied |
| EFL | English as a Foreign Language |
| ELF | English as a Lingua Franca |
| ELT | English Language Teaching |
| EMI | English as the medium of instruction |
| EMU | Eastern Mediterranean University |
| ENL | English as a Native Language |
| ESL | English as a Second Language |
| GAU | Girne American University |
| HE | Higher education |
| L1 | First language |
| L2 | Second language |
| nCt | not Cyprus-tied |
| RoC | Republic of Cyprus |
| TRNC | Turkish Republic of Northern Cyprus |
| UCLan Cyprus | University of Central Lancashire Cyprus |
| UCy | University of Cyprus |

# Introduction

*Jamike smiles. "Cyprus—you know the place?"*
*"No," [Chinonso] said.*
*"I know that you won't. It is an island in Europe. A very small country. Very small, but very beautiful; very beautiful, mehn."*
*…*
*Jamike has painted a portrait of the place where he lives, Cyprus, as a place where everything was in order. Electricity was constant; food was cheap; hospitals were plentiful and free, if you were a student; and jobs, "like water." A student could own a Jeep or an E-class Mercedes-Benz.*

Obioma (2019a: 164–5)

*Cyprus is the solution. … "You can easily go to any other part of Europe, or US. By ship, very cheap. Within two hours! Turkey, Spain, many many countries."*

Ibid. (169–70)

Cyprus—the divided birthplace of Aphrodite with beautiful white beaches and bluer-than-blue water—is a magnet for tourists and, somewhat unexpectedly, for students. Higher education (HE) is of major importance in Cyprus, turning it into an "education island." Since Cyprus cannot rely on oil, gold, or other natural resources, its economy is heavily built on HE and incoming international students. While student mobility and an international orientation, both primarily enabled and reflected by the extensive use of English as a language of instruction and communication, are common features of current and global HE, there is more to the value and use of English in Cyprus. International students, who are often from the Global South, hope for Cyprus's HE to be their stepping-stone to the Global North and Europe. In answering these students' hopes, especially in the Turkish Republic of Northern Cyprus (TRNC)—the occupied northern third of the island, which is only recognized as a country by Turkey—universities are founded like mushrooms. The TRNC, however, is also where some of these hopeful students die; they fall off roofs or balconies, are stabbed or beaten to death, or they just disappear (cf. Agaba 2015; Aygin 2019; Obioma 2019a, 2019b).

Many of the international students in the TRNC—a term used to increase readability, not to make any kind of political statement—are from African countries like Nigeria, Zimbabwe, and Cameroon (see Aygin 2019; Elega and Özad 2017). While some of these students have access to firsthand experiences of friends or family members, others are recruited by for-profit agencies and middlemen that often provide misleading or wrong information about this part of the island. These agencies charge fees for "helping" interested students to get admitted to a university in the TRNC, although they are neither needed to apply at TRNC universities nor do they offer crucial information that students would not have access to otherwise; they represent a new market within HE, which is not concerned with the education itself but with the recruitment of students using the implementation of English as their key argument. This practice of recruiting students, however, does not focus on initiating mobility in local or highly privileged prospective students. It targets young people who are aiming at their future social advancement—the ones who are vulnerable for promises that are "too good to be true," like an extensive use of the English language on and off campus, low study and living costs, and access to well-paid student jobs and Europe. These students are made to believe they were going to a developed country with all the conveniences of the Global North but find themselves in a developing "country" that is politically and ethnically divided and also widely unrecognized. These students are told that English would be spoken widely, their expenses would be low, and well-paid jobs could easily be found. When international students in the TRNC realize their new reality—the fact that they cannot communicate in English and earn their tuition fees easily, while concentrating on their education, as they have been promised—they have often lost money to these middlemen and agencies. Moreover, they cannot bring themselves or cannot afford to return home. Some of these students turn to selling drugs or themselves to earn their living and tuition fees—and some of them do not survive their time in Cyprus. One could say that this, while undeniably tragic, only happens to some of the students in Cyprus's HE and that most are not affected by these deceptions. Furthermore, one might argue that these incidents are rooted in the criminal energy of the middlemen and agencies and are not Cyprus-specific but could happen anywhere. While these arguments contain some truth, there is more to it. Cyprus's HE landscape has developed rapidly into a lucrative business that, rather than counteracting these shady recruiting practices, facilitates the utilization of its students. In this book, the roles and value of the English language in the market of Cyprus's HE and its power to initiate mobility and reproduce social hierarchies are investigated to uncover the hidden dynamics that are at use.

HE has developed into a marketplace constantly reproducing the prevailing social hierarchies it is built on; it neither grants access nor the same chances to everybody. Furthermore, global HE is often rooted in the globally shared value of English and, specifically, in the increasing importance of the language's economic impact as part of its neoliberalization and the effects of the global use of English on the individual students' life trajectories. In Cyprus's HE, English fulfills multiple roles: It is used as the means of communication between a constantly changing group of students, faculty, and local inhabitants; as an advertising tool by universities and recruiting agencies that aim at increasing their income; and as an asset of students, which potentially leads to an improvement of their future perspectives and employability. In assessing the value of English, this book will show that for a comprehensive understanding of the underlying dynamics of these functions, a conceptualization has to go beyond the English language itself and include the social as well as the economic structures it is used in. Following the advance of neoliberalism, languages "constitute a saleable commodity with regard to business and marketing, whilst for the clients they represent an investment in cultural capital which can then be exchanged within the global labour market" (Rassool 2007: 148). The perspective of *value* is a suitable approach to uncovering and understanding this development of the English language from the cultural to the economic capital of users and institutions while considering the individual, social, and institutional motives and advantages of the use of the English language.

In an ideal world, all languages would have the same value. In the current neoliberal, globally connected, and interdependent world, this is what it is set out to be: an ideal, not reality. English is the highest-valued language worldwide, which is, at least part of, the explanation of people's willingness to invest in it. It can transfer its value and valorize its speakers and other commodities it is combined with, as is observable in Cyprus's HE landscape. The job market might serve as an example: A speaker of English is often more valued than a nonspeaker, but it seems to be not only English itself that is valued here but its value combined with the value of its speaker as an employee. The valorization of a person or object, for example, education, through English appears to be only realizable because of the homogeneity in the value ascribed to the language; because speaking English is globally perceived as something "good" or "desirable," people are willing to pay more—or invest more in general. To understand the valuation of English differentiating different types of value is necessary. Following Graeber, value has mostly been used in three different senses:

1. "value" in the sociological sense: conceptions of what is ultimately good, proper, or desirable in human life
2. "value" in the economic sense: the degree to which objects are desired, particularly, as measured by how much others are willing to give up to get them
3. "value" in the linguistic sense, which goes back to the structural linguistics of Ferdinand de Saussure (1966), and might be most simply glossed as "meaningful difference." (Graeber 2001: 1–2)

The power of English and its use as a global language is partly also based on the value it is awarded by us, may we be speakers of English or not. Because speaking English is rated as "good" and "desirable" in most contexts, referring to its sociological value, people invest in mastering it. This investment, which people are willing to offer, is closely related to the economic value of English. Higher-paid jobs are an example, as they are, in most societies, likely to be occupied by proficient speakers of English. In this case, the sociological value of English can easily be transferred into economic value. Finally, the linguistic value of English is naturally given by its ability to express "meaningful differences," that is, its indexicality. The linguistic value has been one of the major foci in twentieth-century sociolinguistic research (see, e.g., Brinck 1997; Hanks 1999; Norton 2000; Romaine 1999). The framework of value presented here does not follow suit fitting this focus but rather understands the value of English to be divided into an ideological, a communicative, and an economic layer. In the first application of this framework, the three layers of value are assessed within the context of Cyprus's HE.

The use of English in Cyprus combines the ramifications of the somewhat untraditional colonial history of the island and the development of the global political economy—it combines, for example, the use of English as a global language in a non-native context, in which parts of the user group maintaining close personal ties to the UK, with the use of English as a first language by users who identify as native users. Cyprus's HE, in turn, is characterized by the extensive use of English as the medium of instruction (EMI) and its users' limited identification with it. English users in this context do not necessarily share a desire to create a somewhat socially and linguistically stable speaker group or to make English "theirs"; students and universities alike commodify the language to capacity. Therefore, the economic layer of the value of English is increasingly important. While the value of the English language is always constructed by all of its layers, the context of its use, the involved users, and the purpose of its use influence the distribution of emphasis on each of its layers. The ideological value of English is rooted in its understanding as a system—constructed, for example, by being used in either the "right" or "wrong" way—and focuses on ideological properties, such as its ownership and cultural embeddedness in its contexts of use. Due to the increasing use of English by traditional non-native speakers, this layer overall appears to decrease in importance and be replaced by the importance of its communicative value. This communicative value is based on the language communicative potential when used as a social practice— aiming at successful communication, reflecting its speakers' identities and social positioning. This layer of the value of English is understood as most important for its global spread and its increasing importance. However, to understand the role of English in HE contexts, the language's ideological and communicative values are not sufficient; its economic potential and instrumental power have to be considered. Incorporating all three layers allows for an adequate understanding of the personal, economic, and social foundation of the value of English in Cyprus's HE and beyond.

English is globally used; it is the language with the highest communicative potential and the highest number of users (de Swaan 2001). Therefore, it is the most attractive language for learners to invest in and is often the only way to communicate in a multilingual environment like HE. Due to the increasing economic orientation of our global society, the English language's global spread and usefulness, however, have led to the increasing importance of the economic value component of the language. This economic value is assessed within, for example, the concept of the commodification of English (cf. Heller 2010; Heller and Duchêne 2016; Park and Wee 2012). Similar to the Marxist commodity, in this concept the value of English is use-based. However, unlike any other commodity, English cannot be consumed and its value does not change inversely proportionally to the number of its users (de Swaan 2001). Furthermore, in Cyprus's HE, an instrumentalization and detachment of the English language from its use is observable, which cannot be fully assessed by the concept of English as a commodity. As it might be detached from its use, the economic value of English is conceptualized as the value of English-as-a-marketable-attribute. This conceptualization is based on three main observations that are utilized in HE in Cyprus and beyond: (1) students do not necessarily have to be competent in English to profit from it; (2) English is objectified and instrumentalized by institutions, businesses, agencies, and students for the sole purpose of future or immediate financial and/or social gain; and (3) the English language is idealized and accepted as a prerequisite of students' future attainment and, therewith, enables illegal activity, crime, and social injustice in the center and periphery of the HE landscape.

The English language is part of Cyprus's colonial history but more importantly part of its current economy and its future development—it is used as a mother tongue, as a learner language, as a lingua franca, and as an attribute to be bought, sold, and benefited from. This book will show that the notion of value is essential for the development of a comprehensive and adequate description of the multiple roles of English. Including the individual students' experiences, biographies, and motives, and using Cyprus's HE as research site, the value of English is conceptualized as divided into three layers—the ideological value, the communicative value, and the economic value—and assessed on three levels—the personal level, the societal level, and the global level.

# Outline

In Chapter 2, the theoretical underpinnings of conceptualizing the value of English are presented. Starting with the ideological value of English (Section 2.2), traditional approaches to describing the use of the English language, such as its ownership and standardization (Section 2.2.1) as well as popular models that use this traditional epistemology (Section 2.2.2), are presented. After discussing why an existing model cannot provide an adequate and comprehensive description of the complex linguistic situation in Cyprus's HE, a poststructuralist perspective in conceptualizing the communicative value of English is taken (Section 2.3). To assess the communicative value of English, language must be understood as a social practice (Section 2.3.1), which, in turn, is the basis for current frameworks such as English as a Lingua Franca (ELF) (Section 2.3.2). The third layer of the value of English is its economic value that represents the aspect of language that has only been focused on quite recently (Section 2.4). Rooted in a zeitgeist of neoliberalism (Section 2.4.1), it allowed for language to be commodified (Section 2.4.3). This chapter ends with the assessment of English-as-a-marketable-attribute and the economic reality of English (Section 2.4.4).

Chapter 3 builds on the framework of value, as developed in Chapter 2, and assesses these layers on three different levels—the personal level, the societal level, and the global level. The value of English on a personal level is created mainly by a person's identification with the language (Section 3.2.1) and its usefulness for them (Section 3.2.2). On a societal level, the value of English is defined by global (Section 3.3.1.1) and local (Section 3.3.1.2) language hierarchies, which depend on the historical, political, or economic status, ambitions, and development of each society, respectively. In addition, language is hierarchized economically, which is approached using Bourdieu's symbolic economy (Section 3.3.1.3). English tends to be of high (economic) value on a societal level. Consequently, because speakers of a language might be categorized as belonging to a certain social group or class, people might be tempted to invest in learning English to initiate or facilitate their social mobility and advancement (Section 3.3.2). Mobility is also facilitated by the use of English on a global level. However, this mobility tends to be physical rather than social and is enabled by the increasing global interconnectedness—by internationalization and globalization (Section 3.4.1). Furthermore, on a global level, the power of English as an unequalizer becomes most obvious. Since language is connected to social structures and used for social advancement, its commodification creates a market of English, which promises that the implementation of English would cause social advancement. This marketization of English, however, results in a reproduction of inequality rather than in less privileged speakers to catch up with their more privileged peers (Section 3.4.2). An exemplary composition of the value of English for three individual speakers is presented at the end of this chapter.

In Chapter 4, the Mediterranean island of Cyprus is introduced—the island's historical, political, economic, and linguistic development as well as its HE landscape. The Mediterranean island of Cyprus is a politically, geographically, linguistically, and economically complex place. In Section 4.2, Cyprus's historical development and the status quo is introduced before the use of various languages in different contexts is assessed (Section 4.3). The use of English in Cyprus's HE is described—as this setting stands out from other educational contexts (Section 4.4)—and its status on the island investigated (Section 4.5), before turning to the methodological considerations of assessing the value of English in Cyprus's HE. This second part of the chapter introduces the research sites (Section 4.6.1), the participants (Section 4.6.2), the research suppositions (Section 4.6.3), and the design of the study (Section 4.6.4) conducted in Cyprus between 2017 and 2019.

In preparation for Chapter 5, a descriptive analysis of the quantifiable data of this study is presented in Section 4.7.

In Chapter 5, the qualitative part of assessing the value of English in Cyprus's HE is focused on. It begins with portraits of not Cyprus-tied (nCt) and Cyprus-tied (Ct) students to comprehensively present their background, situation, and motives for studying in Cyprus. This offers a more detailed assessment of the participants' heterogeneity and the complexity of the value of English, especially, in multicultural contexts of HE. This focus on individual students is followed by an assessment of value, its sources, effects, and ramifications guided by the four research suppositions developed in Section 4.6.3. This assessment clearly shows the three-layeredness of the value of English and enables a depiction of different foci when taking the Ct-students', the nCt-students', or the institutions' perspective. Chapter 6 combines the findings developed in Chapter 5 and the framework introduced in Chapters 2 and 3 (Section 6.3). Furthermore, it presents an initial generalization of the ramifications of the high value of English for the individual speaker (Section 6.4) and the potential it might have to become a source of equalization rather than a tool of marginalization (Section 6.5). Finally, this book concludes in Chapter 7 by suggesting an epistemic change within critical sociolinguistic research so as to create an awareness of the exploitation potential of the global triumph of the English language.

# 1

# The Value of English and Its Three Layers

## 1.1 Introduction

The English language might well be the most studied language around the globe. When assessing English, linguists can access an immense repertoire, that is, they can draw on numerous theories and models, pick and choose from a variety of terminology and subcategories, and compare multiple language characteristics among and across speaker groups. English appears to be the most significant language of our times and, consequently, has been in focus for decades. While all the existing approaches to the English language add valuable insight into the language's use and structure, one aspect has been less focused on—its speakers and their objectives for using English. This most essential aspect of English—and any language really—is often not at the center when philologizing the language. Assessing the value of English closes this gap by approaching the English language from its various and diverging speakers' perspectives and finding that its value is the common denominator in their choosing of "English." The value of English, however, is not uniform but a representation and derivate of the diversity of English speakers, their life trajectories, and life choices. Taking the speakers' perspective, the framework of the value of English accommodates this complexity, when assessing the extensive use of the English language around the globe within a continuum of multicultural and multilingual environments. To understand the power of global English, it is not only important to understand why but rather how and what kind of value is assigned to it in which contexts and systems. To do so, the framework introduced here differentiates between three layers of value—the ideological, the communicative, and the economic value—which are interconnected and vary in their positioning and domination depending on the speaker—or speaker group—and the reality of language use. The ideological value of English is the most traditional layer of value as well as the most limited and restricted one.

## 1.2 The Ideological Value of English

When examining the reasons why people use English, a common reference is the affiliation of language and nations or language and power—might this be the historical power of the British Empire, the current economic power of the United States, or a combination thereof (see, e.g., Crystal 2003; Phillipson 1992, 2009; Saraceni 2015). The academic urge to identify, standardize, and theorize the English language and its varieties has led to more fine-grained questions like the following: Who owns English? What is correct or incorrect English? Which variety/varieties of English is/are the most valuable and desirable one/s? To assess these questions, ideologies have emerged and have built the foundation of the traditional epistemology in English language research. Ideologies, for example, about native-speakerism and language ownership (e.g., Bonfiglio 2013; Crystal 2003) and the concept of standardization (e.g., Da Costa, Dyers, and Mheta 2014) influence the common perception of different speaker groups and their realizations of the English language.

The ideological value of English can be defined as the value that is awarded to the English language based on conscious and subconscious beliefs and ideologies. It is primarily based on long-standing concepts, like standardization and language ownership, and is, as such, incorporated in many popular models of English, that is, Kachru's (1985) Three Circles model or Schneider's (2007) Dynamic Model. While some aspects of the ideological value of English, like the high value of English as a Native Language (ENL), are still unscrutinized, other aspects, like the superiority of traditional Inner Circle speakers' English when compared to Outer Circle speakers' English (cf. Kachru 1985), have been challenged (cf. Hackert 2012 for a detailed elaboration, also Buschfeld 2020 on English in Singapore, Seidlhofer 2005 on English as a Lingua Franca (ELF)). However, adding value to or withdrawing it from a realization of English based on beliefs and ideologies is grounded in a hierarchization of speakers and the belief in monolingualism to be the norm (cf. Gramling 2016), both consequences of the historical development of the British Empire and its practice as a colonizer. The ideological value of English is not based on its actual use by its speakers but builds on the distinction of, for example, varieties of English and their allocation to certain loci and speaker groups.

## 1.2.1 The Value of Ownership and Language Ideologies

As incorporated in its name, the ideological value of English is primarily based on language ideologies. Language ideologies are "representations, whether explicit or implicit, that construe the intersection of language and human beings in a social world" (Woolard 1998: 3). They are often referred to as mediators between language and social constructions (see Piller 2015: 3; Woolard 1998: 3; Wortham 2001: 256). Those social constructions might be found within any size of social grouping—two interlocutors in a conversation, a small community of practice, a bigger people, or even, as is the case with English, among (almost) all global citizens. Because of the different permutations of those social groups in terms of the multiplicity of languages involved, ideologies can refer to beliefs, properties, meanings, and functions of one individual language as well as to a general understanding and interpretation of the concept and functions of all languages. Language ideologies are flexible as they coexist and compete in social structures. They always function bidirectionally as metapragmatic tools to make discourse socially meaningful by serving as a blueprint of both discourse interpretation and production (Wortham 2001: 256). The grating and power tussle of coexisting ideologies might even lead to language change (see, e.g., Woolard 1998: 11–12 on the intersection between language ideology and structure, Irvine and Gal 2000: 39–47 on Nguni languages), which is, at its root, a reflection of value.

Ideologies commonly reflect the value of language—whether referring to language in general or specific realizations or changes of any particular language. When focusing on ideologies concerned with the concept of language in general, the *one nation–one language ideology* (see Hymes 1968 for elaboration) might serve as an example. It is the belief that each language belongs to one people. This understanding serves as a fruitful substrate for the related, albeit wrong, assumption of monolingualism as the "norm" (see Gramling 2016 for an extensive discussion) and the belief of languages as ownable. Both are often the foundation of ideological value. The association of one people with one language has been inverted into an assumed monolingualism of these people, leading to a monolingual ideology. This ideology reflects the hegemony of one language, and therefore of its first language (L1) speakers, in a respective social context and is often reproduced unconsciously as part of "how it used to be." The superiority of the English language and its British L1 speakers in English-speaking contexts in the UK as well as overseas, that is, in former colonies of the British Empire, might serve as an example for the effects of this ideology. Consequently, the ideological value of the English language is high in these contexts. Although in postmodernism, monolingualism and the ideology of it as being the "norm" is scrutinized as incorrect and unfair, it is still in use and its influence can be detected, for example, in education, immigration, language policies, and in any kind of language data collection and evaluation (see, e.g., Gramling 2009; Leeman 2018; May 2001; Pavlenko 2002; Tollefson and Tsui 2014; Wiley 2014). Traditional L1 speakers, in turn, have an interest in defending the ideology of monolingualism and the common belief that English is "their" language. It is a reaction to its global spread and the accompanying changes to the language by its new users. Languages can be shaped by people's language ideologies, and "ideology is always the tool, property, or practice of dominant social groups" (Woolard 1998: 7).

The concept of language ownership is one of the tools associated with assigning value to certain social groups. Based on the ideology of monolingualism, the English language is increasingly objectified, which allows for the assumption that a language can be owned. Any potential ownership is only considered and becomes intellectually possible as a result of the backformation of English from a fluid practice of communication into its perception as an enclosed, objectified, and speaker-external entity (see Park and Wee 2012 on English as an entity). However, English, like any other language, cannot be owned in the same way a pen or any other commodity can be owned. Also, unlike any other commodity, its value is not based on rarity and lack of access. English is neither more valuable with increasing rarity nor can anyone be prevented from using it. Instead, the contrary causality seems to be at work (de Swaan 2001: 27). Still, the English language has to be simplified, generalized, and objectified to argue for any speaker group's ownership and, consequently, for all the other groups not to own it. The concept of language ownership has long been challenged in applied linguistics (see, e.g., Baker 2015; Cook 1999; Davies 2003; Pennycook 2012); among others, it has been criticized for its depiction of English as a monolingual speaker-external system rather than a social practice.

As mentioned before, the potential ownership of English is a systematic as well as a social undertaking since it concerns various speaker groups. The owners of English might differ depending on the perspective taken. From a historical perspective, the English might own the English language because it is "where the language originated" (Widdowson 1994: 377). From an economic perspective, the owners might be the Americans, as they are currently the economically most influential and powerful native speakers of English. From a majority-based perspective, English should be owned by its non-native speakers, as they outnumber the native speakers of English by far (e.g., Crystal 2003: 69; Seidlhofer 2011: 2). Whatever the rational reasons might suggest, the actual perception of who owns English is based on language ideologies (see, e.g., Philips 1998 for a detailed elaboration). It is a common belief that native speakers have the authority over "their" language and are, also, its legitimate owners. Since nativeness is conceptualized as a birthright (Bonfiglio 2013: 30) rather than an accomplishment, its use as the foundation of the ownership of English serves as a threshold against any claims by non-native speakers. It serves as an empowerment of the native speakers of English while, at the same time, leaving non-native speakers completely powerless to change the situation. The "ideology of the native speaker authority" (Bonfiglio 2013: 29) is, like any ideology, a reflection of social power and domination (Woolard 1998: 7) and a tool for the dominating groups to preserve the existing hierarchies. Native speakers of English claim ownership of English to protect the language from misuse only at first sight. At its root, native speakers appear to defend their position at the top of the English speaker hierarchy, to maintain the prestige and high value of their varieties and the resulting economic power of L1 English as a global commodity. However, not all native speakers are at the apex of this English speaker hierarchy. Their position is based on a monolingual assessment of their language use, functioning as the basis of any differentiation of language boundaries or speakers by pointing out deficiencies. The emergence and acceptance of the monolingual native speakers' ownership of English are reflections of the political and economic composition of our global society: rather than appreciating English as a hypercommon good (de Swaan 2001: 31), it tends to be claimed, sold, and, consequently, bought.

While the establishment of ownership might not be of immediate importance for other languages, the rise of English as a global language has multiplied its speakers and, hence, the stakeholders of English. L1 English is traditionally the most desirable and valuable use of English, while the value of other realizations, that is, L2 (second language) English or learner English, depends on the respective context of use, although this impacts the value of English less than the value of other languages or their varieties (see Piller 2016 on local and global language hierarchies). Assigning value to "Englishes" based on ideological beliefs, however, is more complex. Since English is a global language with a constantly increasing number of speakers, it appears to accumulate an extensive body of different realizations. Some of these are recognized as "native," "standard," or "non-standard" varieties; others are looked upon as incorrect or illegitimate alterations of English. Nativeness, for example, used to be the primary factor determining the value of a variety of English, followed by the proficiency of its use. In other words, in, for example, Western non-native contexts, the English of a native speaker is of higher ideological value than the English of a proficient non-native speaker than the English of a nonproficient non-native speaker. However, native varieties of English are not equally prestigious, valued, and desired. Rather than its actual realizations, it is the idea—the concept—of native English that is of high (ideological) value since it is associated with globalization, dominates language hierarchies, and is excessively precious to non-native speakers of English. This concept is commonly referred to as Standard English, making standardization another factor that influences the value of a variety. In the same Western non-native context, the native use of a nonstandard variety might be less valued than a non-native use of a standard variety. A standard variety is often associated with a social group of high status and used in formal contexts (Da Costa, Dyers, and Mheta 2014: 335). While Quirk (1990) leaves his readers under the impression that "*nativeness* and *standard* are conflated to such an extent that they become mutually dependent, indistinguishable, even identical," they are intrinsically independent (Seidlhofer 2011: 53). We used to assume a standardized variety to be native, although, *per definitionem*, this is not a prerequisite. The value of a standard variety, nonetheless, correlates with the value of nativeness as they are ideological in nature. In other words, the positioning of the standard at the apex of the variety hierarchy is justified through the ideological understanding that it is superior to any other variety of a particular language (Piller 2015: 4). This increased value of the standard varieties is not dependent on its reality and use; its value is not based on whether or not the standard is (still) used by native speakers or, in case it is, on the size of the speaker group. This theoretical "standard," consequently, is rather robust in its status and value.

The value of standard native varieties—of English or any other language—is based on (the belief of) their ideological supremacy that locates them at the very top of any value-based ranking. They are the only varieties whose value is almost independent of their contexts of use, and other varieties generally rank below them. The remaining hierarchy of value is context-dependent; however, some tendencies appear to be universally shared: standardized varieties are valued higher than nonstandardized varieties, varieties of the Global North are valued higher than those of the Global South, and native varieties are not always more valuable than non-native ones. Standardization in general allows for the testing and evaluation of language use based on a clear description. A clear description, or "norm," is always based on the existence of a "non-norm," which is often referred to as "the other." This differentiation is based on comparing and evaluating inequalities and, therefore, distinguishing a superior group "us" from an inferior group "them." Rather than functioning as uniting blueprints of language use, standard varieties implicate the possibility of excluding and devaluing speakers—of *othering* (Holliday 2006: 385; Vichiensing 2018). Furthermore, Standard English, similar to ENL, is an artificial construct forced into existence by the desire to describe and objectify a fluid and social practice of communication. Consequently, the hierarchy and any power that comes with it are also artificial and human-made. However, ideologically induced power relations between English speakers as well as the hierarchies of the value of the varieties of English are implicitly or explicitly depicted in the theorizations and models of English.

## 1.2.2 The Traditional Epistemology of Value in Models of English

The evolution of new models is, simplistically speaking, grounded in learning about phenomena that cannot be explained by already existing models. Therefore, the growing insight we have gained in the variability of English, the increasing acceptance of this variation, as well as the changing view of language perceived as an enclosed system toward its social functions might be reconstructed by a diachrony of models of the English language. A first major development has been the acknowledgment of the plurality of English (e.g., Görlach 1990; Kachru 1985, 1990, 1992; McArthur 1987, 1998, 2003; Strang 1970). Furthermore, the potential acceptability of non-native English use as valuable (e.g., Quirk 1985; Widdowson 1994) and the variability of English in postcolonial contexts have been addressed (e.g., Bauer 2002; Kortmann et al. 2004; Mesthrie and Bhatt 2008; Schneider 2007, 2011), as well as its global spread and use (Brutt-Griffler 2002; Crystal 2003; Graddol 1997, 2006, see Kirkpatrick 2007, 2010 on teaching implications). One of the latest rationales in the field of conceptualizing English is the development of ELF (e.g., Jenkins 2000, 2007, 2009, 2014; Kirkpatrick 2010; Mauranen 2012; Mauranen and Ranta 2009; Seidlhofer 2011; Smit 2010). It argues for the rightfulness of the use and variation of English by non-native speakers and is centered around multilingual speakers and social interactions. This approach signals a shift in the conceptualization of English since it is based on an ideological change and is, therefore, discussed in some more detail in Section 1.3.2.

Whenever referring to the English language, there is a commonly shared understanding of what English is. English is the language of the Britons and the

Americans and the language used abroad whenever the local language is not mastered. In most of the everyday encounters with English, one simple fact is neglected: There is no *one* English; there is no one realization of it. Exactly this plurality within English is central in most current models and theorizations of English. They have enriched our understanding of the variations and varieties of English and established the rightfulness of diverse realizations of English when used as a non-native language. However, they are also built on the objectification of English and the idea of its inflexibility, thereby reflecting an underlying monolingual ideology. Three popular models in the field of World Englishes, Kachru's (1985) Three Circles model, Schneider's (2007) Dynamic Model, and Buschfeld and Kautzsch's (2017) Extra- and Intra-Territorial Forces model, will serve as an illustration of how this is implemented. These models differentiate between varieties or loci of English, which leads to an identification and categorization of the respective uses and users of the English language. The notion of value is focused to describe how hierarchies within the introduced models are established and exactly who is considered.

Kachru's (1985) Three Circles model seems to offer a simple and self-explanatory categorization of the location of different Englishes while considering their local function. However, it is not yet able to describe the flexibility and fluidity of the use of the English language, as it is based on the ideology of monolingualism as the norm. The model relates a specific use or variety of English to a specific group of speakers by using national borders as its criteria. In doing so, the Three Circles model values or devalues the various uses of English based on the concepts of nativeness and ownership. This inequality becomes evident, for example, in the English speakers' differing rights concerning the alteration of the norms of English. Kachru's categorization into norm-providing, norm-developing, and norm-dependent varieties reflects a degree of dependence and, therefore, inequality between the three circles. The labeling seems to stress the countries' and, therefore, varieties' hierarchical relations. In addition to the choice of labels, the element of centrality further implements a hierarchy of varieties of English. This might be the reason for the decentralization of the model in later publications (see Kachru 1988).

Hierarchies always coexist with power and value, since hierarchies are reflections of their interdependent relationship. Something might, for example, be more powerful and, therefore, valuable the higher it is depicted within any hierarchical order. Norm-providing Inner Circle varieties that are spoken in the "traditional bases of English" (Kachru 1985: 12) appear to be of higher value than the use of English in the Expanding Circle that does not fulfill any official function. The value of Outer Circle English seems to fall in between the two. Although Kachru's model offers an accessible first insight into the spread of English, it has received some criticism (see, e.g., Bruthiaux 2003; Jenkins 2009; Park and Wee 2012). A main point of this criticism is the model's inflexible correlation of a country's political history and use of English. The allocation of all speakers of one country to one of the three circles results in the exclusion of mixed or borderline cases, like native English speakers in Germany or non-native speakers of English in the UK. One possible alteration of the Three Circles model has been suggested by Park and Wee (2012). They argue that the appropriation of English, that is, its use by speakers of English it "does not belong to," and the included ideologies of allegiance, competence, and authenticity can be visualized by a reconceptualization of Kachru's Three Circles model (Park and Wee 2012: 71). Furthermore, this alteration might be used to reflect the amount of value assigned to English based on language ideologies. Inner Circle Englishes hold, ideologically speaking, the highest value; American and British Standard English are desired and highly valued on the global market, that is, their value is independent of where they are used due to their status as native. Traditional L1 speakers, for example, are often among the most desired language teachers because they offer the "right" English. The value of Outer Circle Englishes, in comparison, is less easily assessed. Speakers of an Outer Circle English variety might be native speakers of English. However, outside their nation, or even community, these new varieties of English might not be perceived as the "right" English. Nonetheless, because of these speaker's identification with English and the oftentimes established standardization of Outer Circle varieties, these varieties as well as their speakers hold a certain value although not as much as Inner Circle English varieties. Furthermore, Outer Circle Englishes appear to be valued more highly on local markets and within, rather than outside, the Outer Circle. The use of English in Expanding Circle countries often reflects education and privilege or the extreme lack thereof. In both cases, it is traditionally described as leaner English or incomplete interlanguage (cf. Brutt-Griffler 2002: 179; see Selinker 1972 on interlanguage). There is no standardization and no variety status awarded to the way English is used in the Expanding Circle; its value can hardly be assessed and reasoned for based on authenticity or nativeness. It might be argued that the value of English within the Expanding Circle differs from its value outside of it, as there might be a certain loyalty among non-native speakers. The true value of Expanding Circle Englishes, however, is in its commodification as a learnable skill, which is further discussed in Section 1.4.4.

Early models of English often provide a synchronic categorization of the various realizations and varieties of English. Consequently, value is assigned to realizations of English in their fixed and "final" form. The development of varieties, that is, the diachronic perspective, and their potential interactions are centered in later theories, like Schneider's (2007) Dynamic Model, Meierkord's (2012) Interactions across Englishes, Onysko's (2016) Language Contact Typology, and, finally, Buschfeld and Kautzsch's (2017, 2020) Extra- and Intra-Territorial Forces model. While these diachronic models incorporate the traditional, ideologically motivated hierarchy of the value of English, they furthermore depict how value is assigned and why it might change.

The Dynamic Model has been the first to comprehensively introduce a focus on the transition of English from non-native to native, describing the development of linguistic diversity and the speakers' growing identification with the language in (post)colonial contexts. It is concerned with the emergence of postcolonial varieties of English in postcolonial contexts and aims to show that they typically undergo the same evolutionary process while passing the stages of *foundation, exonormative stabilization, nativization, endonormative stabilization*, and finally *differentiation*. These stages diachronically cover the initial relocation of the English language to new territory and the following steps of development and alterations that are essential for the new variety to finally be "owned" by the newly developed speaker group. Schneider, furthermore, identifies four parameters, which are observable at each of the stages. He claims that "(1) [e]xtralinguistic factors, like historical events and the political situation, result in (2) characteristic identity constructions [, which] manifest themselves in (3) sociolinguistic determinants of the contact setting" and lead to "specific (4) structural effects to emerge in the form(s) of the language variety/-ies involved" (2007: 30–1). Those parameters specify the evolution of a native variety of English based on linguistic features and their stabilization. The Dynamic Model introduces a developmental perspective, focusing on potential changes and adjustments within the use of the English language. It diminishes, but not yet erases, the gap between the English used in Kachru's Inner and the Outer Circle in terms of their value and prestige by valorizing the newly emerging postcolonial varieties. This valorization of postcolonial Englishes is a by-product of its increasing stabilization and, ultimate, nativization and, consequently, based on the ideological value of "native" English. Specifically, the ideological value of the L1 variety that is initially used by the colonizers, whom Schneider refers to as the *settlers* (Schneider 2007: 31), is partly transferred to the emerging variety that is shared by the indigenous population and the settlers. The increased ideological value of these postcolonial varieties, however, is limited and somewhat locally bound. This reflects the persisting difference between the value of L1 varieties and any nativized or emerging postcolonial variety of English. The latest development within the theorization of English in global contexts is not limited to (post)colonial contexts. Buschfeld and Kautzsch's (2017, 2020) Extra- and Intra-Territorial Forces model is presented as a proxy for these models.

Buschfeld and Kautzsch's (2017, 2020) Extra- and Intra-Territorial Forces model incorporates and assesses the development of postcolonial and non-postcolonial varieties of English while "preserving the parallels but also accounting for the differences between the two linguistic scenarios" (Buschfeld and Kautzsch 2020: 64). It builds on Schneider's model in assuming a uniform development underlying the emergence of new varieties of English, however, can be transferred to account for differences between individual speakers' language use. Buschfeld and Kautzsch hold on to the five stages of the Dynamic Model and add "extra- and intra-territorial forces [that constantly operate] on the development of both PCEs and non-PCEs [viz. postcolonial Englishes and non-postcolonial Englishes]" (2020: 64). Extraterritorial forces are defined as any influence that enters the country "from the outside" (ibid.) and include colonization (only in (post)colonial contexts), language policies, globalization, tourism, foreign policies, and sociodemographic background. Intraterritorial forces are at work on a local or national level and, consequently, "influence the cultural and linguistic development from within the country" (ibid.). They manifest themselves as attitudes toward colonizing power (only in (post)colonial contexts), language policies, acceptance of globalization, tourism, foreign policies, and sociodemographic background (cf. Buschfeld and Kautzsch 2020: 64–5). By addressing the "development from EFL [English as a Foreign Language] to ESL [English as a Second Language] and potentially ENL" (Buschfeld and Kautzsch 2020: 65), this model reproduced the hierarchization of uses of English based on their ideological value. Furthermore, by holding on to Schneider's (2007) five stages, the impact of standardization and categorization is reinforced. However, unlike any earlier models, the Extra- and Intra-Territorial Forces model includes the use of English on an idiolectal level and, hence, includes a narrow scope on English. This change reflects the current ideological shift from focusing on ideology to focusing on communication—from ideological value to communicative value.

## 1.3 The Communicative Value of English

Ideology is one way of assigning and distributing value, communication or communicative potential is another. Unlike ideologies, communication and communicative potential have changed rapidly and immensely in the course of globalization. Communication is inseparable from language and its users; however, the use of English became less dependent on the repercussions of the British Empire, for example, a tradition of speaking English in a certain country or community. Global communication became an increasingly important function of the English language, which soon raised it to a globally unique position. In this role, English is less perceived as representing the culture(s) of its L1 users but as a communicative tool that might be taken up and used by anyone who decides to participate.

The communicative value of English represents the second layer of value. It is based on a paradigm shift from conceptualizing language as a coherent system toward understanding language as a flexible social practice. The understanding of English—or language in general—as a social practice allows for exploring the dynamics of value assignment within social structures. Within these social structures, speakers are considered to use language based on their linguistic repertoires (Busch 2017), a concept that tries to overcome the ideology of monolingualism. The validation of communicative success rather than of achieving native speaker competence has gained importance and has been picked up by popular frameworks focusing on the global use of English like ELF (Jenkins 2007; Seidlhofer 2011). The shift from a focus on nativeness and proficiency toward communication has enabled the rise of the value of English users for whom English is not a native language. This value, however, is not ideological in nature but communicative.

### 1.3.1 Language as Social Practice

"All models are, by definition, reductionist in nature" (Saraceni 2015: 54). They are "artificial constructs" (Schmitz 2014: 376) that can neither include nor explain every aspect, differentiation, or alternation of what they are focused on. For their construction, researchers have to pick and choose aspects of the observed reality that the model can, or should, account for—aspects that fit. Park and Wee argue that models do not incorporate any "magical efficacy in challenging dominant ideologies of English" (2009: 402). They, therefore, initialize a theory-internal debate and do not request the inclusion of all aspects that are observed. To broaden their horizons and enable epistemological change, linguists must disconnect from models and rely on what they observe. In doing so, the conceptualization of language as a system must be renounced and its functioning as a fluid and flexible social practice can be understood.

Language cannot ever be considered independently of its speakers. This a priori connection has been developed from structuralism and the Chomskian view of language as being an innate grammar toward a more usage-based and socially informed approach in poststructuralism (see, e.g., Evans 2014: 16). Following the social turn in sociolinguistics, language is considered as a part of specific communicative situations rather than standardized, theorized, and detached from its actual use. Language users are social performers rather than receptacles of linguistic competence. This perspective allows for a disconnection of language from one specific group of people, for example, its native speakers. Furthermore, it allows for a shift from the value of English being based on language ideologies toward its value being created by its communicative value. This is necessary when engaging with the global use of English.

Rather than referring to speakers within national boundaries, the notion of *communities of practice* has come into use. The term *communities of practice* has been introduced by Lave and Wenger (1991) to offer a new understanding of learning (Cox 2005: 528; Eckert 2006: 683) and has, since then, been commonly used to refer to any group of people engaged in a shared undertaking. In sociolinguistics, it is used to refer to a group of language users without commenting on their proficiency, type of acquisition, nationhood, or any other shared attribute, as

> the value of the notion *communities of practice* to sociolinguistics and linguistic anthropology lies in the fact that it identifies a social grouping not in virtue of shared abstract characteristics (e.g. class, gender) or simple copresence (e.g. neighborhood, workplace), but in virtue of shared practice. (Eckert 2006: 683)

The concept of *communities of practice* is especially suitable to be used in the context of globally used English because it, on the one hand, does not even require the members of the communities to be in local proximity (Lave and Wenger 1991: 98). This independence of *locus* can, for example, account for the emergence of communities via social networks and other technology-induced social groupings. On the other hand, it allows for variety concerning the individual member's position within the communities s/he is a member of as well as the communities' positions within the broader society (Eckert 2006: 683).

For example, in the undertaking of this book the concept of *communities of practice* comprises students at universities involved in traditional in-classroom learning as well as distance learning and can account for individual local and international students' language use as a result of their memberships in several, variously positioned and ranked communities. Due to the new means of determining communities, that is, without focusing on their local proximity and cultural commonness, language ideologies offer little ground to assessing the value of English. When the center of this assessment is the understanding of English as a globally shared social practice, its value must be determined based on communication rather than ideologies.

With the increasing global connectedness, multilanguage use became more and more recognized. This added to the conceptual change in the understanding of communication and language as a social practice. The majority of human beings can identify as speakers of more than one language (e.g., Crystal 2003 on users of English, Grosjean 2010 on bilinguals). In contrast to language researchers, however, language users do not seem to be preoccupied with individual languages—the available potential for communication is more valuable to them, as this is the traditional reason to acquire another language. A notion that reflects the shift from a focus on individual languages to the communicative potential of a speaker is that of the *linguistic repertoire*. A linguistic repertoire is "the collective resources available to anyone at any point in time" (Blommaert 2014: 85) and might refer to speaker groups as well as individual speakers. Gumperz introduced this concept as *verbal repertoire* referring to "all the accepted ways of formulating messages" (1964: 138). It has altered the understanding of languages from being indexical of group membership toward their accumulation in the speakers' repertoire, functioning "as a means of positioning which speakers use in situated interactions" (Busch 2017: 344). Although it has been built on the fundamental assumption that speakers interact within stable speech communities (see Blackledge and Creese 2010; Busch 2017 for criticism), the notion is used in its revised form as aiming "to take into account multilingual biographic trajectories, and to valorize all linguistic resources on which speakers can draw, regardless of whether these are second or third languages, standard, dialectal or other varieties" (Busch 2013: 215). The speakers' active choice to use their linguistic repertoire context-dependently, for example to highlight or hide certain aspects of their identity (Paxton and Tyam 2010), is a key aspect of this concept and reflects the bidirectional relationship of language and social structure.

## 1.3.2 English as a Lingua Franca

ELF emerged around the turn of the century and might be defined as "any use of English among speakers of different L1s for whom English is the communicative medium of choice and often only option" (Seidlhofer 2011: 7). It takes a new perspective on the conceptualization of English—a focus on users of English as a non-native language and their acceptance as rightful rather than deficient users of English (Jenkins 2007: 18; Seidlhofer 2011: 9). The ELF development is rooted in the assumption that English belongs to its users rather than to those who were born in specific environments and, therefore, happen to be native speakers of English—as Graddol states, "Native speakers may feel the language 'belongs' to them, but it will be those who speak English as a second or foreign language who will determine its world future" (1997: 10). The initial aim of ELF has been to identify linguistic features that facilitate non-native speakers' communication and norms that could be used to improve the teaching of English to those speakers (Jenkins 2000: 11, 2007: xii; see Jenkins 2000 on phonological features and the *Lingua Franca Core*; Cogo and Dewey 2012, Dewey 2007, Mortensen 2013, Seidlhofer 2004 on grammatical features; Jenkins 2006, Seidlhofer 2004 on teaching ELF, among others). Research in ELF, subsequently, has developed further to include its sociolinguistic aspects, such as pragmatic strategies and the interrelation of ELF and the speakers' identities (e.g., Canagarajah 2007; House 2003, 2010, 2011, 2012; Hülmbauer 2009; Meierkord 2004; Sung 2015). Furthermore, some research has been conducted focusing on specific settings of use, like ELF in Academic Settings (see, e.g., ELFA 2008; Hynninen 2016; Mauranen 2012) or Business ELF (BELF) (see, e.g., Gerritsen and Nickerson 2009; Murata 2015). Despite the existence of other concepts of English in global use (e.g., EIL, International English, English as a global language, see, e.g., Crystal 2003; Seidlhofer 2011), the concept of ELF is the first one that focuses intensely on the language rights of non-native speakers of English while unifying major aspects of all the other approaches to English in international use.

> ELF emphasizes the role of English in communication between speakers from different L1s, i.e. the primary reason for learning English today; it suggests the idea of community as opposed to alienness; it emphasizes that people have something in common rather than their differences; it implies that "mixing" languages is acceptable … and thus that there is nothing wrong in retaining certain characteristics of the L1, such as accent; finally, the Latin name symbolically removes the ownership of English from the Anglos both to no one and, in effect, to everyone. (Jenkins 2000: 11)

It is estimated that the English language is currently spoken by approximately 300 million native speakers and 1.5 to 2 billion non-native speakers (Crystal 2003: 69; Graddol 1997: 8, Robson 2013: 2). This imbalance and the fact that the majority of English users would traditionally be defined as non-native users (Mauranen 2012: 2) give reason to assume that native English might no longer be the goal of language learners and that the linguistic focus is needed to be shifted on the new majority of non-native users of English and their emancipation. The reflection of the complex composition of the grouping of non-native English speakers in communities of practice (Seidlhofer 2009: 238) and the recognition of their, mostly multilingual, background (House 2012: 174) are among potential strengths of the concept of ELF. ELF is a social construct adjusting to the needs of its users in individual communicative situations. It is highly flexible, emerging "out of and through interaction" presumably without ever achieving "a stable or even standardized form" (Meierkord 2004: 129), reflecting and accepting "the variable use of English in intercultural communication" (Baker 2015: 7). Despite the wide use of the terminology, the proposed inclusiveness, and openness of ELF toward "unconventional" use, one major disadvantage is brought along with its flexibility: ELF is not clearly defined, since the exact nature of ELF, as being "a thing … or a context of use" (Maley 2010: 27), has not yet been fully agreed upon.

The multiplicity of used terminology might reflect the conceptualization of ELF as a thing since researchers might study ELF, ELF varieties (ELFs), or Lingua Franca English (LFE) (cf. O'Regan 2016; Park and Wee 2012; and Prodromou 2008 for more detailed discussions). Although Jenkins and Seidlhofer state that ELF is not a variety of English (Jenkins 2006: 161; Seidlhofer 2011: 77), they sometimes argue as if it was. Jenkins, for example, points out that ELF is not, but should have been, mentioned in Bolton's (2004) survey of the world's Englishes (2006: 161) and that "it is now conceived, i.e. as an emerging English that exists in its own right" (Jenkins 2007: 3), while Seidlhofer identifies linguistic features of ELF (2004: 220). However, a variety is defined as "a set of language habits that is shared by a certain group of speakers for use in certain contexts" (Schneider 2011: 16). This does not apply to ELF "because its speakers do not belong to particular primary communities, and its non-conformities are assumed to be too irregular" (Seidlhofer 2011: 95). The advantages of ELF—its applicability to various settings, its usability by everyone, and its linguistic adaptability to its various users' needs—prohibit the accordance of variety status, as a variety is, for example, bound to a specific location or speaker group (see, e.g., Schneider 2007). Canagarajah reasons along the same lines when he differentiates between

ELF and LFE, claiming that it is LFE that "is intersubjectively constructed in each specific context of interaction" (2007: 91). Consequently, ELF appears to constitute a context of use rather than a specific variety of English, and the shift in ELF research from core-linguistic toward sociolinguistic aspects of ELF follows this recognition. Hence, ELF as a context of use—for example, of a random combination of multilingual and/or multicultural users of English—allows for "the use of its non-conformist variations" (Seidlhofer 2011: 95) because it is not concerned with a potential standardization.

Although the concept of "ELF does not exclude NSs [native speakers] of English, … they are not included in data collection, and when they take part in ELF interactions, they do not represent a linguistic reference point" (Jenkins 2007: 3). ELF, instead, is concerned with "expert speakers" of English (Jenkins 2006: 169) who are "highly competent" (Seidlhofer, Breiteneder, and Pitzl 2006: 14). ELF, therefore, does not refer to the use of English by just anybody but remains a discourse of deficiency. The hierarchy and relevance of the various groups of English speakers are nonetheless altered within the development of ELF. Based on being concerned with this speaker group of "experts" and the fact that native speakers of English have become a global minority among English users, this framework obviously elevates the power of ELF speakers, meaning to proficient non-native speakers of English, and weakens that of speakers of native English, in questioning their solitary ownership of English. However, ELF does not explicitly equalize native and non-native speakers of English, since "ELF researchers specifically exclude mother tongue speakers from their data collection" (Jenkins 2006: 160). Moreover, less proficient non-native speakers are widely neglected, which further contradicts the antihegemonic stance proclaimed by ELF researchers (cf. Park and Wee 2012: 45–6). ELF is only applicable after speakers have gained a certain, but unspecific, level of proficiency—after they are above the "threshold level … required to join this invisible community" (Canagarajah 2007: 91).

Although the ELF development has taken a step into a more liberated approach to English, it still does not reflect the reality of its use. ELF is claimed to conceptualize English from a practice-based perspective and researchers argue for its neutrality. Nonetheless, it appears to shed light only on some users and uses of the English language, excluding those who are affected by the repercussions of its global spread as well as the negative side effects of privilege. Advertising a high level of inclusiveness and a presumed neutrality (see House 2003; Jenkins 2006; Seidlhofer 2004), ELF speakers are often conceived as people who *choose* to use English. This understanding romanticizes the influence of the English language—its boldness and inescapability. This inescapability is what less privileged English users—those who do not have access to typically elitist ELF settings, like discourse in global business, science, technology, media, and politics (Seidlhofer 2004: 211) and cannot *not choose* to achieve a certain goal—suffer from. Romanticizing the influence of English draws a whitewashed picture of its use by non-native speakers, neglecting the people's investment of time, money, and effort to learn the language, thereby reaching a certain level of proficiency and the economic benefit generated by those who commodify it. The conceptualization of the value of English in such commodified contexts requires the addition of an economic layer to the framework.

## 1.4 The Economic Value of English

The third layer of the value of English is its economic value. Among the three layers of value, it is the layer with the most recently increased importance. While communication and systematicity, that is, the idea of language as a social practice and language as a system, are, by-now, inherent parts of the English language, its monetarization and economization are more recent aspects of the language's assessment and value. Concepts like neoliberalism (Gray, O'Regan, and Wallace 2018; Holborow 2015) and language commodification (Heller 2010; Heller and Duchêne 2016) reflect and build the foundation for this development as they depict our global society's perception and utilization of English. While social and ideological approaches are part of the official narrative of language, the economic considerations that increasingly influence the English language's narrative are often located just below the surface. Despite its concealment at first sight, the economic value of English is essential and increasingly important for a comprehensive understanding of the language.

The economic value of English is closely intertwined with its increasing use. One context in which this linkage is clearly observable is global higher education (HE). For locally bound universities around the globe, adding English as one medium of instruction is a necessity to create a prominent aspect of internationality (Lasagabaster 2015). This "internationality through English" leads to a higher number of potentially interested students who might even be willing to pay higher student fees, which universities profit from (cf. Section 4.3.2). Hence institutional internationality in HE, and the consequential loss of local boundedness, is primarily rooted in the economic value of English—which is appreciated and utilized by universities and students alike—rather than by the communicative value of English, for example, its usefulness for international collaboration and exchange. The concept of *English-as-a-marketable-attribute* (Section 1.4.4) is developed to illustrate the assessment of English as a primarily economic resource that is potentially independent of its actual use.

## 1.4.1 Neoliberalism

The foundation of any valuation of language is the social and economic structures its value is assigned and accepted within. Today, as it is commonly argued, we live in a neoliberal society (see, e.g., Block 2015, 2018b; Block, Gray, and Holborow 2012; Harvey 2005; Holborow 2012, 2013, 2015; Pennycook 2010). Therefore, the valuation of English is based on the structures imposed by neoliberal ideologies. To identify the reasons and the mechanisms at work that maintain and reproduce the global hegemony of English, those ideologies as well as the role of language in neoliberalism must be scrutinized.

"Neoliberalism is a contemporary social and political phenomenon" (Holborow 2015: 1) that coins "the common sense way many of us interpret, live in and understand the world" (Harvey 2005: 3) and is "a term used by those critical of its effects" (Holborow 2015: 2). Although neoliberalism is based on an "economic doctrine" (Shin and Park 2016: 443) that puts "individualized human capital at the centre of a competitive market world" (Holborow 2015: 16) and promotes, for example, the privatization of state-owned industries, the perception of human value as marketable skills, and extensive entrepreneurial freedom as advancing human well-being (Harvey 2005: 2–3), it has also developed into a linguistic phenomenon (ibid.; Gray, O'Regan, and Wallace 2018: 471). The linguistics of neoliberalism are reflected by "the language of neoliberalism itself, and … the role of certain languages *under* neoliberalism" (Gray, O'Regan, and Wallace 2018: 473). The language of neoliberalism is characterized by an extensive and apparently common and justified use of economy-related terminology in other domains and fields (ibid.: 474; Holborow 2015: 3). This "adoption of the market metaphor" (Block 2018a: 5) is observable in the use of words like *intellectual property*, *innovation*, *enterprise*, *knowledge transfer*, or *human capital* (ibid.; Holborow 2013: 233, 2015: 4). This change of terminology is especially relevant in the domain of education as it welcomes and establishes the influence of the economy as a driving force of education. Furthermore, the language of neoliberalism has introduced the conceptualization of individuals as "mini-replicas of corporations" (Holborow 2015: 2). This use of neoliberal language is the result of the ideological transformation of "humans as social beings to humans as individuals" (Block 2018a: 5, based on Foucault) and imitates the value shift from societal or group accomplishments to individual accomplishments of the "neoliberal citizens" (Block 2018b: 578). A person is recognized as a bundle of skills (Shin and Park 2016: 447), as human capital, and, in his or her ideal form, as *homo economicus* (Foucault 2008).

The concept of languages under neoliberalism is based on their use as neutral skills (see Park and Wee 2012: 161); the use of language is a skill that can be attached and, consequently, adds to the speaker's, or bearer's, value on the global market (Shin and Park 2016: 446). This objectification is ideology-based and serves "to rationalize social organization"—as language ideologies always do (Piller 2015: 7). Language ideologies that view "language as a set of flexible skills that may be detached from a person as decontextualized medium of communication illustrate ways in which language functions as an essential part of the mechanism that sustains neoliberalism" (Shin and Park 2016: 450). The detachment of language from its cultural and social predispositions allows for a neutral assessment of language as a communicative tool. This neutrality is, of course, only theoretical, as language can never be used without cultural or social implications. Nonetheless, language learners and teachers are no longer focused on studying and teaching languages to become proficient users of them in all domains of life. Rather, languages serve to enlarge their skill sets so that, as they are bearers of the languages, their demand on any respective job market increases. Although all languages are potentially valuable on those markets, English holds a special role under neoliberalism. "A language ideology associated with neoliberalism is the belief in the need for a global language and the belief that using English for business or education will increase competitiveness (Piller & Cho, 2013)" (Piller 2015: 8). Phillipson (2009: 84–5), who refers to the European context, has discussed, for instance, the emergence of English as a necessary component within academia. This extended use of the language, furthermore, introduces a third level of occupation to HE—positions that are neither entirely academic nor entirely administrative. Those mixed positions are located in the neoliberal university's "Third Space" (Holborow 2015: 3–4). For these jobs, English is essential, since they are commonly based on contact with (international) students and have developed due to the increasing use of the English language as a commodity in HE.

## 1.4.2 Language Commodification

The commodification of languages is based on neoliberal ideologies and the objectification of language. Neoliberalism accounts for the gaining importance of the economy in traditional noneconomic fields. The objectification of language is the cognitive construct that serves as the prerequisite and the key assumption of its possible commodification (see Park and Wee 2012: 124). The idea of a possible commodification of language is based on the Marxist definition of a commodity as the product of labor that has its value in its use. Commodities in this traditional sense might be a pen for writing or a knife for cutting food (Block 2019: 125). Language, as de Swaan points out, differs from other economic commodities in so far as it cannot be consumed and it is not limited (2001: 27). He argues that nobody can be prevented from using a specific language the way people can be prevented from owning or using material items. In contrast to those material commodities, the use of a language does not limit its supply or reserves. It rather increases its value since every speaker increases the communicative potential of the language for all speakers (de Swaan 2001: 28). Language is not a commodity in the traditional sense. Its commodification is based on its perception as an "autonomous system" (Heller and Duchêne 2016: 139) and the conceptualization of language as serving two functions: it might either serve as a learnable (technical) skill that adds value in the global marketplace or it might be a reflection of authenticity (Heller 2010: 102; Heller and Duchêne 2016: 139; see also Coupland 2003; Urciuoli 2008). The neoliberal value shift "from primarily use value to exchange value in addition to use value" (Block 2019: 123) has facilitated the acquisition of a commodity status for language (Agha 2011: 25). Objects or competencies are no longer valued to be used but to be owned and have the potential to be exchanged. English can be used and exchanged on a global scale and, therefore, appears to fit right into this concept of neoliberal commodification. The specific exchange value of English is, however, determined by the context and demand—the specific market.

The exchange value of the English language might, furthermore, be approached through its speaker-internal or its external potential. The speaker-internal potential of language is also referred to as a language's indexicality (see Silverstein 1976) and relates to its realization and its contexts of use. Heller uses the example of the standard variety as a sign of intellectuality or good school education (2010: 102). This speaker-internal potential is no longer treated as a quality of the speaker but also "as directly exchangeable for material goods, and, especially, for money" (ibid.). The external potential of language is reflected by the shift of, for example, job requirements. It works hand in hand with the "tertiarization" of the neoliberal economy (Heller and Duchêne 2013: 9) and is characterized by a shift toward focusing on linguistic resources. Both potentials result in an increasing importance of language throughout various domains and are, ultimately, always transformed into money.

The foundation of a possible commodification is always the idea of language as an autonomous system or entity (Heller and Duchêne 2016; Park and Wee 2012). However, Park and Wee argue that the "indexicality of English as it lives and transforms in everyday practice and discourse is the very site where the value of English is formed" and that "the value of English as a commodity is not formed solely in the marketplace of exchange" (2012: 124). The discursively negotiated and constructed indexicality of English initiates its constant reevaluation within various indexical fields (cf. Agha 2011; Eckert 2008). This link between the semiotic and economic value is how the value of English is constructed. In the context of HE, the value of English is evaluated, negotiated, and confirmed by its speakers' use of it. The value of English seems to be a self-fulfilling prophecy: it needs to be considered to be valuable in order to be chosen for use in various contexts and for economic value to be assigned. Because of its economic value and the resulting speaker behavior, however, it is deduced as valuable in the first place (see Grin 2002: 20–1). The initial origin of the unparalleled global value of English, therefore, might very well be its historical spread (see Phillipson 1992 on linguistic imperialism) and the accompanied forceful valorization.

The value of any language depends on the specific features of the respective market, the proficiency level of its users, and the standards of use, to name just some influential factors (Heller and Duchêne 2016: 148). While those factors might be manageable in small or strongly regulated contexts of language use, they are not equal, or equally important, across the field of global international HE. However, an assessment of the value of English has to be developed consciously without falling into the trap of assumptions based on language ideologies. The concept of commodification has variously been criticized (see Heller and Duchêne 2016 for a categorization of criticism). One major point of this criticism has been the vagueness of the concept underlying the terminology used and the approach taken (Grin 2014; McGill 2013). McGill (2013) argues for the misuse of the Marxist term *commodity* by scholars like Heller and Duchêne when used to refer to languages and their relations to *markets*. Commodities are defined as being bound to specific markets, with identifiable conditions, in which they are produced and consumed. The effects of those conditions, so

McGill (2013), have to measurably change the exchange value of linguistic ability. English, therefore, cannot just be called a commodity just because it appears to be connected to economic variables. Furthermore, following Grin, the economic perspective on language is only metaphorically assessed by the framework of language commodification as "it offers no economic angle—it simply happens to formulate propositions with reference to a macro-level context that presents some economic features" (2014: 18–19). The framework of language commodification appears to be only pseudo-economic in nature. Although it seems to not have been fully developed yet, the concept of the commodification of language, especially English in a global context, offers accessible insights into a first conjunction of language and economy. This link is investigated from a theoretical economics perspective in the field of *language economics* (cf. Grin 2002, 2014; Grin and Vaillancourt 2012), which will be looked at again in Section 1.4.4. Before doing so, a contextualization of the commodification of English is offered by approaching the field of HE and investigating the utilization of English within this field from a value-based perspective.

## 1.4.3 English in Higher Education

In HE, which can be described as voluntary, mostly university-based, tertiary education (e.g., Merriam-Webster 2018; Shkoler and Rabenu 2020), English fulfills multiple functions; it grants access to knowledge, attracts international students and academics, boosts these students' future employability, and potentially improves the institutions' positions within international rankings (Lasagabaster 2015: 265–6; Wilkinson 2013). From a neoliberal perspective, English, furthermore, is the key to internationality and success for both the university and its students (Lasagabaster 2015: 258; see also Holborow 2013; van der Walt 2013). More than 70 percent of the universities named English as their favorite language of communication and teaching (Maringe 2012: 22), resulting in various research studies focusing on the level of proficiency of faculty and students (see, e.g., Benzie 2010; Chen and Goh 2011; Durant and Shepherd 2009; Murray 2016; Oliver, Vanderford, and Grote 2012). The extensive use of the English language is, furthermore, a key aspect of the transformation of HE into a global enterprise (Murray 2016: 1). This trend reflects the shift from English functioning as the subject of study to serving as the language of instruction and communication in this setting. Traditionally, the content of study has been taught in the language(s) of the country in which the university was based. The study of languages, that is, the language as the subject of study, for example, "English

Studies" or "French Studies," however, is traditionally not bound to the location of the university but taught "in English" or "in French" around the globe. In the course of globalization and the increasing global connectedness and mobility across national borders, English, especially, has lost its restricted function as a subject of study, functioning furthermore as the medium of instruction, *id est* the vehicle of the transfer of knowledge. The teaching of any content, consequently, has developed to be potentially context and location independent, as it might be taught in English anywhere by anyone to anyone, provided the necessary individual competences are available.

The use of English in academia, its threat to local languages, and the difficulties it causes in terms of language testing have been widely discussed (see, e.g., Björkman 2013; ELFA 2008; Gunnarsson 2000; Jenkins 2014; Mauranen 2012 on English in academia; Baker 2012; Hall 2010; Jenkins and Leung 2014; McNamara 2014 on challenges in English language testing, Phillipson 2009 on domain loss). English, furthermore, is the dominant language in academic publishing, for student and staff mobility, and as a language of instruction (cf., e.g., Brock-Utne 2001, 2007; Curry and Lillis 2018; Ferguson 2007; Murray 2016). Rather than concentrating on a specific field of implementation and occurring challenges, this book is concerned with the underlying political, social, and economic reasons for the implementation of English at universities. A university's decision to introduce the use of English in all or some academic branches is oftentimes a strategic decision to enhance their international character and attract international scholars and students rather than an affiliation to the language itself or its traditional speaker groups' cultural or social customs (Ferguson 2007: 13; Jenkins 2014: 5; Murray 2016: 1). Although it might appear to be a free choice, in virtue of "the globalisation and commodification of HE in a competitive, market-driven world characterized by the increased mobility of academics and students, and by the increased ease of international communication" (Ferguson 2007: 14), English has to be included into a university's offerings to remain attractive and prestigious, which is often represented by respective positions in university rankings. The use of the language, especially as the medium of instruction, is essential for a university to remain lucrative within the global market of HE since English is identified with high-quality education (Lasagabaster 2015: 266). In addition, the implementation of English is a fruitful way "to seize part of the major English-speaking countries' market share of international students" (ibid.: 265) and increase the institution's economic profit, as these students often pay higher fees than local students (see Holborow 2013: 233 on EU versus non-EU students).

Due to the shared belief that English is essential for a university's internationalization, the favorite language of teaching and learning, and, due to the influence of language policy in education on future employers and employees, dominant on the global job market, English cannot be bypassed in HE (Lasagabaster 2015: 258; Maringe 2012: 22, see also van der Walt 2013). While the use of English is an essential part of a university's internationalization strategy, a mere increase of its use does not suffice for its successful internationalization (Doiz, Lasagabaster, and Sierra 2014; Lasagabaster 2015: 268). Foskett (2012) developed a categorization of universities and identifies five types of universities based on their internationalization strategies based on a survey of twenty-three universities in the UK and Asia. He differentiates between domestic universities, imperialist universities, internationally aware universities, internationally engaged universities, and internationally focused universities (2012: 44–5). While domestic universities accept international students who apply, they mainly focus "on their own national and regional context" (ibid.: 44). English, here, might serve as a subject rather than as a crucial tool of communication and cooperation. In contrast, imperialist universities have a strong focus on recruiting international students and might have to rely on the use of English, in case no other language is shared. The implementation of English as the medium of instruction (EMI) study programs might be the only concession to the process of internationalization, as they will have done relatively little to change their organization, facilities, or services "at home." The use of English, therefore, seems to be partially guided by the financial advantages of accepting fee-paying international students rather than by advocating international culture and cooperation in research (Ferguson 2007: 13). International students are expected by and large to "experience college life in just the same way as home students" (Foskett 2012: 44). International universities located in mainland Europe appear to belong to this category as not only intuition fees but also prestige and other secondarily financial advantages are connected to being perceived as international (Ferguson 2007: 13–14; Jenkins 2014: 3; Murray 2016: 1). Those, mostly Anglophone, universities open satellite or branch campuses abroad that focus primarily on local inhabitants as indirectly international students, like the University of Central Lancashire (UCLan Cyprus) in the Republic of Cyprus (RoC), the Florida State University in Panama, or the Middlesex University London in Dubai, Malta, and Mauritius. However, they tend to implement their home, meaning Anglophone, structure. Foskett continues to differentiate between three types of universities that are internationally committed. Internationally aware universities have changed "their organization and culture to have a profile that is international"; furthermore, "they recognize the global nature of economy and society and even of higher education, but have not yet engaged with 'overseas'" (Foskett 2012: 45; see Section 4.4.1 for the categorization of the research sites). Internationally engaged universities operate "in international arenas, for example through institutional partnerships and student recruitment, but [also pursue] an internationalization agenda 'at home'" (ibid.). For both of these university types, the implementation of the English language is essential for international communication and prestige. Finally, Foskett identifies a smaller number of internationally focused universities as institutions "where the level of progress and achievement in internationalization is strong in many dimensions" and a transformational change of the institution's culture (ibid.). Furthermore, he states that the categorization of universities should consider a "gap" between their aspirations in terms of internationalization and the achieved reality—universities might aim and advertise a level of internationalization, often via the use of the English language, that they have not (yet) achieved from an external perspective (Foskett 2012: 45–6). In these cases, the institutions' internationalization efforts might serve as a smokescreen for their actual goal that is globalization.

Globalization represents, following van der Walt (2013), the understanding of HE "as a commodity and academics and students as tradable products from a neoliberal and market-related discourse perspective" (Lasagabaster 2015: 256). It, furthermore, reflects the capitalistic interest of stakeholders, like the government, in the internationalization of universities (Holborow 2013: 249). However, this interest is often hidden behind the traditional autonomy and the altruistic privilege of HE to serve as a society's common good. Universities, as Maringe (2012: 21) states, habitually decide what they teach to whom and in what way. This traditional authority has been transformed into a practical, market-related business decision that might be crucial for an institution's survival—language choice has become an important economic factor in HE. The decision to implement English, as has been shown, is traditionally a political and economic top-down instruction (Haberland 2014: 258; Jenkins 2014: 74; Lasagabaster 2015: 257) that neglects the reality of academic classrooms and occurring challenges when put into practice. English therefore might be at use only theoretically, due to, for example, a lack of language proficiency on the part of students or staff (Murray 2016: 3). Crucial to the realization of English in HE is the fact that it, due to globalization and the increased mobility of people, involves comparatively few users of ENL (see, e.g., Jenkins 2014: 42; Murray 2016: 12), especially when the institution is not located in a traditionally English-speaking country, such as Cyprus.

Although the English language holds a major role in the internationalization and globalization of HE, the specific realization of English in academic settings is most likely not a native variety. Furthermore, stakeholders of HE in traditional non-native English-speaking countries do not share *one* variety of English but realizations that are influenced by a mix of other languages—especially students who use English primarily for successful communication and to increase their future employability. For these students, potential alterations from ENL norms are common and not understood as obstacles. The function of English as the language of international communication, cooperation, and (paid-for) mobility has initiated a shift from a focus on native proficiency toward realizability, successful communication, and economic potential. Although this development brings along major difficulties in the field of language testing, diverging from the testing benchmarks of native speaker standards, it potentially also raises the value of English users for whom English is not a native language. As Mauranen, Pérez-Llantada, and Swales state, "Most research in academic English is oriented towards … native speakers of English" (2010: 638), as native speakers still occupy an "expert position" that functions as the benchmark for all speakers of English. A speaker's proficiency in English, and therefore his/her value, used to be assessed by comparing it to native English use, although there is no one English that is relevant and used in academia collectively (cf. Davies 2003; Hyland 2009; see Holliday 1994, 2005; Vetter 2012; Widdowson 2012 on teaching ESL/EFL). Furthermore, and as stated earlier, nativelikeness is no longer the most valued aspect of English in HE.

Assessing English in HE based on a value-based framework enables a comprehensive understanding of the multiple, complex, and diverging contexts of its implementation. It can account for the high popularity of universities in native English-speaking countries with students around the globe who appreciate the ideological value of English in its traditional homes. Furthermore, it can account for the increasing acceptance of alternative realizations by students and faculty alike whenever the communicative value of English outranks its ideological value. However, it also shows that in all of these scenarios, the economic value of English is always coexistent. In addition, the English language does not only contain value but can also apply value to its associates, whether speakers, objects, or study programs. Holding a university degree in an English-medium study program or university might considerably increase the holder's employability, that is, his/her value for potential employers. The value of this degree is likely to be seconded only by a degree from an L1 English-speaking university. This objective of *having* English might even lead to an overobjectification of the language, separating its economic value from the reality of its actual use.

## 1.4.4 Buying into English: English-as-a-Marketable-Attribute

In addition to the investigation of the value of the English language itself from an economic perspective, the value that is added by and from English to other commodities should be considered, since both aspects are essential for the global success and continued spread of English. As Heller shows, languages can be commodified in two different ways: as a skill and as a sign of authenticity (2010: 102). This also holds true for the English language. Furthermore, both uses rely on and construct the value of English at the same time. As well as the construction of the value that is assigned to the English language itself from various perspectives has to be theorized, the effect of this value on other entities, constructs, or people must be considered. In so doing, the field of language economics appears to be fruitful. Language economics, following Grin and his elaborations, can be described as being concerned with the mono- and bidirectional effects of economics and linguistics on one another and the use of economics as a framework to investigate the linguistic changes (2014: 8). Economics, and especially its specific lexicon, is widely used to explain the use and development of linguistic resources. Here, the focus will not lie on creating an argument about the correctness of the use of those terms and framework (see, e.g., Grin 2014; McGill 2013 for criticism) but on examining the relationship between economic variables and language use. As mentioned previously, the high valuation of English might be perceived as a self-fulfilling prophecy: the English language is valued because of its influence that, in return, affects its valuation. The economic underpinnings of social class represent one way of investigating the causal direction from economic variables to linguistic resources. The use of English by people of high social status and economic power might, for example, lead to a valuation of their specific realization or variety of English, which is independent of its conformity with native or standardized use in this specific context or market. The effects of linguistic variables on economic developments are to be theorized in this section.

While the English language can add value to other commodities and constructs when commodified as a sign of authenticity, it can also add value to its non-native users when it is commodified as a skill rather than an identity trait of a socially positioned persona. Starting with the value of English as a sign of authenticity, it might add value to its native users. However, it is often used to add value to other commodities or constructs, like language teaching, since the native speaker is still accepted as the desired goal of language learning. The amount of value added by the English language when used to signal authenticity might be reflected by a reconstruction of Kachru's Three Circles model, as suggested by Park and Wee (2012: 71–5).

Park and Wee argue that the appropriation of English—its use by speakers of English it "does not belong to"—and the included ideologies of allegiance, competence, and authenticity can be visualized by a reconceptualization of Kachru's Three Circles model (2012: 71, see Section 1.2.2). Furthermore, it might be used to reflect the amount of value added by English used as a sign of authenticity on the global market, since authenticity is constructed through a combination of nation-bound speaker ideology and identification with English. Inner Circle Englishes add, ideologically speaking, the highest value "due to the speaker's 'inner essence' as an English speaker" (ibid.: 72–3), that is, their speakers' nativeness and identification with the English language. Therefore, certificates from "native English" institutions are more valuable on the global job market than EMI degrees from other universities, even in professions that are not based on the use of English. The fact that Inner Circle Englishes are at use adds value to the degree or study program that is independent of the content's quality. The value added by Outer Circle Englishes, in comparison, is more content-dependent as it decreases outside local contexts. Outer Circle English varieties—despite being L1 varieties—tend to be less highly valued on global markets as these new varieties are often not perceived as the *right English*. Nonetheless, due to their speakers' identification as native speakers of English, they add value to them, although not as much as Inner Circle English varieties to their speakers. The use of English in Expanding Circle countries tends to be the reflection of the speaker's education and privilege or the extreme lack thereof. As it is based on L1 English, no variety status is awarded and the value it adds to its speakers cannot be rooted in concepts like nativeness or authenticity. Although these uses of English might be valued more highly by non-native speakers than by native speakers, the true value added by English to its non-native users is rooted in its commodification as a learnable skill—a skill that represents communication as well as internationality and valorizes its bearers.

Although the conceptualization of language has developed toward promoting multilingualism, on the global market, this growing interest in multilingualism is "mainly concern[ed with] access to English, but it also has room to develop commodifiable local or regional authenticities (Alcaras et al. 2001, Pujolar 2006, LeMenestrel 1999)" (Heller 2010: 107). While in the traditional epistemology of English, only native speakers are authentic and legitimate speakers of "their language," the commodification of English as a skill, among other factors, has supported the valorization of non-native English and the advocacy of its speakers as legitimate. English as a skill is "focused on performances (notably communicative ones) as skills that are marketable commodities rather than as expressions of true selves or relatively good or poor accomplishments of socially located personae" (Heller 2010: 103). This use of English is, in theory, detached from English in its function as part and reflection of the speaker's identity. Due to this detachment, the language can be conceptualized as a skill, adding value to its non-native speakers (ibid.). However, this concept of English-as-a-skill does overlook cases in which performing English is not even needed. Therefore, in the following, it is argued that people are stakeholders, who invest in the acquisition of English-as-a-marketable-attribute, valorizing their commodifiable public personae "on paper" as well. Furthermore, English-as-a-marketable-attribute does also add value to any other commodity due to its translatability that "requires the marshaling of controlled, proprietary content from language to language and from market to market" (Gramling 2016: 216). The gain of the objectivity of English, due to its perceived independence from its speaker's private identity, facilitates its translatability. Gramling (2016) argues that translatability, furthermore, determines the value of a language. Within the *linguascene* English, commodified as speaker identity independent, should, therefore, add more value to any commodity or construct than the opulent language of a native speaker.

The commodifications of English and their added value rely on the convertibility of language and the transferability of commodities and their value between different neoliberal markets. This, however, implies changing power relations between English users and shifting emphasis on the standardization or the variability of the English language. The value added by English as a sign of authenticity is based on the standardization of native English and the associated ideologies. This is the reason students might pay more for a "British" EMI education than for a French one—it is a symbol for an education in the *right English*, which makes native speakers powerful stakeholders of the preservation of those ideologies and the existing power relations. However, more than the native use of English, its non-native use reflects privilege or the lack thereof—the privilege of an educated population using English voluntarily, stressing their internationality, and the lack of privilege of the non-elite needing English to earn a living, for example, in the tourism sector. Bourdieu states that the linguistic relation of power is not completely determined by the prevailing linguistic forces alone: by virtue of the languages spoken, the speakers who use them and the groups defined by possession of the corresponding competence, the whole social structure is present in each interaction. (1991: 67)

The English language in use, therefore, adds the value of the associated social structure to each interaction, might it be commodified as the identity trait of native users or the learnable attribute of privileged non-native users. This might be reflected in the tendency to not assess powerful speakers' use of English as critically as that of the powerless. Utterances "are ... *signs of wealth*, intended to be evaluated and appreciated, and *signs of authority*, intended to be believed and obeyed" (ibid.: 66). The commodification of English appears to allow for a separation of these two functions—identity and attribute—concerning the value added to speakers of English. The valuation of English can be transferred, across unified markets, to people and commodities, resulting in an alteration of their respective value while the differentiation between different realizations and uses of the English language persist and often remain unmentioned and undistinguished.

## 1.5 Summary

The English language has been researched for decades and a lot has been learned about the language, its users, and the contexts of its use. Over time, English became a global language and increasingly shared. This development and the growing linguistic insight have led to multiple shifts in the language's value. The chapter at hand has introduced a three-layered framework to assess this value, which can account for the various contexts of use, for the multitude of user groups, as well as for the varying reasons for their choosing of English.

It has been shown that the value of English can be subdivided into ideological, communicative, and economic value. The ideological value is based on common beliefs of what realization of English is *right* and *correct* and who might speak and own it. This layer of value finds hearing in many models of English and reflects the long-standing valuation and advancement of its traditional native speakers. For non-native speakers of English, the communicative value of English might be more important when they decide to learn the language. When the systematicity of English was superseded by its communicative power, language became to be understood as a social practice that, in turn, allowed for new frameworks like

ELF (e.g., Jenkins 2007; Seidlhofer 2011) to develop. The third layer of value that has been introduced in this chapter is the economic value of English. The increasingly strong influence of neoliberalism on most aspects of society and life has led to the acceptance of *English-as-a-marketable-attribute*. The accompanied objectification and commodification of the language has developed a reciprocal relationship, for example, with the implementation of English in global HE. To create a comprehensive understanding of the global role of English, the reasons for its continued spread and implementation in various contexts, and, finally, the individual speakers' choices, this framework will now be applied to the personal, the societal, and the global level.

# 2

# Assessing the Value of Language

## 2.1 Introduction

In a perfect world, all languages have the same value. In reality, some languages are valued more than others, and English is currently one of the highest-valued languages in the world. In this chapter, the variation within the value of English for its users is assessed and analyzed, presenting the factors that affect this value on a personal, societal, and global level, that is, the angle that is taken on the language's validation or the involved users. While, for example, an individual speaker might not want to learn or use English, on a societal level, English is often introduced in the early years of school education and considered to be inevitable. In global settings, English often appears to be valued more highly than any other language. However, some dialects or accents of English are even more valuable than others. The hegemony of the native speaker (cf. Section 1.2.1) is reproduced on a global level more intensely than on a societal or personal level.

The concepts depicted in this chapter are essential for a comprehensive understanding of the complex dynamics involved in assigning value to languages in general and the English language specifically. Furthermore, they can account for the variability of the value of English, for example, in different settings, by various user groups, and based on its users' varying objectives and mobility trajectories.

## 2.2 Personal Value

Traditionally, a person's first language (L1) (or L1s) tends to be the most highly valued language within his/her linguistic repertoire, as the speaker usually identifies most strongly with this language and uses it very frequently. However, the rise of global mobility has enabled an increasing heterogeneity of L1s in a given local setting. This disconnection of speakers from their traditional linguistic origins influences the valuation of languages based on the frequency of their use as well as their usefulness. On the global job market, for example, the English language tends to be more useful than any other language that, in turn, influences the personal value of English for the individual speaker. These examples show that the value of a language differs for each speaker and is primarily influenced by factors like, for example, the speaker's identification with the language and the frequency of its use. The following elaborations depict to what extent the three layers of value are represented and interrelate in the assessment of the value of English on the individual speaker's level. Furthermore, it is shown how this valuation might be influenced by the value of English on its other levels of use, that is, in social groups or societies.

## 2.2.1 Language and Identity

"Identity is the social positioning of self and other" (Bucholtz and Hall 2005: 586) with language functioning as the means and marker of this positioning. While early approaches assumed stable identities to be automatically assigned to individuals, poststructural approaches argue for their social construction and reflection of power relations (Bucholtz and Hall 2005: 587; Pavlenko and Blackledge 2004: 13). As a consequence thereof, the assumed one-to-one correlation between language and identity, which is based on the conceptualization of "individuals as members of homogeneous, uniform, and bounded ethnolinguistic communities" (Pavlenko and Blackledge 2004: 5), has been replaced by the view of identity as "a discursive construct" (Bucholtz and Hall 2005: 587). Identities are conceptualized as constantly constructed and negotiated via social interactions (Pavlenko and Blackledge 2004: 14), using language to "co-construct [its users'] everyday worlds and, in particular, their own social role and identities and those of others" (Hall 2012: 41). Identities are negotiated in a bidirectional discourse utilizing language as the armamentarium—the medium—of negotiation and as the index of the users' chosen identities (Pavlenko and Blackledge 2004: 14). The concept of identity is multiple, multifaceted, fluid, social, and contextual in nature (Hall 2012: 33, 41), which aggravates the formulation of a universally valid definition. Omoniyi and White (2006), therefore, moved on to compile commonly shared positions on identity. They state:

1. that identity is not fixed;
2. that identity is constructed within established contexts and may vary from one context to another;

3. that these contexts are moderated and defined by intervening social variables and expressed through language(s);
4. that identity is a salient factor in every communicative context whether given prominence or not;
5. that identity informs social relationships and therefore also informs the communicative exchanges that characterize them;
6. that more than one identity may be articulated in a given context in which case there will be a dynamic of identities management. (Omoniyi and White 2006: 2)

An individual's various identities appear to reflect and be rooted in his/her multiple social roles and their contexts of use. The construction, or negotiation, of those identities is always intertwined with language use and, therefore, closely connected to language ideologies and other socialization of the social group a speaker belongs to or wants to belong to, that is, customs, traditions, and social roles (cf. Hofstede 1991; Spencer-Oatey 2012). The value of language used as part of an individual's various identities is primarily composed of the ideological value of a language. This ideological value is assigned in cooperation with the other members of the respective social construction based on, for example, shared or juxtapositional expectations of language use. When the shared expectations are met, the respective identity and the assigned value of the used language are mutually accepted; when the expectations are juxtapositional or not met, identities and the value of the used language(s) are negotiated.

Following Pavlenko and Blackledge (2004), identities might be allocated into three categories: *imposed*, *assumed*, or *negotiable* identities. Imposed identities are ascribed to the individual by others and not negotiable in a particular setting. Identities that are accepted and, consequently, performed by an individual are assumed identities. These are not negotiated and are often highly valued. Identities that are not accepted are negotiable and negotiated since the individual aims at replacing them with other, more preferred identities (cf. Pavlenko and Blackledge 2004: 21). One means of negotiation is language use, as language is an identity marker (e.g., Ferris, Peck, and Banda 2014: 410; Omoniyi 2006: 20). Omoniyi argues along these lines in stating that "identity options are always co-present" (2006: 20) and so is linguistic choice. Based on this multiplicity, he proposes a hierarchy of identities that is based on their salience in a given situation. "The most appropriate or lucrative identity option is foregrounded," while "alternative languages [that are] not chosen in a given moment within an interaction would be alternative identities that are backgrounded" (ibid.). In the given situation, the languages of a foregrounded identity are more highly valued than those of backgrounded identities. Language, in general, is a performative means (Ferris, Peck, and Banda 2014: 413), and its appropriateness and lucrativeness as such are based on the power relations that social conventions or language ideologies are rooted in. Therefore, identity choice is similarly based on social power relations and the respective value assigned by those relations.

The power and value of a language influence the power and value of the connected identities and vice versa, as "language choice and attitudes are inseparable from political arrangements, relations of power, language ideologies, and interlocutors' views of their own and others' identities" (Pavlenko and Blackledge 2004: 1). Individuals, therefore, negotiate their identities and use or acquire linguistic resources to construct identities they perceive as desirable in the respective time and space—they perform a desired and valuable identity until they are identified as such by others. While this negotiation of identity can be based on group identities, the desire to show sameness and having become a member of a chosen group, they can also aim at separating oneself from a group in showing uniqueness (cf. Joseph 2004 on individual and group identity). In times of global economy and connectedness, the appropriateness and lucrativeness of certain language use might, however, have become disconnected from its user groups' identities. Although Norton argues, following Bourdieu (1977), that "the value ascribed to speech cannot be understood apart from the person who speaks, and the person who speaks cannot be understood apart from larger networks of social relationships" (2010: 350), the value of the English language might be disconnecting from its speakers.

In poststructuralism, language use shapes and is shaped by identity options and their value; since language is ideological in nature, it is often based on the legitimacy of its users—for example, being accepted as rightful speakers of a certain language, members of a certain group, or social class rather than impostors (Bourdieu 1977: 650). In the case of English, its global use results in it "rapidly losing its national cultural base" (Dörnyei, Csizér, and Németh 2006: 9); the legitimacy of speakers and their identification with English is also changing. The global use of English is supplemented by disconnection and separation of language and identity, resulting in speakers of non-native English no longer necessarily aiming at the identification with this cultural base or native speaker groups. Since "multilinguals are able to use English for shared purposes while not losing their values and identities" (Canagarajah 2007: 90), English might not necessarily be part of what Bourdieu (1990) calls a speaker's *habitus*—"a set of bodily dispositions acquired through extended engagement in our everyday activities that dispose us to act in certain ways" (Hall 2012: 36). English, in its global use, is rather valued as a generic add-on to an individual's global identity than in the traditional culturally induced way as part of a speaker's local identity. Identification with English, consequently, does not only influence the value of English on a personal level but also affects its value on a societal level.

In global settings, the use of English is not necessarily linked to the speakers' identification with the language. In settings like, for example, the use of English as the medium of communication in business meetings or international—and often multilingual—conferences, the cultural aspects and ideological value of (L1-)English are mostly neglected. However, English, in these settings, alters its speakers' identities when being used as a marketable attribute, realizing the economic layer of its value. Simultaneously, the communicative layer of value is realized when English is used as a communicative practice that is socially shared but independent of any other, momentarily backgrounded, languages. These aspects of the value of English are, however, less based on the speakers' identification with the language but on its relevance and frequency of use. A useful framework to illustrate the languages that are most relevant for a speaker is Aronin and Singleton's (2012) *Dominant Language Constellations* (DLCs).

## 2.2.2 Dominant Language Constellations

Frameworks like the *linguistic repertoire* (see Section 1.3.1) represent a conceptual shift within linguistics. This shift aims at conceptualizing the linguistic means a speaker has access to as singular and inclusive and languages as connected and interwoven rather than separated. Furthermore, the concept might be interpreted as flattening language hierarchies, as it is often used as opposed to "discrete, hierarchically distributed languages" (Lüpke and Storch 2013: 77). However, communicative skills are ranked within a speaker's linguistic repertoire depending on their usefulness and value in specific situations. This hierarchy of value and usefulness might be represented by the concept of DLC. While a linguistic repertoire "can be imagined as the sum or the storage of available language varieties and/or skills, registers and styles and language assets accumulated in one's life," the DLC "denote[s] a group of one's most expedient languages, functioning as an entire unit, and enabling an individual to meet all needs in a multilingual environment" (Aronin 2016: 4). DLCs highlight the understanding of linguistic resources as a unit in the center of various orbits determined by the contexts of use. Like linguistic repertoires, DLCs are indexical, for example, concerning the users' cultural or geographical heritage. However, in contrast to linguistic repertoires, they are flexible enough to instantly reflect sociolinguistic changes in the speaker's life (Aronin and Singleton 2012: 65–6). DLCs reflect a combination of dominant skills or languages that are of the highest value for the individual speaker in a particular space and time. Hence, this value might be ideological, communicative, or economic in nature—or a combination thereof, depending on the reason a language is part of a speaker's DLC, that is, for professional reasons, for religious purposes, or to read a specific book in its original version. The linguistic resources that become less important for the speaker's daily needs remain part of his/her linguistic repertoire but leave the DLC and move to the orbits at the repertoire's periphery. Since the value of a language is determined by the individual speaker's situated needs, all layers of value can be included. The extent of a language's (combined) value is indicated by the positioning of a language on one of the variously distanced orbits. Since speakers' communicative needs are always codependent on their interlocutors' needs and abilities, the number of speakers of a language appears to indirectly influence its value. English as a globally used language might be part of various DLCs primarily for its availability, that is, its communicative and economic value rather than for its ideological value. The concept of DLC allows for an objective assessment of the relative importance and value of the English language for its users without necessarily including any emotionally or culturally laden perspective. However, it is most informative when it illustrates the personal level of the use and value of English and other languages to their speakers. To assess the societal value of English, other frameworks are more fruitful.

## 2.3 Societal Value

Assessing the value of English on a societal level must take a different approach than assessing it on a personal level. First, the frameworks and concepts that the assessment on the personal level is based on, that is, the speaker's identification with English and its frequency of use, can easily be transferred to any other language than English. Second, while societies might differ from one another, many societies share a much stronger focus on the economic and communicative value of English than its ideological value, which is still very important on the personal level of value. Third, social groups of a certain size—or societies—are inherently limited in the pace of their assimilation to given changes. Consequently, the value assigned to English, or any other language, on a societal level is quite stable and not as easily changed as the value on a personal level.

On a societal level, language hierarchies, for example, based on the status of a language as official or unofficial, as well as social class and potential social mobility, determine which languages are more or less valuable than others. English appears to have a somewhat special position in societies as it is often introduced to their members in educational contexts, for example, as the first obligatory foreign language or the medium of instruction.

### 2.3.1 Language Hierarchies

Languages are assigned or ranked in societies more firmly than in global or personal contexts. The language hierarchies introduced in the following represent an approach to assign and determine the value of English on a societal level. However, some, for example, de Swaan's (2001) approach to systematizing languages, has been designed for and can be transferred to a broader global scale. At this point, the introduced hierarchies will be presented from the societal level to discuss their impact on assigning ideological, communicative, and economic value to the English language.

#### *2.3.1.1 De Swaan's Global Language System*

De Swaan (2001) uses the picture of a galaxy or solar system to visualize the different concentric layers languages can belong to. The more central a language the more valuable it is argued to be. As a point of reference for the assessment of a language's value, he chooses to use the languages' communicative potential, thereby going back to the essence of language. He differentiates between four types of languages: *Peripheral languages* are located at the most outside layer of the galaxy and at the bottom of this hierarchy. These are local, often nonstandardized varieties or languages that are used for oral purposes. "They are the languages of conversation and narration rather than reading and writing, of memory and remembrance rather than record" (de Swaan 2001: 4). Together, peripheral languages represent approximately 98 percent of all languages and are used by less than 10 percent of people. *Central languages* occupy the subsequent, more central, position. De Swaan argues that most, if not all, communication between speakers of different peripheral languages is realized through central languages, and he, therefore, groups peripheral languages around each of the approximately one hundred central languages.

Central languages are national and often official languages that are written and used in formal education. In sum, they are used by some 95 percent of the global population (ibid.: 4–5). These languages are the building blocks of nation-states: all people share the official language or languages and might speak a more locally bound language or the language of their ancestors. With the increasing interconnectedness of nations, people became multilingual "by choice" or necessity to communicate across national boundaries or with authorities of any kind. The most common form of educated multilingualism, therefore, is upward oriented. People tend to learn languages spoken by more rather than fewer people, strengthening the hierarchy of languages. Those multilingual speakers of central languages often choose to learn a *supercentral language*. Those languages are spoken internationally and often hold a colonial history and are used in power positions like politics, law, and HE. De Swaan (2001: 5) names Arabic, Chinese, English, French, German, Hindi, Japanese, Malay, Portuguese, Russian, Spanish, and Swahili as current supercentral languages. As he points out, each language, except for Swahili, has more than one hundred million speakers, since every nation relies on at least one of these languages for international communication and negotiations (ibid.). Conclusively, speakers of supercentral languages will learn an even more valuable language to communicate with speakers of other supercentral languages: English. English is the only *hypercentral language*, singled out by its global use (ibid.: 6). English is the most central and most valuable language that is at the heart of the twelve supercentral languages' solar systems. The increase in the value of a language like English can be reconstructed using de Swaan's analogy: English has started as a peripheral language, being spoken only. Following its speakers' history of peaceful or enforced demographic expansion and trade, English became a central language. Furthermore, from the beginning of the twentieth century, the spread of English has been supported by formal education and, therefore, the language has become more closely related to the using nations' politics, economy, and culture. It has become a supercentral language. Some fifty years ago, the expanding globalization and the increasing need for international and intercultural communication and collaboration, among other factors, have led English to become the hypercentral language.

The communicative value of English closely links its societal and global settings of use as the global usefulness of English or any other language—its centrality—often leads to an increased valuation of it on a societal level. This, in turn, causes their introduction into the educational system and a positive connotation toward their acquisition and use in general. This usefulness is reflected primarily by the communicative value, which, following de Swaan, can be measured through a language's communicative potential. In his theorization, he defines the communicative potential of a language by the number of its speakers. He stresses that, although the composition of a particular language's speaker group is altered through migration, it changes more rapidly through language acquisition (ibid.: 25-6). People cannot be kept from learning any language, since language is a free and hypercollective good (see de Swaan 2001: 27-33 for details). Furthermore, the utility, range, and value of a language increase with each additional user. This, likewise, causes others to acquire the language resulting in an uphill helix of value and power. De Swaan (2001: 33) uses the notion of *Q-value* to refer to the communication potential of a language and the resulting attractiveness of a language to a potential language learner. To determine the Q-value of a language, he incorporates its prevalence and centrality: its prevalence reflects "the proportion of speakers ... in the overall language constellation," and its centrality is its connectedness with other languages via the share of multilingual speakers within its prevalence (ibid.). Together, prevalence and centrality compose a language's Q-value by reflecting potential instances of use in a certain constellation. In addition to individual languages, this combination of prevalence and centrality can also be used to identify the Q-value of linguistic repertoires—to determine how useful certain combinations of languages are in a certain linguistic environment (ibid.: 35-6). From a global perspective, English appears to have the highest mean value as it has the highest number of competent users, native or non-native. Furthermore, there are few scenarios in which the acquisition of English is not useful and many in which it is most useful, since it is globally connected to languages of all types. It offers the widest range and highest potential of communication and is, therefore, very attractive for language learners to invest in. While he refers to specific constellations and specific speakers, de Swaan also describes languages from a universal and global perspective, centering the communicative layer of value. However, this communicative value of English is often linked to its economic value, especially in a local context, and when compared to other local languages. In these settings, it might differ considerably from its high global value. To comprehensively understand the language hierarchy on a societal level, the unique local dynamics need to be considered. In the following, the island of Cyprus will be used as an example whenever a specific society has to be referred to.

## 2.3.1.2 Piller's Language Hierarchy

Piller (2016) has developed a local language pyramid to reflect the relation between private and public language use since the usefulness and prestige of languages might vary in these contexts. To describe the local use of languages, Piller differentiates between three types of languages used in a local setting: *home languages, public but unofficial languages,* and *public and official languages* (2016: 16). Home languages are used solely within the speakers' households. Those languages might also be called *heritage languages* and have the potential to reflect a population's diversity. They are the highest in number in a given society but often the lowest in prestige and value. Home languages form the bottom layer of the local language pyramid. The subsequent layer holds public but unofficial languages. Those languages are "languages that can be heard on the street and languages that are visible in public space, such as on commercial signage" (ibid.). These languages are often connected to the respective society for historical or economic reasons. Public and official languages "that are used on official signage (e.g. street names, directional signs to public institutions such as schools or train station) and that are used in education and bureaucratic communication" (ibid.) occupy the top layer.

As in de Swaan's (2001) global language system, languages can be assigned to more than one layer of the pyramid, reflecting the range of their use. A home language, therefore, might also be a public and official or public but unofficial language and carry ideological, communicative, and economic value. It bears mentioning that Piller used Auburn, a suburb of Sydney, Australia, as the basis of her model. Australia is considered an inner circle country with native use of English and, consequently, English holds a superordinate position a priori especially when the ideological value of English is concerned. To understand the uniqueness of the English language's global reach and importance, a country with traditional non-native use, and, consequently, assigning less ideological value to English, should serve as an example. To effectively visualize the global influence of English in traditional non-native countries the local language pyramid offers a valuable blueprint but also should be modified, as English might not be part of the top layer but, is nonetheless, highest valued. In the following, the Mediterranean island of Cyprus will serve as an example of a traditional non-native English-speaking country (for a detailed presentation of Cyprus see Sections 3.2–3.5).

The value of English differs in each part of Cyprus respectively and should be assessed individually. English serves as a home and public but unofficial language in both parts—the Republic of Cyprus (RoC) and the Turkish Republic of Northern Cyprus (TRNC). British Cypriots often returned to Cyprus with their children, after having migrated to the UK during the island's time under British rule. They bring English as a home language to their respective ethnic group of origin in (Northern) Cyprus. Furthermore, English, like in many other countries, is used in public conversations, advertisements, and tourism. While in the TRNC, English is accepted in public use, its value decreases when used as a home language by British Turkish Cypriots. Apparently, since the language of the household is most closely connected to the cultural and historical origin of the users, using English is perceived as a sign of dissociation (Excerpt 4a). However, a decrease in value from its public to its private use does not seem to occur in the RoC (receptionist at Tsialis Hotel, Larnaca, RoC, personal communication, March 14, 2017). Remarkable is the use of English on official signage, like road signs, although it is not one of the official languages of Cyprus. This use is partly a remnant from British colonization; partly it reflects the current importance of the English language. In the RoC, the official public use of English has been continued and caters to international visitors, who arrive multitudinously due to, for example, the simplified mobility across EU member states. While the RoC is closely connected to other European countries, since the Turkish invasion in 1974 the TRNC is highly dependent on Turkey and rather isolated from the remaining countries in Europe. Hence, the former dominator Britain has lost its power and, as a result, the TRNC should have abandoned its language in official displays. The fact that it continues to use the English language on official signage reflects the global rather than the local value of English. Therefore, the value of English can only be assessed when incorporating global and local contexts.

### *2.3.1.3 Bourdieu's Symbolic Economy—English as Capital*

For a comprehensive understanding of the value of English in a global context, the different senses of value—sociological, economic, and linguistic—need to be considered. De Swaan (2001) and Piller (2016) base their hierarchies mainly on the sociological and partially on the linguistic value of a language. However, Bourdieu (1977, 1986, 1991) bases the value of a language on its economic worth. In his framework, like in Piller's local language hierarchy, the context of a language is elementary. The value of any language or other entity is, in almost all cases, context-dependent. For English, for example, its linguistic value is stable; the sociological and economic value, however, differs from context to context, society to society, or even from speaker to speaker (Botsis 2018; Bourdieu

1991; Heller and Duchêne 2016). In sociolinguistics, the notion of *linguistic markets* has been used since the linguistic turn to refer to the "exchange" of language in diverse contexts and to link the concept of value to those language exchanges (see Kelly-Holmes 2016 for a short theorization of the linguistic market). Bourdieu (1991) used the concept of linguistic market to interrelate power, language ideologies, and language use from an economic perspective. He perceives economics as being the foundation of everything and claims that the economic perspective has been neglected in linguistics because it perceives "language as an object of contemplation rather than as an instrument of action and power" (Bourdieu 1991: 37).

Bourdieu's take on value is that it is created through and developed by various types of capital that might be material or symbolic in nature (1986: 21). Since capital can be symbolic or material—it can be sign-based or concrete—it can be part of the material or symbolic economy. He distinguishes between three types of capital—*economic capital, cultural capital,* and *social capital*. Economic capital is the only form of capital that is part of the material economy since it refers to material wealth and exists physically. It is "immediately and directly convertible into money" and might be institutionalized as buildings, gold, or even only property rights (Bourdieu 1986: 16). Social capital and cultural capital, on the contrary, are part of what Bourdieu calls the symbolic economy. Social capital is determined by people's membership in social networks or groups, for example, social class or heritage—it is "made up of social obligations ('connections')" (ibid.). Cultural capital is determined by cultural practice and "can exist in three forms: in the *embodied* state, i.e., in the form of long-lasting dispositions of the mind and body; in the *objectified* state, in the form of cultural goods (pictures, books, dictionaries, instruments, machines, etc.) …; and in the *institutionalized* state" (Bourdieu 1986: 17), that is, academic qualifications. Language can be part of a user's social capital since it might, for instance, be a sign of belonging to a specific social class (for social variability in language, see, e.g., Labov's 1966 New York study; on social class cf. Section 2.4.2). However, for Bourdieu (1986: 20, 1991: 61) it is at the heart of the cultural capital since it serves, for example, as the transmitter and reflector of education or cultural practice.

Bourdieu (1986, 1991) argues that capital can be converted from one form to another within a specific field or market—under certain conditions immaterial capital can be represented by or converted into material capital and vice versa. In other words, cultural capital and social capital can be converted into economic capital. This convertibility reflects and allows for a comprehensive description of the conversion of language into economic capital. The exact conversion of the symbolic value of language into economic, and hence material, capital appears to be defined in the context of specific conditions—specific markets. The value of a specific language—within a specific market—might even be depicted by a stable conversion rate between symbolic and material capital (Bourdieu 1986: 21). A devalued language would be reflected by an unbalanced conversion rate of symbolic and economic capital, and a highly valued language by a rather balanced conversion rate. In Bourdieu's framework, economic capital is "at the root of all the other types of capital and … these transformed, disguised forms of capital … conceal the fact that economic capital is at their root" (ibid.: 24). He advocates that

> linguistic exchange … is also an economic exchange which is established within a particular symbolic relation of power between a producer, endowed with a certain linguistic capital, and a consumer (or a market), and which is capable of producing a certain material or symbolic profit. (Bourdieu 1991: 66)

The value of a language in a certain context is determined by power, which is most often realized in the form of money. The value or price of a language depends on the context it is used in. Bourdieu refers to those contexts of use as *fields* (1986, 1991). "A field is an ideologically structured system reinforcing the forms of capital beneficial to the preservation of that field" (Botsis 2018: 42). The value of a language, therefore, is not fixed. It differs on a macro level, so between fields, and on a micro level, meaning within a field over time. The difference in the value of English between fields in Cyprus might be evident in the fact that English is less valued in private contexts than in educational ones and on the (global) job market. However, because of the gatekeeper function of the English language to this job market, the value of the language also rises in educational contexts. Although only the public value of English appears to be changing, people are willing to invest private resources, such as money and time, for good—meaning English as the medium of instruction (EMI)—education. This illustration shows more than the different valuations of English in various fields—it shows the interrelatedness of value across fields. The valorization of English in professional life influences the value, and therefore use, of English in the field of higher education. This interconnectedness, furthermore, affects the development of value within a specific field—English became more valuable in HE because of the increasing demand on the job market. The understanding of fields as "reinforcing the forms of capital beneficial to [their] preservation" (ibid.) relates them to the notion of power. The powerful will preserve their power by assigning value in a way that supports and stabilizes their social and economic positions—their power. The value of the linguistic capital—or linguistic competence—of a speaker, therefore, depends on the benchmark implemented by the members of the most powerful group since they define the field's underlying paradigm. Linguistic resources, as symbolic capital, "acquire a value of their own and become sources of power and prestige in their own right" (Heller 1994: 7). The fact that English is increasingly valued, and hence used, in the field of HE reflects its benefit for this field to maintain its power. As power equals the summation of various forms of capital, the value of English must bring capital to the field of higher education. As Bourdieu's capital is, at its root, always economic, and consequently directly translatable into money, the value of English is essentially monetary. When applied to the context of Cyprus, the use of English is irrevocably interwoven with the economy in both parts of the island. Bourdieu's theoretical framework offers guidance for a specific understanding of the value of English in Cyprus since it enables a description of power relations based on the value of language.

## 2.3.2 Social Mobility and Social Class

Social structures are often expressed via social class, which is only one axis of the prevalent societal division into subgroups. People are labeled and differentiated in terms of, for instance, gender, race, religion, nationality, and social class. All these categorizations differentiate people and function as identity dimensions (Block 2015: 3). In addition to gender and race, social class is a major operator of separation and hierarchization and essential for the production of social power relations (Kergoat 2010: 63–5). It is relational, constructed via the comparison of social actors (Wright 2015: 33). "Social class is a multi-dimensional construct [and] classes are not merely economic phenomena but are also profoundly concerned with forms of social reproduction and cultural distinction" (Savage et al. 2013: 223). Block names eleven key dimensions of social class, including property, wealth, occupation, education, symbolic behavior, mobility, and life chances (2015: 3). In these dimensions, a clear shift from the Marxist view of labor-based class divisions toward a social stratification based on prestige, status, and different capital is reflected (cf. Leung 2017: 2707). While all these dimensions interdepend and correlate, two are of special importance in this study: education and mobility.

Education is one of the most valuable forms of cultural capital (Bourdieu 1986, cf. Section 2.3.1.3) and often serves as the foundation for the accumulation of other forms of capital, potentially leading to social advancement (Leung

2017: 2708; Waters 2006b). Due to the advancement of globalization, education is increasingly interwoven with human mobility. (Higher) education becomes increasingly inclusive, as it is no longer offered exclusively to the elites (Marginson 2018). Due to this inclusivity, the (higher) education itself is no longer the prestigious factor. Instead, the institution and its location are decisive for the social recognition of a person's educational achievements, which requires geographical human mobility (cf. Section 2.4). As "class has been found to be an important factor in determining who is able to move, made to move, how one moves, where to, how far s/he manages to get to and how her/his migration experience will unfold" (Leung 2017: 2706), people in more privileged positions have more of this mobility (e.g., Brooks and Waters 2009; Waters 2006a; Waters and Brooks 2010 on student mobility). In addition to human geographical mobility, education is also decisive for social mobility—a person's change between levels in a social system (cf. Iversen, Krishna, and Sen 2017; Jöns, Heffernan, and Meusburger 2017). The privileges of high social status or class—"the unearned benefits of socially dominant groups" (Piller 2016: 208)—enable geographical mobility for education, which, in turn, is supposed to result in upward social mobility; this education is supposed to represent the pathway to becoming a member of the "global elite" (cf. Mazlish and Morss 2005; Sklair 2001). However, while social mobility is usually directed upward, it is potentially bidirectional and contradictory at the same time.

Mobility is "a process through which class and other social positions and identities … are negotiated in an on-going manner" (Leung 2017: 2705). While the possession of certain capital, for instance, a certain education or language use, might lead to access to a higher social class in one context, it might not change the social position, or even decrease it, in another context. This is especially true for mobility from the Global South to the Global North (ibid.: 2714), leading to a contradiction of the mobility trajectories (Parreñas 2001)—while the financial status might increase in the new environment, the social status decreases (cf. Leung 2017 on Asian scholars in the Global North). This decrease is referred to as downward social mobility (see, e.g., Leung 2017 about academic mobility, Legewie and Bohmann 2018 about gender (in)equality, and Ponzo 2018 about socioeconomic mobility).

One aspect of the value of English is its potential for upward social mobility through education. The initial social positioning of a speaker might be bypassed utilizing linguistic proficiency and the associated linguistic privilege. This, in turn, might enable access to another social class—upward social mobility—and ensures the characteristic further increase of social privilege, since this increase is an ideology-based result assimilating to the social hierarchy. A certain way of using language is indicative of a speaker's membership to a certain social class and reflects privilege in class dimensions. As mentioned before, language ideologies represent the interests of the members of certain, primarily high-level, social groups (Piller 2015: 4) and, therefore, reflect social division and power relations within society. This ideological representation of biased and unilateral interests also leads to the reproduction of those social inequalities and ensures the maintenance of the present privilege distribution as they favor the gainers. Language, being indexical of social structures, holds especially true in its spoken form—it is always a reflection of its user and receiver as well as the social conditions of its use (Bourdieu 1991: 67). Privileges associated with the gainers in these social structures often remain hidden to those who benefit from it: white privilege is mainly experienced by people of color, male privilege by women, and linguistic privilege by non-native or less proficient speakers of a dominant language. Due to its historical and current powerful origins, the English language cannot ever be separated from power and privilege adding to its ideological value as represented in social structures. The extent of these privileges is, again, mainly experienced by those who are not included.

On a societal and global level, the dividing properties of the global use of the English language appear to be camouflaged to a point that might leave them unnoticed by the affected users. The ideological domination of English in the global social fabric is subliminally accepted and universally practiced. Occasionally, it is discussed and questioned (see LaDousa 2014; Vandrick 2014); however, it assists in maintaining and even strengthens the existing social hierarchy. The supremacy of English appears to be a self-fulfilling prophecy: the more English is perceived as reflecting education and power, as international and beneficial, to name just a few connotations, the more it is used on the societal and global level. The more it is used, the more it is perceived and accepted as the language of education and power, as international and beneficial. This is not an entirely smooth process, as ideologies are always coexisting and competing in any form of society. The language used by a speaker reflects his/her social, economic, and ideological belonging, along with the associated privilege and power. The ideological value of a language, and the economic value that results from it through power and privilege, depends on the social structures it is used in. However, English is often connected to members of higher social classes with economic power. Therefore, the economic power of this class is transferred onto English increasing the language's economic value. Furthermore, the extensive use of English increases the language's communicative value, especially on a global level.

## 2.4 Global Value

The English language is unique on a global scale. No language is more important in our globalized and interconnected world than the English language, and no language is currently more valuable. The global use and spread of English is another self-fulfilling prophecy: The more people use it, the more people invest in learning it and vice versa. While the ideological value of English decreases on the global scale, its communicative value increases and takes a central position. The communicative value of English is one of the reasons to introduce the language as a—often obligatory—foreign language into educational systems, expanding and manifesting its globally shared use. This shared use, furthermore, not only enables mobility and connectedness but also multiplies potential areas of social injustice.

### 2.4.1 Globalization and Mobility

The advancement of globalization—the increasing international connectedness and the extensive use and spread of English—supports and facilitates mobility, for example, in the fields of HE, tourism, and employment. The use of English in global HE is no longer remarkable but a global common denominator—something that equalizes countries and people and which can be used as a tool of their emancipation. Implementing the use of English might aim at universities' internationalization—the increasing mobility of students and faculty as well as the increasing ease of research collaboration—as well as their globalization—the commodification of HE as a neoliberal product and the resulting income (cf. van der Walt 2013: 3 for her definitions of each term). In both contexts, English attracts mobility more than any other language while ideologically signaling high-quality education for public and private institutions (Lasagabaster 2015: 266). The maintenance of this ideology is "of the utmost importance" (Holborow 2013: 267), because it results in an easier-to-meet requirement—language choice instead of quality education—for the university to be attractive for prospective students. Especially private universities, which cannot sustain themselves through government funding, have to attract paying students (Holborow 2013: 233). This attraction might follow a direct approach, for example, through advertisement, or an indirect one, for example, via a university's high position in international university rankings. The implementation of English and the offer of EMI programs are decisive factors in both approaches to increase universities' attractiveness, especially for international students. Following Knight (2012: 4), mobility within the area of HE developed into three generations. Broadly summarized, the first generation of mobility in HE aims at human mobility, that is, students move to foreign countries for educational purposes. The second generation focuses on institutional mobility, that is, the transfer of study programs or institutions to foreign grounds, for example, by opening branch campuses. The third generation incorporates both types of mobility by aiming at education hubs, that is, the movement of students, researchers, institutions, and/or study programs to certain countries to concentrate and agglomerate knowledge and research. While the first two potentially increase internationalization, that is, global connectedness, the latter form of mobility creates focal points of HE, which individual universities or countries with fewer opportunities to focus on HE cannot compete with.

Globalization and mobility convene in HE contexts, like in Cyprus. This link is often created through the implementation of English as the language of communication and teaching. The value of English in these contexts, however, is not limited to its communicative potential but constitutes a combination of its three layers. In some cases, the English language holds ideological value, either as being used in one of its traditional homes, that is, the UK, the United States, and so on, or as being used in a rightful setting, that is, postcolonial countries that used to be "English-speaking." The recognition and appreciation of the ideological value of English are shared and transferred due to globalization and result in mobility toward these "rightful" contexts, especially but not exclusively by (prospective) students. In addition to the ideological value of English in HE, the language holds communicative value due to its shared use. Therefore, universities use the language to transport knowledge, to increase the graduates' employability in local and global job markets, and to attract international academics and students (see Lasagabaster 2015: 265–6). The communicative value is, due to globalization and internationalization, increasingly independent of the geographical location of the university but an essential prerequisite for global (student) mobility. While this mobility is mostly based on the communicative value of English, it is often accompanied by an economic profit for the institutions when high-paying international students are attracted. This adds economic value to English, utilized through EMI education resembling a possibility "to seize part of the major English-speaking countries' market share of international students" (Lasagabaster 2015: 265). Global mobility is essential for some HE landscapes to persevere, as they depend on the economic power of international students. Cyprus, for example, is the only southern European country that offers a comparable degree of English use and number of EMI programs to northern European countries (ibid.: 266), having built markets of HE based on the value of English and global student mobility. In contrast to the ideological value, the communicative and economic value of English is utilizable in (almost) all contexts of globalized HE. Whether the economic or communicative value of English is targeted, its respective counterpart is always brought along, since both are (almost) inseparable in settings of globalization.

Human mobility is essential in a globalized world, especially for HE economies as it provides for a constant current of incoming international students (see, e.g., Brooks and Waters 2011; Findlay et al. 2012; Holloway, O'Hara, and Pimott-Wilson 2012; Leung 2017; and Waters 2012 on student mobility). Often, a tendency of movement from the Global South to the Global North exists, as international students move "northward" to improve their economic and social position (cf., e.g., Odeh 2010 on economic differentiation of Global South and Global North; Almeida 2020; Gürüz 2011; Hertz et al. 2007; Jalan and Murgai 2008; Shkoler and Rabenu 2020 on mobility in education). Inhabitants of the economically weaker Global South aim for the economically more developed Global North (see, e.g., Khattab and Mahmud 2018; Odeh 2010). This movement of people, however, is based on the use of English as it is the only linguistic resource shared by all involved parties. English, as an international language of communication rather than the standardized language of (a) certain people, functions as an equalizer of these students. Unfortunately, this is no more than a surface function since its use is often evaluated based on well-known neoliberal factors—power, prestige, and, ultimately, money. Mobility, however, is not always related to (higher) education.

Similar to educationally motivated mobility, mobility for touristic reasons mostly holds positive connotations. However, when mobility is initiated by economic or employment reasons, it is perceived as a double-edged sword. Mobility is not always a privilege—the privilege of choosing to be (im)mobile—but a necessity or compulsion. Since mobility on a global level is most strongly increased and eased by the English language, certain groups of people might feel they must speak English to survive or succeed in their local markets. Other groups might choose to speak it to increase their mobility and communicative reach and still others might have the privilege of choosing to not use English at all. Therefore, English does not offer the same benefits for each of its speakers but reproduces locally rooted social stratification on a global level.

## 2.4.2 Language and Social Injustice

English has become the most widely used language of our time (Park 2009: 16). This might appear as if the spread of English has been "the people's choice." However, its spread reflects the interests and ideologies of members of powerful classes and, therefore, imposes a certain social structure. The often-assigned property of ideologies to sustain asymmetrical power relations, that is, to maintain domination (e.g., Thompson 1984: 4), results in an ostensible validity and invariability of those social inequalities. Social inequalities are always copied to language use, which then can cause economic and linguistic inequality. While powerful and privileged members of society can choose English—or not choose it —less powerful members might not have this choice, either through not having access to English or through not being able to afford not to learn it as English would add value to them. When examining the relation of English and social injustice, the value of the English language itself as well as the value it adds to its speakers and other commodities should be considered since both aspects are essential for the global roles of English. As Heller shows, languages can be commodified in two different ways: as a skill and as a sign of authenticity (2010: 102). Both of these ways are based on the ideological or communicative value of English while, at the same time, constructing all three layers of value on a global level. However, the global inequality reproduced by English language use and its valuation is essentially economic, as social and ideological inequality are displayed by economic means (for a detailed investigation of the relation between economic means and linguistic resources from an economic perspective, see, e.g., Grin 2014 on language economics).

As mentioned previously, the high valuation of English might be perceived as a self-fulfilling prophecy: the English language is valued because of its influence that, in return, affects its valuation. Following Grin's (2014) take on language economics, the economic underpinnings of social class represent one way of investigating the causal direction from economic variables to linguistic resources. Language use reflects not only its speakers' identities and their position in a social environment but also the prevailing language ideologies that highlight or blur social differentiation (Piller 2015: 5). In so doing, they influence the construction of communities and relations of power (Park 2009: 14–15). In other words, language ideologies are a crucial aspect of the creation and reproduction of social class and, therefore, social inequality. The use of English by people of high social status and economic power might, for example, lead to a valuation of their specific realization or variety of English, which is independent of its conformity with native or standardized use in this specific context or market. As Park points out, "There is no reason to think that any kind of linguistic variable should inherently be associated with a particular social variable" (2009: 14). Therefore, the particular relation between language and social group—and consequently social injustice—needs to derive from speaker interpretations rather than language features (see, e.g., Eckert 2000; Irvine 2018; Woolard 1998).

Social injustice can interrelate with the English language on multiple axes. One might be the discrepancy of power over the linguistic properties of English between native and non-native speakers. Another might be the varying potential of English for social or economic advancement for speakers who are more or less privileged. The native speakers' assumed ownership of English serves as both evidence of their legitimate use of English as a Native Language (ENL), which results in its high ideological value, and their license to share it ad libitum—as seen fit. ENL appears to be more valuable than any other of its "reproductions" due to the legitimation of its speakers and the understanding of ENL being the historical source of any other variety of English. Therefore, traditional native speakers are often believed to have more power over English—even when used in global contexts—than any other users. The high value of ENL is not only ideological, that is, its acquisition is most desired and invested in by non-native speakers, but also economic. The values of other realizations of English are less stable and depend on their contexts of use. More fruitful than focusing on artificial constructs like standardized language use or distinct language varieties, however, might be a focus on English speakers. Therefore, three examples of potential compositions of the value of English for different speakers of English are presented below.

The first scenario is visualized in Figure 2.1. The speaker is British, living and working in the UK, and English is her only language. On a personal level, the ideological value of English is dominant, since she identifies only with the English language and the "British" culture. Since she is monolingual and her life develops within an English-speaking context, the language holds also communicative and economic value for her. However, on a personal level, the language does not tend to represent economic or communicative opportunities for a speaker like this. The value of English is increased by its value in societal contexts. Especially the economic and ideological value of English is cherished on this level, since (1) the UK is the traditional and ideological home of English and, (2) therefore, British

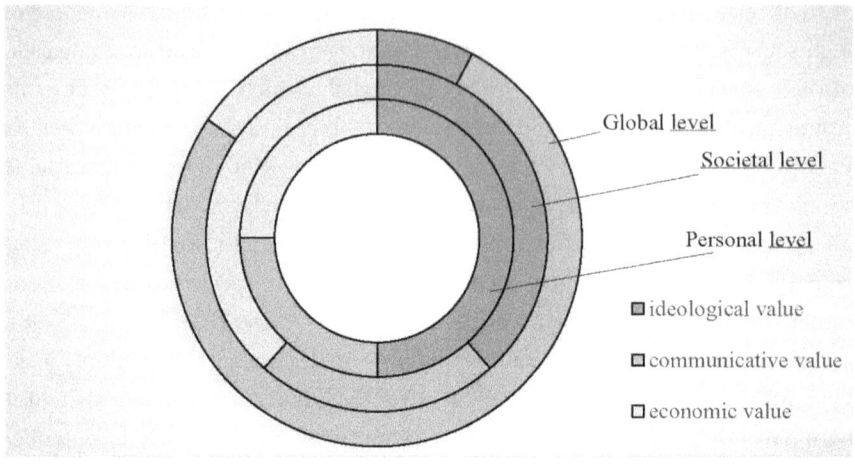

**Figure 2.1** The value of English (ENL speaker).

ENL is a commodity of high demand. For this speaker, the value of English on a global level might be primarily communicative, especially, if the speaker is not dependent on the language in her professional life but leaves her home country primarily for vocational purposes.

The second scenario is represented in Figure 2.2. This speaker shall be a monolingual speaker of another language than English, living and working in the Global North. This speaker could be characterized as an "EFL-speaker" for whom English is not the most valued language. He learned English in school, but the language is rarely used in his everyday life. Consequently, on a personal level, the value of English is mainly communicative for this speaker. He enjoys watching videos online in English and playing video games with their original (English) sound. In his society, English is primarily used for international and political communication and, thereby, brings along economic profit, that is, trade agreements with other nations, and so on. Since "British English" is taught in school, some ideological value of English on the societal level is added to his composition. The global value of English, for him, is also mainly communicative as it, for example, enables communication with locals during holidays and ordering goods from abroad.

The last example is a bilingual speaker of English and another language who has been born in the Global South, as shown in Figure 2.3. She identifies with English only to a certain extent, since the language she is culturally connected to more closely is her other first language. For her, English has been brought to her country as part of colonization and is not the "native" language. On a personal level, the ideological value of English is, therefore, less important

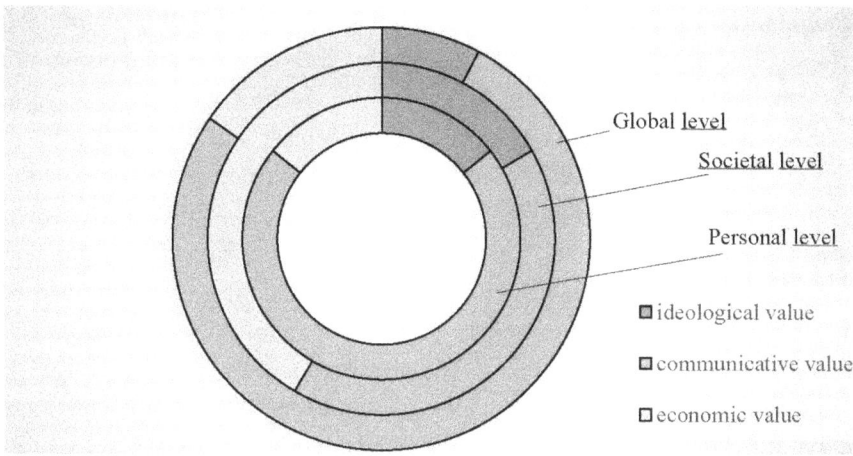

**Figure 2.2** The value of English (EFL speaker).

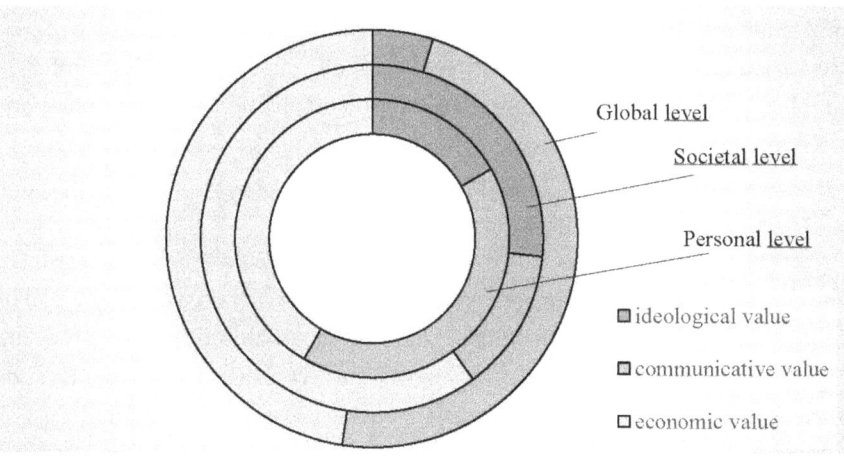

**Figure 2.3** The value of English (ESL speaker).

than the communicative and economic value; from her perspective, she has to speak English to find adequate employment. On a societal level, ideological and economic value is added to English. The ideological value of English is reflected, for example, by the people in the respective society officially claiming native speaker status as speakers of English as a Second Language (ESL). Economic value is added via trade with or support by other social groups or countries. While in bigger social groups, English might serve as a unifying language of communication, in smaller social groups it is often not used for everyday communication. On a global level, the economic value of English is predominant, as speaking English offers social and economic advancement in another country, for example, in the Global North.

Although these distributions of value are exemplary and simplified in many aspects, they show that the value of English is speaker-dependent and that the composition of this value might be more or less complex and is likely to vary, depending on, for example, the speaker's interests, the size of the dominant social groups, and the speaker's current life situation. However, as long as they are the solitary legitimate owners of English, monolingual native speakers of English are the custodians of an infinite globally requested resource as well as the gatekeepers of its access. Although the native speakers' authority is increasingly questioned and challenged, for example, in the English as a Lingua Franca (ELF) movement (see Section 1.3.2), for the time being, it persists. The shift in the composition of value for speakers in the Global North compared to speakers in the Global South from being primarily ideological to becoming predominantly economic reflects how English reproduces existing global inequalities between the various speaker groups. As discussed earlier, the use of English can initialize mobility and grant access to different, and potentially higher, social circles. For users of English who are less privileged on a societal level, the language can serve as an enabler of social and economic advancement in local settings. This also holds for, on a societal level, more privileged users of English and might, furthermore, be reproduced in international contexts. For English users from the Global North, there is less difference between the advancement potential of English in national or international contexts. For privileged speakers from the Global South, the use of English in international contexts and outside local or national markets might cause downward social mobility (cf. Section 4.3.3), as the value of their use of English might be lower in international than in local contexts. English, therefore, is not necessarily a useful enabler and equalizer but might be used as a reason to reproduce colonial power structures.

## 2.5 Summary

In this chapter, the value of English has been assessed on three levels of its use: the personal, the societal, and the global level. For each of these levels, concepts and frameworks have been presented that might be useful when investigating the value of language in general and English specifically on the respective levels of use. Furthermore, it has been shown that the value of English always constitutes a combination of ideological, communicative, and economic value, while the significance and impact of each of these values is highly context- and speaker-dependent. On a personal level, the value of English for a speaker might be assessed through his/her identification with the language and the language's importance in the speaker's everyday life. On this level, the value of English is often mainly ideological or communicative and can change comparatively simply, for example, if the life situation of the speaker changes, that is, through migration or change in employment. On a societal level, the value of English is more stable and not as easily changed. Language and speaker hierarchies that are implemented in the social or political structures of a society influence or even determine the value of English for an individual speaker within this level of use. Furthermore, the speakers' social position within these structures might determine their access to English. On a societal level, the value of English tends to be primarily communicative and economic. On a global level, the value of English has been shown to be closely linked to its speakers' mobility. Speaking English is often chosen to facilitate mobility but rarely offers equal opportunities and possibilities for all of its speakers. Now that a comprehensive conceptualization of the value of English has been introduced, the settings of its first implementation are presented in the next chapter.

# 3

# Cyprus: A Case Study

## 3.1 Introduction

After the theoretical underpinnings of conceptualizing the value of English have been discussed, this chapter will introduce the island of Cyprus as a possible setting for its application. The uniqueness and fruitfulness of a value-based assessment of English roots in its flexibility and its potential to depict complex and changing compositions of the language's value in various contexts. Cyprus's higher education (HE) landscape is such a complex context of English use. In this chapter, the politically and linguistically turbulent history of the divided island as well as the economies and HE sectors of each of its parts will be presented. It will become clear that the use of English in Cyprus's HE cannot be depicted by any of the prevailing models of English without neglecting the sometimes diverging motives of the involved social groups. Furthermore, the methodological considerations of assessing the value of English in Cyprus's HE landscape will be introduced. While the assessment of value, and consequently the following study, must take a qualitative focus, relevant findings from the study's quantitative assessment of the participants' language use and attitudes will be depicted at the end of this chapter.

## 3.2 Cyprus in the Global South–Global North Trajectory

The island of Cyprus covers an area of 9,251 square kilometers and is the third-largest island in the Mediterranean Sea, following Sicily and Sardinia. It is located at the intersection of Europe, Asia, and Africa, at the eastern edge of the Mediterranean (Hadjioannou, Tsiplakou, and Kappler 2011: 503; Ker-Lindsay 2011: 1; Poew 2007: 9; Tsiplakou 2006: 337). Its neighboring countries are Turkey, Syria, Lebanon, Israel, Egypt, and Greece, which locate Cyprus at the edge of the Global North and in immediate proximity to the Global South. In 2018, the estimated population on the island of Cyprus was 1,250,000 people, 372,500 of whom are located in the Turkish Republic of Northern Cyprus (TRNC) and 876,000 in the Republic of Cyprus (RoC) (CYSTAT 2019; State Planning Organization 2020).

The two main ethnic groups native to the island are Greek Cypriots and Turkish Cypriots, speaking Cypriot Greek and Cypriot Turkish, respectively. In 1960, at the last census that covered both parts of the island, Cyprus's population was composed of 77–78 percent Greek Cypriots and 18 percent Turkish Cypriots. In 2016, the RoC's Statistical Service estimated a division into 74.6 percent Greek Cypriots and 9.2 percent Turkish Cypriots (CYSTAT 2017b: 11; Ker-Lindsay 2011: 2). The numbers provided by the RoC's Statistical Service do, however, exclude "illegal settlers from Turkey" (CYSTAT 2017b: 11), which are estimated to represent 20 percent of the population in 2016 (ibid.; State Planning Organization 2018). In 1960, the remaining 4–5 percent of the population was represented by the three constitutionally recognized groups at the time of the census, namely Armenians, Maronites, and Latins, as well as an unrecognized Roma community (Ker-Lindsay 2011: 8). Nowadays, in addition to these four minorities, several other communities are at home in Cyprus, resulting in 18.1 percent of foreign residents in 2019 (CYSTAT 2020a: 4). As a consequence of Cyprus's history, Greek, Turkish, and British citizens, along with their respective languages, are well represented in Cyprus. Immigrants, guest workers, or foreign students from Russia, Serbia, Sri Lanka, the Philippines, Poland, Hungary, and other countries make up further communities (Ker-Lindsay 2011: 8). Because of its location, "Cyprus has become a hub for illegal immigrants seeking to enter the EU" (ibid.) since its entrance into the European Union (EU). In addition to immigration, the history of Cyprus is the foundation of its emergence as a diverse and multilingual island.

### 3.2.1 Cyprus under British Rule

Due to its strategically valuable location at the intersection of the Global North and the Global South—Europe, Asia, and Africa—Cyprus has been interesting for and ruled by various nations and colonial powers (Hadjioannou et al. 2011: 503; Kanelakis 2006: 13–25; Karoulla-Vrikki 2004: 21; Ker-Lindsay 2011: 11–14; Poew 2007: 10–15; Tsiplakou 2006: 337). The British Empire has been the last colonial power that de facto ruled the island from 1878 until its independence in 1960. In 1878, power over Cyprus was offered to the British

Empire by the then ruling Ottoman Empire in exchange for Britain's support against Russian aggressions after the Russo-Turkish War (1877–8). English was introduced to the island by the new ruling class. When the Ottoman Empire sided with Germany in the First World War, the British Empire annexed Cyprus in 1914 (cf. Ker-Lindsay 2011: 14–16; Poew 2007: 14). British rule finally became legal under the terms of the Treaty of Lausanne in 1923, when the Republic of Turkey, as the successor of the Ottoman Empire, officially renounced any claims to Cyprus. In 1925, Cyprus became a crown colony, completing its integration into the British Empire (Ker-Lindsay 2011: 17; Poew 2007: 14) and thereby implementing the English language on the island.

The Greek Cypriots perceived the change of rule in 1878 as the liberation from three hundred years of Ottoman rule and, at the same time, as a helpful development toward *enosis*—the unification with Greece (Buschfeld 2013: 16, 19; Kanelakis 2006: 16–20; Ker-Lindsay 2011: 14–15). This perception reflects the social division and social hierarchy that have been at work in Cyprus all along— the Greek Cypriot majority's restrained acceptance of the Turkish Cypriots as equals. Britain rejected the possibility of a unification with Greece, provoking anti-British sentiment in the Greek Cypriot community, which culminated in violent conflicts in 1931. Britain's previously moderate rule became autocratic and the already existing tensions between the British Empire and the Greek Cypriot population rose. Increasing their control over the Cypriots' language use was only one way in which the British reacted to this rising anti-colonialism movement (cf. Tsiplakou 2009: 76–8). The conflict reached its apex when the Greek Cypriot underground organization Ethniki Organosi Kyprion Agoniston (EOKA—National Organization of Cypriot Fighters) violently led off the fight against the British authorities in 1955 (Kanelakis 2006: 20–5, 117; Ker-Lindsay 2011: 17; Poew 2007: 15–18). The Turkish Cypriots first supported the British administration in fighting the EOKA. In 1957, they founded their own violent underground organization—*Voltan*—later restructured and renamed Türk Mukavemet Teskilati (TMT—Turkish Resistance Movement), aiming at *Taksim*—the division of Cyprus (Buschfeld 2013: 16; Kanelakis 2006: 25–8, 118; Ker-Lindsay 2011: 21–2; Poew 2007: 17–18). Although the British administration has always treated the Cypriot population as divided, serious conflicts began to develop between the two groups only during this period of decolonization and fighting for independence, as each group wished for different outcomes.

In the subsequent efforts to pacify the situation in Cyprus, three parties with different interests emerged; while the Greek Cypriot community, supported by Greece, argued in favor of *enosis*, the Turkish Cypriot community, in turn, supported by Turkey, argued against *enosis* and in favor of a division of the island (Buschfeld 2013: 17; Kanelakis 2006: 27–8; Ker-Lindsay 2011: 22–5). Great Britain supported the idea of a partial self-government of Cyprus while wanting to guarantee that both ethnic groups partake in its realization. After rejecting initial potential solutions, the Greek and Turkish governments met in Zurich in January 1959 and agreed on the independence of Cyprus and the division of powers between the two communities. The confirmation of this agreement by Great Britain, known as the Zurich-London Agreement, led to the independence of Cyprus in 1960 (Buschfeld 2013: 17–18; Kanelakis 2006: 28–9; Ker-Lindsay 2011: 25; Poew 2007: 19–20). This change of power naturally brought along a change of prestige and use of language. During British rule, English was the ruling class's language and was used as a lingua franca. Therefore, as it is common in colonized contexts, it was more prestigious than the local languages. Since language is a crucial aspect of identity (see, e.g., Pavlenko and Blackledge 2004 on the complexity of the relation between language and identity, cf. Section 2.2.1), the adjustment of the value of the languages used in Cyprus reflected a changing identity of its citizens. Crucially, it diminished English and expressed both communities' closeness to their so-called motherlands Greece and Turkey rather than reflecting an independent and united Cypriot identity.

### 3.2.2 Independence, Division, and Status Quo

On August 16, 1960, the RoC officially came into existence. Although Cyprus, from this point on, was to be ruled by Greek and Turkish Cypriots concertedly, Britain, Greece, and Turkey functioned as guarantor powers under the Treaty of Guarantee (Kanelakis 2006: 30; Ker-Lindsay 2011: 25; Poew 2007: 17–18). Firstly, the explicit involvement of both communities as disjoint groups was also specified in Cyprus's Constitution and aimed at preventing the influence of the smaller Turkish Cypriot community from being bypassed by the much larger Greek Cypriot community (for details on the exact division of powers in the Constitution of Cyprus see Kanelakis 2006: 30–3; Ker-Lindsay 2011: 25–8; Poew 2007: 20–2). Secondly, the continued influence of Britain, Greece, and Turkey in Cyprus was established. This influence was enforced in the Treaty of Alliance that allows Greece and Turkey "to maintain small military contingents on the island" (Ker-Lindsay: 2011: 28; cf. Treaty of Alliance 1960: Article IV), and the Treaty of Establishment adjudicated the two sovereign base areas, Dhekelia and Akrotiri, to the UK and thus consolidated the continued use of the English language on the island (cf. Treaty concerning the Establishment of the Republic of Cyprus 1960: 10). This substantial involvement of Britain, Greece, and Turkey was perceived as limiting the independence and sovereignty of Cyprus; the Greek Cypriots were especially reluctant because, along with their obligation to protect the independence of Cyprus, the guarantor powers received the right to intervene in case this independence was challenged on an intra- or international level (Ker-Lindsay 2011: 27), which impeded their wish for *enosis*.

The formation of a government under the agreed-upon Constitution appeared to be difficult and by 1963, all efforts to govern Cyprus mutually had failed, which caused tensions between the two ruling parties to rise. President Makarios's proposal of thirteen constitutional amendments (known as the "13 points") and their following rejection by Turkey are widely recognized as the end of any further efforts to form a constitutional administration (Kanelakis 2006: 33–4; Ker-Lindsay 2011: 30–4; Poew 2007: 22–4). The tension between both groups developed into a violent conflict in December 1963, causing hundreds of casualties on both sides and the escape of the Turkish Cypriots to the north of the island. This caused the geographical and linguistic separation of the two communities and, at the same time, the transfer of all de facto political power to the Greek Cypriot community, as the Turkish Cypriots had abandoned all political positions. Promising talks about a possible reunification resumed only in 1968 when both communities were prepared to compromise (Kanelakis 2006: 33–6; Ker-Lindsay 2011: 34–41; Poew 2007: 24–9). However, after an underground organization of pro-*enosis* Greeks and Greek Cypriots expelled Makarios from Cyprus and occupied his office, from the Turkish Cypriots' perspective, *enosis* became unavoidable (Kanelakis 2006: 36; Ker-Lindsay 2011: 41–2; Poew 2007: 30–2). After the diplomatic efforts undertaken by Turkey to convince Britain of a collective intervention under the Treaty of Guarantee failed, the Turkish military invaded Cyprus on July 20, 1974. Within a few days, Cyprus was divided and the military junta overthrown, enabling the negotiations to resume. However, the second wave of Turkish militia arrived in Cyprus on August 14, 1974, and permanently captured more than one-third of the island (Kanelakis 2006: 37; Ker-Lindsay 2011: 42–4; Poew 2007: 32–5). While the first invasion is argued to have been legal under the Treaty of Guarantee, the second is mostly argued to have been illegal, transgressing international law as well as the Treaty of Guarantee (e.g., Kanelakis 2006: 37–8; Ker-Lindsay 2011: 44–6; Richter 1997: 314–15; for an extensive legal discussion of the topic cf. Poew 2007: 72–82).

As a result of the Turkish invasion, an estimated 160,000 Greek Cypriots and 50,000 Turkish Cypriots were relocated and had to abandon their properties in the respective part of the island. The abandoned land in the North was given to Turkish settlers, who arrived soon afterward (Ker-Lindsay 2011: 47–8), and the Green Line, a demilitarized buffer zone between the two parts that is supervised by the United Nations (UN), was installed. Negotiations regarding a possible reunification started again, this time more seriously, in 1977. Although several agreements were made and published regarding the terms of such a reunification, the Turkish Cypriot administration declared independence on November 15, 1983 (Kanelakis 2006: 39; Ker-Lindsay 2011: 49–51; Poew 2007: 38). The TRNC, as the new state called itself, has been recognized solely by Turkey, while the UN Security Council put a resolution in place prohibiting its recognition (Kanelakis 2006: 43; Ker-Lindsay 2011: 52; Poew 2007: 39–40). While the reasons for this surprising declaration are not clear, it resembled the final separation of the Cypriot population and their languages, thus causing much grief. In the years thereafter, several reunification proposals, plans, and ideas have been developed, all without changing the divide of Cyprus. The most successful so far has been *The Comprehensive Settlement of the Cyprus Problem*, the so-called Annan Plan (United Nations Peacemaker 2004), which aimed at the reunification of Cyprus prior to its entrance into the EU on May 1, 2004 (ibid.; Kanelakis 2006: 43–50; Ker-Lindsay 2011: 61; Poew 2007: 55–6). In April 2004, it caused the first positive and peaceful encounter of Greek Cypriots and Turkish Cypriots in almost thirty years when the Green Line was opened at three checkpoints. However, for various political and emotional reasons, the majority of Turkish Cypriots voted in favor of it and the majority of Greek Cypriot against it when both groups were to vote on the final version of the Annan Plan simultaneously a week before Cyprus was to become a member of the EU (cf. Kanelakis 2006: 50–2; Ker-Lindsay 2011: 64–71; Poew 2007: 186, 205–22 on details of the Annan Plan V). The result of this referendum is widely perceived as a turning point of the international perception of the conflict and led to the stall of further communication (Ker-Lindsay 2011: 71; Kanelakis 2006: 52). Although talks resumed in 2008, the negotiations stalled in 2017, leaving the Cyprus problem unsolved and the island still divided.

Due to the former British rule, Cyprus and the UK still have a strong connection and many Cypriots in both parts of the island have family in the UK. Furthermore, an increasing number of retirees from Great Britain use Cyprus as their winter or primary retirement residence (Hadjioannou et al. 2011: 519). This bond has most likely contributed to the continued use of English by Cypriots, especially in the TRNC.

## 3.3 Languages in Cyprus

Cyprus has always been a multilingual island (Karoulla-Vrikki 2004: 22–3). It is furthermore "home to a complex mixture of different nationalities and ethnic groups" (Ker-Lindsay 2011: 11). During British rule, a small number of languages, namely English, Greek, Turkish, and the local varieties of Greek and Turkish, were predominantly used (Annual Colonial Reports 1937: 4). After the independence of Cyprus in 1960, two official languages, namely Greek and Turkish, were chosen, which were to represent the two major ethnic groups of the island (CYSTAT 2019; Tsiplakou 2009: 78). Migration and geopolitical changes have brought further ethnic groups and their languages to Cyprus, for example, a considerable number of Russians (Karpava, Ringblom, and Zabrodskaja 2018: 117; Ker-Lindsay 2011: 10–11; also Evripidou and Karpava 2016). However, the English language has remained significant, especially in educational, legal, and other official affairs as, for example, all but the Treaty of Alliance have been written in English (Tsiplakou 2009: 78–9, Treaty concerning the Establishment of the Republic of Cyprus 1960, Treaty of Guarantee 1960). While the global market of English appears to be well represented in Cyprus, the true uniqueness of English is its function as a political vehicle language. It ensures communication between the UN and Cyprus and, most importantly, between the two parts of Cyprus, as Cypriot Greek is on its way to extinction in the TRNC (Kappler in Hadjioannou et al. 2011: 536; McEntee-Atalianis and Pouloukas 2001).

### 3.3.1 Language Use, Recognition, and Prestige

Various languages are currently in use in Cyprus. Although they differ in the level of prestige they reflect, each contributes as a dimension of social class and to the construction of identities (Block 2015: 3). The Turkish Cypriots settled in Cyprus during the Ottoman rule (1571–de facto 1878) and encountered an environment originally settled and still dominated by Greek Cypriots and the Cypriot Greek variety. Despite their century-long coexistence, the Greek Cypriot and Turkish Cypriot communities have remained rather separate from each other and so have their languages and varieties; Cypriots had not developed into a bilingual community speaking Greek and Turkish before the partition of the island. Before the division of the island, Turkish Cypriots, however, often spoke both varieties, Cypriot Greek and Cypriot Turkish (Annual Colonial Reports 1937: 4; Goutsos and Karyolemou 2004: 5). With the Turkish invasion in 1974 and the following separation of the two main ethnic groups, both varieties lost each other as the respective major contact variety. While Cypriot Greek was then almost only spoken in the Southern part and influenced by Standard Greek, Cypriot Turkish was used almost exclusively in the North and influenced by the Anatolian varieties of Turkish (Kappler and Tsiplakou: 2018: 76, 85).

Turkish is the official language of the TRNC. Since the Turkish Cypriots mostly speak the Cypriot Turkish variety, the convergence of Cypriot Turkish to Standard Turkish has variously been discussed (see, e.g., Menteşoğlu 2009; most publications on the Turkish Cypriot variety have been written in Turkish: see Osam and Kelepir 2004). While many have concentrated on the differences between the two varieties (see, e.g., Evripidou and Çavuşoğlu 2015 on attitudes, Kappler 2008 on syntactic variation, Kızılyürek and Gautier-Kızılyürek 2004 on the effect on identity, Pehlivan and Osam 2010 on lexical differences, and Sultanzade 2013 on phonetic changes), more recently, the mutual influence of Cypriot Turkish and Standard Turkish on each other and a potentially emerging "mixed" variety has been discussed (see, e.g., Demir and Johanson 2006; Kappler and Tsiplakou 2018 on emerging koinai). The attitudes toward the Cypriot Turkish variety used to be rather negative and denigrating; however, Cypriot Turkish as well as the emerging variety are now perceived as rather prestigious (Demir and Johanson 2006: 3; Kappler and Tsiplakou 2018: 76). The rising prestige of Cypriot Turkish is not based on the number of its speakers, as Turkish immigrants are believed to outnumber Turkish Cypriots in the TRNC (Research Centre on Multilingualism 2004). It rather seems to be a result of the Turkish Cypriots' continued use of their variety to distinguish themselves from the Turkish immigrants (Kappler in Hadjioannou et al. 2011: 538) and might, furthermore, reflect a change of identification of the Turkish immigrants as becoming "more Cypriot." This changed attitude toward the local variety led to the transition of the school curricula from Turkey-focused to Cyprus-focused in 2004. However, it did not change the fact that the official language of instruction remains Standard Turkish (Kappler in Hadjioannou et al. 2011: 541).

The two official languages of the RoC are Greek and Turkish, although Turkish "has attained a *zero degree of use* within the Greek-Cypriot community since it no longer responds to any real communicative need" (Karyolemou 2001: 27). Variations within the Cypriot Greek variety as well as its approximation to the standard variety have nevertheless been widely discussed (see, e.g., Hadjioannou et al. 2011; Kappler and Tsiplakou 2018; Newton 1972; Papapavlou 1994; Rowe and Grohmann 2013; Tsiplakou 2011; Tsiplakou et al. 2016). Cypriot Greek used to reflect locality. After 1974 and the resulting recomposition of local communities, this tendency decreased toward a leveled variety (Kappler and Tsiplakou 2018: 85). Resembling the emergence of the Cypriot Turkish koine, the new social structures have enabled the development of a Cypriot Greek koine (e.g., argued for in Kappler and Tsiplakou 2018; Rowe and Grohmann 2013; Tsiplakou, Armosti, and Evripidou 2016). Standard Modern Greek has a strong influence on this emergent mixed variety, due to the migration of Greeks and the use of Standard Modern Greek in formal and written contexts, and as the language of instruction in the Greek Cypriot education system (Kappler and Tsiplakou 2018: 85). Cypriot Greek is not stigmatized but perceived as prestigious, as is Standard Modern Greek (Rowe and Grohmann 2013: 131–3). In contrast to the competing varieties in the TRNC, it seems like the Greek Cypriot community neither favors nor fights the standard variety. One reason for this might be the fact that Greek Cypriots, in contrast to Turkish Cypriots in the North, represent the major ethnic group in the South (Research Centre on Multilingualism 2004: 18). Therefore, they might not feel the need to defend their variety or protect it from being erased. Consequently, both communities are multiglossic, using the standard and local varieties of Greek and Turkish, respectively (Kappler in Hadjioannou et al. 2011: 536–8; McEntee-Atalianis and Pouloukas 2005: 214).

Since 1878, speakers of both communities might have added the English language to their language repertoires if it had been necessary (cf. Karoulla-Vrikki 2004; Tsiplakou 2009). Although English had been introduced as part of primary education, neither Greek Cypriots nor Turkish Cypriots became bilingual in English and their native variety during British rule. The use of English in Cyprus did not change drastically after Cyprus's independence and the establishment of Greek and Turkish as the island's official languages; while the introduction of English in primary education was revoked, it remained the main language of formal public documents and the legal system (Davy and Pavlou 2001: 211–2; Tsiplakou 2009: 79). However, the Turkish invasion and the separation of the island introduced a turning point concerning the use of English and the attitudes toward it. Prior to 1974, English was used as a mediator language in a "linguistically heterogeneous population" (Davy and Pavlou 2001: 211). In both parts of Cyprus, the environment and the community changed drastically in 1974, making a mediator language redundant (Kappler and Tsiplakou 2018: 76; Tsiplakou 2006: 337). However, the sentiments against the English language increased in the South—potentially because the Greek Cypriots perceived a preference by the British toward the Turkish Cypriot community. Britain's lack of support against the Turkish invader might have substantiated the Greek

Cypriots' feelings (cf. Karoulla-Vrikki 2004: 24; Ker-Lindsay 2011: 29–30). As a result of these sentiments and the ensuing public discourse, English was slowly removed from official domains in the late 1980s and early 1990s (Davy and Pavlou 2001: 211–12; Tsiplakou 2009: 79). While the use of English for official purposes decreased, it was and still is extensively in use in private, unofficial contexts. Although Greek Cypriots had perceived English as endangering Cyprus and the Cypriot Greek variety during the British rule, they nowadays show broadly positive attitudes toward the English language (cf. Buschfeld 2013; McEntee-Atalianis and Pouloukas 2001; Sciriha 1996).

In addition to the official languages and the local varieties, various minority languages are used in Cyprus. In the RoC, the languages of the officially recognized minorities are Cypriot Arabic and Armenian. Those two speaker groups, in addition to the recognized minority group of Latins, moved to the South in the course of the partition of Cyprus in 1974 because they had traditionally been speakers of Cypriot Greek, as an additional or only language (Hadjioannou et al. 2011: 507–8). The de facto Constitution of the TRNC does not recognize any minority languages (Kappler in Hadjioannou et al. 2011: 536); however, the unrecognized Roma community has settled down in the North (Hadjioannou et al. 2011: 509). Other languages have been brought to the island based on migration. In the RoC, migrants came, for example, not only from former USSR countries, like Poland and Bulgaria, but also from Sri Lanka and Cambodia. One group that was increasingly visible in public life were the Pontic Greeks, who spoke Russian, Georgian, Pontic Greek, Turkish, or any combination of them (see Tsiplakou and Georgi 2008) and brought these languages to Cyprus (Hadjioannou et al. 2011: 519). Russian has primarily been used as a lingua franca in these communities and is nowadays, due to continued immigration and maintenance of the language, the language of the largest group of immigrants in the RoC (ibid.; Karpava 2015: 35, 2017: 235). The high number of Russian speakers in Cyprus, combined with its high potential in touristic purposes and Russians' past and current financial impact, leads to an increase in the language's prestige (Karpava, Ringblom, and Zabrodskaja 2018: 108–9). Following Kappler (in Hadjioannou et al. 2011: 536–7), the major immigrant languages in the TRNC are Kurdish and Arabic.

### 3.3.2 English in Educational Contexts

Nowadays, English is one of the few remaining linguistic links between the TRNC and the RoC, since English has been and still is a compulsory subject in both parts' primary and secondary education. The RoC currently has a fourfold educational system, divided into compulsory and free—if public—preschool, primary, and secondary education and voluntary tertiary education. English is introduced in primary school and continued throughout junior and senior high school (Tsiplakou 2009: 81). As a result of this education and the colonial history of the island, Greek Cypriots are able and willing to communicate in English in all age groups (Buschfeld 2013; Tsiplakou 2009: 83).

The population in the TRNC appears to be less proficient in English, although Kappler states that native speakers of English are located around the cities of Girne and Kapta and that bilingual Turkish-English speaking Cypriots might occasionally be found (Kappler in Hadjioannou et al. 2011: 537). This might be due to the substantial change in the Northern Cypriot society—initialized through migration from and by Turkey—which led to Turkish becoming the shared language of the major inhabitant groups and caused a lack of necessity to use English in public life. However, English is widely used in education. The education system in the TRNC consists of mandatory and free preschool, primary, and secondary education and voluntary tertiary education (The Public Relations Department 2014: 38). English is introduced in first grade and is continued throughout secondary education (Kappler in Hadjioannou et al. 2011: 542; TRNC Ministry of National Education and Culture 2005: 16-17). Although the use of English in each part's education system appears to be quite similar, the reasons for the use and implementation of English in their HE landscapes are more complex.

## 3.4 English in Cyprus's Markets of HE

In the RoC, HE is provided by fifty-five, private or public, institutions. In 2018, 31.5 percent of the 47,169 students in tertiary education were enrolled in free public institutions and 68.5 percent in private ones that are to be paid for (CYSTAT 2020b: 4). Almost 80 percent of those 47,169 students attend one of the three public and five private universities: the University of Cyprus (founded in 1992), the Open University of Cyprus (founded in 2006), and the Cyprus University of Technology (founded in 2007) are public universities; the European University Cyprus, the University of Nicosia, the Frederick University (all founded in 2007), the Neapolis University (founded in 2010), and the UCLan Cyprus (founded in 2012) constitute the sector of private universities (ibid.: 10, 16). UCLan Cyprus is a satellite campus of a British university. Its opening appears to, on the one hand, reflect the opportunities of globalization and, on the other hand, to restore British regency, former colonial structures, and hierarchies in the educational system of Cyprus. It offers a highly prestigious education for those who cannot afford—or who do not wish to—study in a traditional native English-speaking country.

While in the academic year of 2015/2016, 56.4 percent of the students in the RoC's tertiary education were Cypriots and 43.6 percent were international students, in 2017/2018, for the second consecutive year, more students were international (51.3 percent) than Cypriot (48.7 percent) (CYSTAT 2017a: 13, 2018: 4, 2019: 13). Within the overall numbers of students in Cyprus, the share of Cypriot students has decreased while the number of international students has continuously increased. This caused a shift in relevance toward international students as they currently represent the majority of students in the RoC (CYSTAT 2018: 9, 2020b: 9). The open borders within the EU facilitated the movement of people and goods and, therefore, for students to study abroad. This is a bidirectional movement, as international students come to Cyprus, for example, attracted by the University of Central Lancashire's satellite campus in Cyprus, and Cypriots move abroad for their tertiary education. Although comprehensive numbers are not available, the RoC's Ministry of Education relies on the European Statistical Service when stating that in 2016/2017 a total of 22,197 Cypriot students studied in other European countries (CYSTAT 2020b: 12). An education outside Cyprus might be an attractive alternative for some Cypriots, and Greece and the UK appear to be especially attractive destinations—the former due to the shared language and the latter because of the high prestige of the there-obtained degree ("Cypriot certificates are [not] any bad, but British are more recognized and accepted all over the world"; Excerpt 7a). For students who cannot afford to go to the UK, such a prestigious British certificate can be obtained while residing in Cyprus and attending UCLan Cyprus.

In the TRNC, HE is the only voluntary and cost-entailing form of education and is provided primarily by universities (State Planning Organization 2018: 142; The Public Relations Department 2014: 38). The number of universities continuously increases—in 2014, ten universities were available (The Public Relations Department 2014: 39), while in 2016, fifteen universities (State Planning Organization 2017: 33–4), and in 2018, twenty universities (State Planning Organization 2020: 33–5) were located in the TRNC. In the academic year 2018/2019, almost 103,000 students were enrolled in those universities (State Planning Organization 2020: 33), of which 12,507 (12.1 percent) were Cypriots, 54,966 (53.4 percent) were Turks, and 35,480 (34.5 percent) were of other nationalities (ibid.: 33). The fast growth of the market of HE is, furthermore, reflected by the development of the number of students compared to the number of inhabitants. From 2014 to 2018, the number of universities grew by 100 percent, from ten to twenty universities, and the number of students grew by 34.5 percent, from 76,600 to almost 103,000. However, in the same time, the population grew by only 16 percent, from 321,000 to 372,500 (ibid.: 3, 33–5). Furthermore, while from 2016 to 2018, the number of Cypriot students decreased by 2,150 students (14.7 percent), the number of international students, excluding students from Turkey, increased by 9,600 students (34.9 percent) (ibid.: 33). Therefore, HE in the TRNC appears to be focused on international rather than on local students. The continuous inflow of these students is triggered and catered for by the universities' offer of instruction in English—only one university does not offer an EMI program (The Public Relations Department 2014: 39). A negative result of this inflow might be that students are the occupation group committing second to most crimes in the TRNC, with an increasing number almost every year from 2012 until 2017 (State Planning Organization 2018: 196–7, more recent numbers are not available). To study abroad, Turkish Cypriot students most often choose Turkey (2,382 out of 3,328) and the UK (ibid.: 142, 159), likely due to the shared language(s) and the interconnected histories.

As has been shown, the small island of Cyprus is home to twenty-eight universities—eight in the RoC and twenty in the TRNC (as well as other tertiary education institutions, e.g., colleges that are not incorporated here; see CYSTAT 2020b: 16; State Planning Organization 2020: 33–5). The high number of universities reciprocates with the importance of HE for the economies of both parts of the island. In the TRNC, HE is a "priority sector" (The Public Relations Department 2014: 35) and experiences rapid growth. In 2016 it received an approximately €7.8 million investment (ibid.; State Planning Organization 2017: 15). In the RoC, the branch of HE generated 6.7 percent (€1,061,420,700) of the GDP in the same year (CYSTAT 2017a: 16). This economic aspect of HE is closely related to and based on the above-described student mobility and the income international students bring to the island. In the TRNC the inhabitant/university ratio is 18,600/1, meaning that there is one university for every 18,600 inhabitants, while in the RoC this ratio is 175,200/1. Hence, especially in the TRNC, locals can only represent a small percentage of students. The majority of students are international, traveling to Cyprus solely to enroll in HE. At first sight, tertiary education abroad appears to be both desirable and beneficial—and for some students it is. However, a significant number of international students do not choose Cyprus voluntarily. Their first choice would be the UK, the United

States, or another native English-speaking country. Cyprus might be their second choice, at best, and sometimes the only realistic one, due to the unaffordability of native English education (Excerpt 2b). HE in Cyprus is affordable and visa regulations are less strict than in other countries. Furthermore, Cyprus is the only southern European country that is equally successful in offering EMI-HE as northern European countries (cf. Lasagabaster 2015: 266). Therefore, students perceive it as a suitable option (Excerpt 1b). For those international students who are not of Turkish or Greek origin, being taught in English is a fundamental prerequisite and the only reason Cyprus ever became an option. English is essential for these students in two ways. First, it facilitates communication, as English is internationally learned and spoken. Second, English functions as a kind of "add-on" to their education, making it even more valuable. English is no longer necessarily connected to its native speakers in Cyprus's HE but perceived as an attribute or asset that is detached from its original use. Maybe the monetary rewards granted under British rule to secondary school that would teach English more in the 1930s "have led to the sociocultural construction of English as linguistic and social capital" (Tsiplakou 2009: 78); however, it is certainly used as capital in Cyprus's HE nowadays, as is shown by the rapid increase of universities and their English programs. Its use and value are shared by both parts of Cyprus; the implementation of English and its realization as an asset and as the medium of HE, however, differs.

English is part of Cyprus as the language of education, the media, and political representation (McEntee-Atalianis and Pouloukas 2001). It functions as the bearer of power and the medium of discussions and negotiations with the UN, the EU, and, perhaps socially most important, between the two states (see McEntee-Atalianis and Pouloukas 2001). The use of the English language is, therefore, not a choice but a necessity for Cyprus's political survival and global partaking. It is, in addition, the most important foreign language for Cyprus's economic development and success.

## 3.5 The Economies of English in Cyprus

The research site of Cyprus's HE appears to provide a fruitful hub created by unique circumstances: Cyprus combines an enclosed environment of an island, a priori multilingualism, a colonial history that introduced the English language to the island, and political and cultural separation in times of a neoliberal global economy in a contact area of the Global North and the Global South. Due to these unique circumstances, the use of the English language in Cyprus cannot be comprehensively described by any one existing model. It can neither be easily classified as postcolonial, being part of the Outer Circle, nor does it fit neatly into the common definition of Expanding Circle Englishes. The concept of ELF might be useful but does not consider the unique situation at hand in a divided Cyprus. This can only successfully be done by comprehensively depicting the interrelation between language and the economy, which is part of assessing the value of English.

The role of English in Cyprus is manifold. As McEntee-Atalianis and Pouloukas (2001) point out, English infuses the Cypriot societies as a language of education, the media, political discussions, and economic negotiations. It maintains the leading position in tourism and trade, which it inherited during British rule and is, therefore, a key element within Cyprus's economy. To illustrate the economic implications of the use of English, the natural link between the prestige or social value of a language and its economic value needs to be recognized. By analyzing and comparing previously undertaken studies of the attitudes and use of languages in Cyprus (e.g., Buschfeld 2013; Eracleous 2015; Hadjioannou et al. 2011; Karpava, Ringblom, and Zabrodskaja 2018; McEntee-Atalianis and Pouloukas 2001; Papapavlou 2005 on language use and attitude in the RoC; see e.g., Kappler in Hadjioannou et al. 2011; Tum, Kunt, and Kunt 2016 on the TRNC, as well as personal email exchange with students, university teachers, and linguists from both parts of Cyprus), and combining them with the findings of this study (see Chapter 4), a ranking of languages in both parts of Cyprus and their respective prestige has been developed. The rankings in Tables 3.1 and 3.2 illustrate the importance of the English language and its role in society in comparison to the other languages that are in use.

Both parts of Cyprus use the English language but relate to it differently. While they were equally familiarized with English during Cyprus's colonial history, their exploitation of English differs. In the RoC English is used, similarly to other European countries, as a language of international relations, tourism, and globalization. English in the RoC implicates the cultural aspects of English, by maintaining its connection to the UK, as well as the economic and disconnected aspects by using the language to sell, for example, university degrees. However, by and large, the use of English as an attribute or asset appears to be most openly used in liaison with international students in HE (cf. Table 3.1). In the TRNC, the exploitation of English is differently weighted: Only when related to family ties in the UK, English is used as a cultural good. In all other instances, English is regarded as an economic good, to be utilized as needed (cf. Table 3.2). In the

Table 3.1 Languages in the RoC and Their Prestige

| Order of Prestige | Language/Variety | Attitude | Use |
|---|---|---|---|
| 1 | Standard Modern Greek | Educated, formal, precise, expressive, attractive, ambitious, modern | Formal and official contexts and writing, language of formal education, media |
| 2 | Cypriot Greek | Friendly, uneducated, inferior, inexpressive, incomplete | Local and unofficial contexts, often home language |
| 3 | English | Educated, former danger to Greek and Cypriot Greek, modern, important | Academia, tourism, international relations, media, private education |
| 4 | Russian | | Tourism, banking, increasing public use |
| 5 | (Cypriot) Arabic | Endangered | No frequent public use, only among native speakers |
| | Other | | Among immigrants |

Table 3.2 Languages in the TRNC and Their Prestige

| Order of Prestige | Language/variety | Attitude | Use |
|---|---|---|---|
| 1 | Standard Turkish | Educated, formal | Formal and official contexts and writing, language of formal education |
| 2 | English | Language of identity theft and the former colonizer | Academia, tourism, international relations |
| 3 | Cypriot Turkish | Uneducated, informal, nonacademic | Informal, local and unofficial contexts, tool to express Cypriotness |
| 4 | Arabic | | Among immigrants |
| 5 | Kurdish | | Among immigrants |
| | Other including Cypriot Greek | | Among immigrants; Cypriot Greek: (native) use by older Cypriots |

following examination, the use of English in both parts of Cyprus is scrutinized, illustrating its rootedness within the economic value of English used as an attribute. The disconnection of language and speakers opens the floodgates for its commodification and the reproduction of social inequalities based on wealth rather than on nationality.

## 3.6 The Study

As discussed in the first part of this chapter, Cyprus is a unique context of English use. It combines an unconventional history of British colonialism with a unique political, social, cultural, and linguistic situation. In addition, it is located at the edge of the Global North; this location and the differing visa regulations of the TRNC and the RoC make Cyprus's HE offerings interesting for international students, as Cyprus is geographically and bureaucratically (more easily) accessible for them. The extensive economics markets of HE rely on English. This holds true especially in the North, where HE often appears to be primarily aimed at and seized by students from outside Cyprus. An appropriate assessment of this complexity of the significance and roles of English exceeds the possibilities of quantitative research and therefore requires a qualitative approach. The investigation at hand offers the opportunity to explore the underlying reasons for the involved students' investment in English while paying attention to the students' individuality as well as the complex situation of Cyprus. Including these characteristics, this study is the first investigation of Cyprus's HE in both parts of the island as well as the first value-based approach to a comprehensive investigation of the role of English in these contexts.

Due to the colonial history of the island and its inhabitants' strong connection to their so-called motherlands Greece and Turkey (cf. Section 3.2.1), many non-Cypriot students have ties to the island prior to pursuing their HE there. Therefore, a differentiation of students with and without existing ties to Cyprus has been found to be most productive and accurate in developing a comprehensive depiction of the roles and values of English from the students' perspective. Universities in both parts of Cyprus were identified, so as to uncover Cyprus-tied (Ct)- and not Cyprus-tied (nCt)-students' experiences in Cyprus as well as their motives for choosing one of the four universities that are included here.

### 3.6.1 The Research Sites

The present study includes students of four universities in both parts of Cyprus. The universities vary in their backgrounds and affiliations, student body composition, advertisement strategies, and study program offers to approach a comprehensive description of Cyprus's HE landscape. The following four universities will be included: the University of Cyprus (UCy) in the Southern Greek part of the capital city Nicosia; UCLan Cyprus in Pyla, located within the demilitarized zone between the South and the North; Eastern Mediterranean University (EMU) in Famagusta, Northern Cyprus; and Girne American University (GAU), located in Girne, Northern Cyprus. While the first three universities have been visited personally, the GAU students volunteered to participate based on direct or indirect personal relationships with the researcher (cf. Milroy 1980: 53, 1987: 66, on the "friend-of-a-friend" approach).

#### *3.6.1.1 UCLan Cyprus*

UCLan Cyprus is a satellite campus of the University of Central Lancashire in Preston, UK. Consequently, it is a British university that follows a British structure in administration and teaching. This is, furthermore, its rationale for using English as the exclusive official language both inside and outside the classroom. The university's ties to the UK are especially prestigious in Cyprus, as they build on the island's colonial history. UCLan Cyprus is a rather new university that opened in October 2012, with its campus, student accommodation, sports center, and other facilities situated in Pyla, a small village in the district of Larnaca (UCLan Cyprus 2019). Pyla, in turn, is one of the last remaining mixed Greek Cypriot/Turkish Cypriot villages and is located in the demilitarized UN-governed zone that separates the North and the South. Located within Cyprus's buffer zone and in a mixed village—geographically, linguistically, and politically between the two parts—UCLan Cyprus is accessible and also attractive for Greek Cypriots and Turkish Cypriots. This provides UCLan Cyprus with an extraordinarily composed Cypriot part of its student body in a unique local environment, which is why it has been chosen for this study. However, this is not mentioned in UCLan Cyprus's advertisement. Instead, the university highlights its Britishness as a gatekeeper to internationality for graduate students (see, e.g., ibid.; UCLan Cyprus 2017e, 2017i).

Each graduate of any of the university's twelve undergraduate and twelve postgraduate study programs obtains a Cypriot as well as a British certificate (UCLan Cyprus 2019). While the university highlights its Britishness and issues British university degrees, the English language requirements are moderate. The minimal requirement for admission to undergraduate English Language Studies is "5.5 IELTS [International English Language Testing System] or equivalent," while for all other undergraduate study programs only a "knowledge of [the] English Language" is required (UCLan Cyprus 2017a). For admission to any postgraduate study program, however, an "IELTS 6.5 level and above, or any other equivalent" is required (ibid.). Furthermore, the university offers an entrance examination for proficient students who are not able to present any official documentation of their language proficiency and issues interviews with "the Head of School of the program of study they are applying for" to students "who do not meet the above minimum entry criteria" (ibid.). Although no student numbers have been published, UCLan Cyprus appears to attract Greek Cypriots, Turkish Cypriots, and students from outside Cyprus who are interested in a British degree and/or being taught in English.

UCLan Cyprus aims at innovation, internationality, and excellence, which is advertised widely (e.g., UCLan Cyprus 2017g, 2017i, 2019). However, other than the university-internal exchange with the mother campus in the UK and its participation in the Erasmus+ program, an EU-based student and staff mobility program, limited international collaboration had been announced at the time of the study (UCLan Cyprus 2017b, 2017f). UCLan Cyprus is a private university and is conceptualized as an "enterprising British University delivering educational and training programmes to local and international students" (UCLan Cyprus 2017h). Consequently, and like any other private university, its management follows an economic objective and is based on income in the form of the students' tuition fees. The university uses extensive advertisements to reach prospective students, promoting the university, its quality programs, facilities, and equipment, as well as the quality of living in Cyprus all valorized through the prestige of being British.

### *3.6.1.2 University of Cyprus*

UCy is Cyprus's first public university in the southern part of the island, located in its divided capital Nicosia (UCy 2018). As a public university, its official languages are the languages of Cyprus—Greek and Turkish—while most classes are taught in Greek. UCy was chosen to be included in this study because it offers (mostly) free HE and it is strongly tied to Cyprus and to serving the island's population. It is the only university in this study that does not focus, mainly or partially, on including international students. UCy follows a traditional and humanistic orientation rather than an economic agenda (ibid.). It offers thirty-nine undergraduate and eighty-seven postgraduate study programs in six faculties, mostly using Greek as the language of instruction (UCy n.d.-e, n.d.-h). At the time of the study, UCy had a student body of about 5,300 undergraduate and 1,850 postgraduate students (UCy 2017, 2018) and employed 729 faculty and 500 administrative staff members (UCy n.d.-a, n.d.-b).

At UCy, English is used as the exclusive medium of instruction in seventeen postgraduate programs; it is used in the five postgraduate study programs of the Department of English Studies and twelve postgraduate study programs in other departments (UCy n.d.-e, n.d.-h). For some postgraduate study programs, prospective students have to prove competence in the English language. This can be demonstrated "through a certificate from a recognized examining board" (UCy n.d.-g; cf. UCy n.d.-c). Although the English language is not the major language of administration and teaching at UCy, it is important in a variety of international collaborations and cooperation agreements. The university lists 119 non-Cypriot institutions with whom agreements of cooperation have been signed—only seven of which are Greek (Agreement of Cooperation with Institutions Abroad n.d.). Furthermore, the university participates in the Erasmus+ and Erasmus+ international programs, facilitating student and staff mobility (UCy n.d.-f). As it has no primary economic orientation, UCy does not use advertising to attract prospective students but appears to rely on its local reputation. Furthermore, the RoC absorbs the tuition fees for all undergraduate studies of EU students (UCy n.d.-i); non-EU students pay annual fees and postgraduate students pay program-based tuition fees (cf. ibid.; UCy n.d.-d).

### 3.6.1.3 EMU

EMU opened in 1985 in Famagusta, on the eastern coast of the TRNC, and became a public university in 1986 (EMU Web Office n.d.-c). Its home city of Famagusta used to be very popular with tourists and, therefore, was economically important prior to the Cyprus conflict and the Turkish invasion in 1974. EMU was chosen for this study, as it is an underexplored but prestigious and well-recognized university, located in the direct vicinity of this historically important and politically conflicted area. Furthermore, its geographical and political location appears to be removed from the university's policy, reputation, and any research connected to it.

The university is rather big, having a student body of 20,000 students and a faculty of 1,100 academics (EMU Web Office n.d.-a). It does, however, not publish the number of nonacademic employees or the year of counting. EMU lists eighty-nine undergraduate and ninety-five postgraduate programs, while 133 study programs are taught in English as the medium of instruction and fifty-one use the Turkish language (EMU Web Office n.d.-d). Although the major language at EMU is English, prospective students are required to show a "copy of proof of English Proficiency [only] if any [exists]" (EMU Web Office n.d.-f). In the case that students cannot meet this requirement, the university offers an in-house language proficiency examination, which results in either an exemption from language classes or the requirement to attend them prior or simultaneous to the chosen study program. Again, although the main language of teaching at EMU is English, the proficiency requirements are moderate; for most study programs a threshold of 60 percent of the in-house language tests is announced for entry to the language classes and, subsequently, enter the desired study program. However, students who score 50–59 percent are interviewed by the language school and, when announced as successful, are also admitted to EMU's language classes and, later, study programs (EMU n.d.-a; cf. EMU n.d.-c for a summary of accepted certificates, offered language classes, and the English proficiency-based admission process). A directive of what "to be successful" includes, is not available.

At EMU, the English language functions primarily as the medium of instruction and communication on campus, rather than of international collaboration. In contrast to public universities in the RoC, all students at EMU pay tuition fees. Citizens of the TRNC pay the lowest fees, while Turkish citizens pay twice as much, and other international students four times as much as local students. The university uses online advertising on its webpages, social media, and, indirectly, via university rankings to attract prospective students. This reflects both the university's and the TRNC's interest in the economic benefit of prospective students. Furthermore, international students are billed in U.S. dollar, which is a more stable and internationally more highly valuable currency than the local Turkish Lira (TL). To convince prospective students to enroll at EMU, the use of the English language as the medium of instruction and the international accreditations of the offered study programs are shown off as the university's main assets (EMU Web Office n.d.-a). Apparently independent of EMU, for-profit agencies and businesses make extensive use of advertising in various countries, so as to benefit from the international students' desire to pursue their education in Cyprus.

### 3.6.1.4 GAU

GAU was founded in 1985 and claims to be the oldest private university in the TRNC (GAU 2019c). It is located shortly outside Girne (also called Kyrenia) on the northern coast of the island. GAU was chosen for this study primarily for two reasons: it includes "American" in its name and it is located near the only airport in the TRNC—Ercan—and to a direct ferry connection to Turkey (cf. TRNC Public Information Office 2018 for an elaboration Girne's transport connections). Both are convincing arguments for international students to enroll at GAU, as they expect convenient access to education that is culturally connected to one of the English language's traditional homes, in this case, the United States.

While the university had around 5,800 students a decade ago, it claims to teach 20,000 students at the time of the study (Bingham 2010; GAU 2019c). The university does, however, not provide any numbers of the academic or nonacademic staff. It offers fifty-four undergraduate and twenty-eight postgraduate study programs in twenty faculties, institutes, or schools. Thirty-eight undergraduate and twenty-seven graduate programs are taught in EMI (GAU 2019a, 2019d, 2019i). Furthermore, the university maintains an English language school (GAU Foundation School 2019). For admission to GAU's EMI study programs, students are required to present proof of their English-language proficiency in the form of certificates of specified tests. These students are then admitted directly to their desired study program. Prospective students who cannot provide the university with the required certificates have to take the in-house proficiency examination with comparably low thresholds; for the majority of study programs, a threshold is set to 60 percent in this proficiency examination. Students who meet this threshold are transferred directly to their desired study programs, while those students who do not achieve the threshold are required to attend language classes prior to starting in their desired study programs (cf. GAU 2019j, 2019g for more details on specific certificates and exceptions).

The university states it is "a global university with 7 international campuses in 3 continents"—with two campuses located in Anglophone countries—and that it educates "students from 135 countries around the world" (GAU 2019c). Furthermore, it claims to have developed "educational partnerships [in] India, Kazakhstan, Pakistan, Sri Lanka, Kyrgyzstan, Turkey, the USA, the UK, the Czech Republic, Hong Kong and Moldova," which offer potential mobility for students during their studies (GAU 2019e). The internationality of GAU is further supported by the claim that it leads "more than 200 academic collaborations signed with prestigious universities around the world" (ibid.), although none is referred to by name (cf. GAU 2019b). GAU advertises the use of English as a medium of instruction and communication on- and off-campus and further highlights its internationality (GAU 2019d, 2019g). The university pursues an economic objective and aims mainly at international students. Furthermore, and most interestingly, GAU maintains "regional offices"; these are seventy-five contact persons or organizations—all in the Global South—which are presented with contact details and visitors' addresses. These agencies are used as direct contact between prospective students and GAU and represent another part of the university's economic orientation and objective (cf. GAU 2019k). While they seem to facilitate convincing international students of enrolling at GAU, further details on them are not offered. In addition to GAU's "regional offices," external for-profit agencies and businesses benefit from GAU. Although unnecessary for the enrollment and admission process, these agencies pretend to be go-betweens, promising international students facilitated access to GAU and high-quality education in exchange for additional payment (e.g., Goldenchips Educational Services International 2019; Study in North Cyprus n.d.).

### 3.6.2 Participants

During multiple visits to Cyprus, the author had the opportunity to attend various classes and spent time on the campuses of EMU, UCy, and UCLan Cyprus. While spending time with students, open interactions and conversations were possible, so as to learn about the students' biographies and experiences and to build trusting relationships. Based on these relationships and casual encounters, some participants offered or were asked to partake in in-depth conversations. Because using this practice created a heterogeneous participant sample, many different perspectives, experiences, intentions, and motives for investing in the value of English in Cyprus's HE were included. For these reasons, 125 Ct-students and 80 nCt-students of various study programs, ages, and backgrounds constitute the participants of this study.

Participants who indicated having had existing ties to Cyprus before entering HE, and who were familiar with the environment of the context of the respective part of Cyprus, are defined as Ct. These ties might be represented directly by the students having spent all their lives in Cyprus or indirectly through family ties or migration and long residence in Cyprus prior to their admission at any of the universities. Students who lack these ties and often moved to Cyprus not long before starting their HE or primarily to receive their HE, and without being familiar with the geopolitical situation of the island, are defined as nCt. In the study at hand, the majority of the nCt-students (87.5 percent) arrived in Cyprus in the same year in which they commenced their HE, most often without adequate or with misleading knowledge of the local contexts. This confirmed the choice of using the students' ties to Cyprus as the initial level of comparison. For the division into Ct- and nCt-students, the participants' biographic information was used (see Appendices 1.1 and 2.1). More specifically, the answers to the questions presented below needed to show the Ct-participants' ties to Cyprus, as they indicate residence, nationality, and family relations prior to their admission to the respective university. The answers included—but were not limited to—the following examples:

1. Why did you come to Cyprus?—I was born here; for family reasons
2. Since when have you been in Cyprus?—Year of birth; always
3. Nationality—Cypriot; Turkish Cypriot; Greek Cypriot
4. Place of birth—Cyprus:

Students whose answers did not indicate existing ties to Cyprus prior to their arrival were identified as nCt-students.

Table 3.3 offers a partial overview of each of the participants' biographies and their reasons for pursuing their HE in Cyprus, as needed for a division into Ct- and nCt-students. In this table, the nationality "English" refers to an officially English-speaking country, like the UK or Nigeria. Furthermore, "0" signals missing information, while "Y" refers to any language other than the two official languages of Cyprus—Greek and Turkish—and English; "X," however, reflects any language but English.

Although the analysis of the participants' age is based on their year of birth, it provides a general overview and similarities and differences of the various subsamples are observable. Almost half of the participants (47.5 percent) were born in the years 1996 to 1998, with a mean age of 21.02 years (SD 3.59). Of the participants, 56.6 percent are female, while 43.4 percent are male, and the majority (50.7 percent) were born in Cyprus, with 57.1 percent being of Cypriot nationality. Furthermore, 13.7 percent of the participants claim to identify as native speakers of English, while the majority describe their English language skills as "advanced" or "near-native"—62 percent in speaking, 64.3 percent in listening, 60 percent in writing, and 71.2 percent in reading, respectively (cf. Appendices 2.1 and 2.2). Of these 205 students, 30 volunteered, in addition, to participate in voluntary semi-structured interviews. A more obvious tendency and focus emerge within the distribution of the participants when grouped by university.

Table 3.3 Participants

| No | University, Interview | Ties | Part | Place of Birth | Nationality | Why in Cyprus | Time in Cyprus | Native Language(s) |
|---|---|---|---|---|---|---|---|---|
| 161 | UCLan | Ct | RoC | English | Cypriot | Born in Cyprus | 2001 | Greek |
| 162 | UCLan, yes | Ct | RoC | Cyprus | Cypriot | Born in Cyprus | 1995 | English+X |
| 163 | UCLan | Ct | RoC | Cyprus | Cypriot | 0 | 1996 | Greek |
| 164 | UCLan | Ct | RoC | Cyprus | Cypriot | 0 | 0 | Greek |
| 165 | UCLan | Ct | RoC | Cyprus | Dual | 0 | 0 | English+X |
| 166 | UCLan | Ct | RoC | English | Cypriot | 0 | 1996 | English+X |
| 167 | UCLan | Ct | RoC | Cyprus | Cypriot | 0 | 0 | Greek |
| 168 | UCLan | Ct | RoC | Cyprus | Cypriot | 0 | 1996 | 0 |
| 169 | UCLan | Ct | RoC | Cyprus | Cypriot | 0 | 1993 | 0 |
| 1610 | UCLan | Ct | RoC | Cyprus | Cypriot | Born in Cyprus | 1995 | Greek |
| 1611 | UCLan | Ct | RoC | Cyprus | Cypriot | 0 | 1998 | Greek |
| 1612 | UCLan | Ct | RoC | Cyprus | Cypriot | Born in Cyprus | 1993 | Greek |
| 121 | UCLan | Ct | RoC | Cyprus | Dual | 0 | 0 | Greek |
| 122 | UCLan | Ct | RoC | Cyprus | Cypriot | 0 | 0 | Greek |
| 123 | UCLan | Ct | RoC | Cyprus | Cypriot | Other | 1998 | Turkish |
| 124 | UCLan | Ct | RoC | English | Cypriot | Born in Cyprus | 0 | 0 |
| 125 | UCLan | Ct | RoC | Cyprus | Cypriot | Born in Cyprus | 0 | 0 |
| 126 | UCLan | Ct | RoC | Cyprus | Cypriot | 0 | 0 | Greek |
| 127 | UCLan | Ct | RoC | Cyprus | Cypriot | 0 | 0 | 0 |
| 128 | UCLan | Ct | RoC | Cyprus | Cypriot | 0 | 1998 | Greek |
| 129 | UCLan | Ct | RoC | Cyprus | Cypriot | 0 | 2001 | X+X |
| 1210 | UCLan | Ct | RoC | Cyprus | Cypriot | 0 | 0 | Greek |
| 1211 | UCLan | Ct | RoC | Cyprus | Cypriot | 0 | 0 | Greek |
| 1212 | UCLan | Ct | RoC | Cyprus | Cypriot | 0 | 1998 | Greek |
| 1213 | UCLan | Ct | RoC | Cyprus | Cypriot | 0 | 0 | English+X |
| 1214 | UCLan | Ct | RoC | Cyprus | Cypriot | 0 | 0 | English+X |
| 1215 | UCLan | nCt | RoC | Other | Other | Other | 2014 | Y |
| 1216 | UCLan | nCt | RoC | Other | Other | Other | 2014 | Y |
| 111 | UCLan | Ct | RoC | Cyprus | Cypriot | Born in Cyprus | 0 | Cypriot Greek |
| 112 | UCLan | nCt | RoC | Other | Other | Other | 2015 | Y |

**Table 3.3** (continued)

| No | University, Interview | Ties | Part | Place of Birth | Nationality | Why in Cyprus | Time in Cyprus | Native Language(s) |
|---|---|---|---|---|---|---|---|---|
| 113 | UCLan | Ct | RoC | Cyprus | 0 | Born in Cyprus | 1995 | 0 |
| 114 | UCLan | Ct | RoC | Cyprus | Cypriot | 0 | 0 | 0 |
| 115 | UCLan | Ct | RoC | Cyprus | Cypriot | 0 | 0 | Greek |
| 116 | UCLan | Ct | RoC | Other | Cypriot | 0 | 1998 | Greek |
| 117 | UCLan | Ct | RoC | Cyprus | Cypriot | 0 | 0 | X+X |
| 118 | UCLan | Ct | RoC | Cyprus | Cypriot | 0 | 0 | Y |
| 119 | UCLan | Ct | RoC | Cyprus | Dual | Born in Cyprus | 1996 | Greek |
| 1110 | UCLan, yes | Ct | RoC | English | Cypriot | 0 | 2000 | Y |
| 1111 | UCLan | Ct | RoC | Cyprus | Cypriot | 0 | 0 | Greek |
| 1112 | UCLan | nCt | RoC | Other | Other | Other | 2015 | Y |
| 1113 | UCLan | nCt | RoC | Other | Other | To study | 2016 | Y |
| 1114 | UCLan | Ct | RoC | Cyprus | Cypriot | 0 | 0 | Cypriot Greek |
| 1115 | UCLan | Ct | RoC | Cyprus | Cypriot | 0 | 0 | Greek |
| 1116 | UCLan | Ct | RoC | Cyprus | Cypriot | Born in Cyprus | 1998 | English+X |
| 1117 | UCLan | nCt | RoC | Other | Other | Other | 2010 | 0 |
| 1118 | UCLan | Ct | RoC | English | Dual | 0 | 2003 | English+X |
| 1121 | UCLan | Ct | RoC | Other | Cypriot | Other | 2002 | Greek |
| 1122 | UCLan | Ct | RoC | Cyprus | Cypriot | Born in Cyprus | 1996 | Greek |
| 131 | UCLan | Ct | RoC | Cyprus | Cypriot | Born in Cyprus | 0 | Turkish |
| 132 | UCLan | Ct | RoC | Cyprus | Cypriot | Born in Cyprus | 0 | Turkish |
| 133 | UCLan | Ct | RoC | Cyprus | Cypriot | 0 | 0 | Greek |
| 134 | UCLan | Ct | RoC | Cyprus | Cypriot | 0 | 0 | Greek |
| 141 | UCLan | nCt | RoC | Other | Other | To study | 2016 | X+X |
| 142 | UCLan | Ct | RoC | Cyprus | Cypriot | 0 | 0 | Greek |
| 143 | UCLan | Ct | RoC | Cyprus | Cypriot | 0 | 0 | Greek |
| 144 | UCLan | Ct | RoC | Cyprus | Cypriot | 0 | 0 | Greek |
| 145 | UCLan | Ct | RoC | Cyprus | Cypriot | 0 | 0 | Greek |
| 146 | UCLan | Ct | RoC | Cyprus | Cypriot | Born in Cyprus | 0 | Greek |

Table 3.3 (continued)

| No | University, Interview | Ties | Part | Place of Birth | Nationality | Why in Cyprus | Time in Cyprus | Native Language(s) |
|---|---|---|---|---|---|---|---|---|
| 147 | UCLan | Ct | RoC | Cyprus | Cypriot | To study | 1998 | English+X |
| 1123 | UCLan, yes | Ct | RoC | Other | Other | Other | 2000 | X+X |
| 1512 | UCLan, yes | Ct | RoC | Cyprus | Cypriot | 0 | 0 | 0 |
| 1125 | UCLan, yes | Ct | RoC | Cyprus | Cypriot | Born in Cyprus | 1996 | Greek |
| 1124 | UCLan, yes | Ct | RoC | Other | Dual | Other | 1999 | 0 |
| 151 | UCLan | Ct | RoC | Cyprus | Cypriot | 0 | 0 | Greek |
| 152 | UCLan | Ct | RoC | Cyprus | Cypriot | 0 | 0 | 0 |
| 153 | UCLan | Ct | RoC | Cyprus | Cypriot | 0 | 0 | 0 |
| 154 | UCLan | Ct | RoC | Cyprus | Cypriot | Born in Cyprus | 1996 | Greek |
| 155 | UCLan | Ct | RoC | Cyprus | Cypriot | 0 | 0 | 0 |
| 156 | UCLan | Ct | RoC | Cyprus | English | 0 | 0 | Greek |
| 157 | UCLan | Ct | RoC | Cyprus | Cypriot | Born in Cyprus | 0 | 0 |
| 158 | UCLan | Ct | RoC | Cyprus | Cypriot | Born in Cyprus | 1993 | 0 |
| 159 | UCLan | Ct | RoC | Cyprus | Cypriot | 0 | 0 | 0 |
| 1510 | UCLan | Ct | RoC | Cyprus | Cypriot | 0 | 0 | Greek |
| 1511 | UCLan | Ct | RoC | Cyprus | Cypriot | 0 | 1997 | Greek |
| 148 | UCLan, yes | nCt | RoC | Other | English | Other | 2015 | Y |
| 1126 | UCLan, yes | Ct | RoC | Cyprus | Cypriot | 0 | 1998 | Greek |
| 1127 | UCLan, yes | Ct | RoC | Cyprus | Cypriot | 0 | 1996 | 0 |
| 1128 | UCLan | Ct | RoC | Cyprus | Cypriot | Born in Cyprus | 1998 | Greek |
| 149 | UCLan, yes | Ct | RoC | Cyprus | Cypriot | 0 | 0 | Greek |
| 1410 | UCLan, excluded | Ct | RoC | Cyprus | Cypriot | Other | 1998 | Greek |
| 1411 | UCLan, yes | nCt | RoC | Other | English | To study | 2016 | X+X |
| 1613 | UCLan | Ct | RoC | Cyprus | Cypriot | 0 | 0 | Greek |
| 271 | UCy | Ct | RoC | Cyprus | Cypriot | 0 | 1996 | Greek |
| 272 | UCy | Ct | RoC | Cyprus | Cypriot | 0 | 0 | Greek |
| 273 | UCy | nCt | RoC | Cyprus | Cypriot | To study | 2014 | Greek |
| 274 | UCy | Ct | RoC | Cyprus | Other | 0 | 0 | Greek |
| 2751 | UCy | nCt | RoC | Other | English | 0 | 2015 | Greek |

Table 3.3 (continued)

| No | University, Interview | Ties | Part | Place of Birth | Nationality | Why in Cyprus | Time in Cyprus | Native Language(s) |
|---|---|---|---|---|---|---|---|---|
| 275 | UCy, yes | Ct | RoC | Cyprus | Cypriot | 0 | 0 | Greek |
| 276 | UCy, yes | Ct | RoC | Cyprus | Cypriot | 0 | 1997 | Greek |
| 281 | UCy, yes | Ct | RoC | Cyprus | Cypriot | 0 | 1995 | Greek |
| 277 | UCy, yes | Ct | RoC | Cyprus | Cypriot | 0 | 0 | Greek |
| 282 | UCy | Ct | RoC | Cyprus | Cypriot | 0 | 1995 | Greek |
| 283 | UCy | Ct | RoC | Cyprus | Cypriot | Born in Cyprus | 1990 | Greek |
| 284 | UCy | Ct | RoC | Cyprus | Cypriot | 0 | 1993 | Greek |
| 285 | UCy | Ct | RoC | Cyprus | Cypriot | 0 | 1996 | Greek |
| 286 | UCy | Ct | RoC | Cyprus | Cypriot | Born in Cyprus | 1996 | Greek |
| 278 | UCy | Ct | RoC | Cyprus | Cypriot | Born in Cyprus | 1996 | Greek |
| 279 | UCy | nCt | RoC | Other | English | To study | 2015 | Greek |
| 2710 | UCy | Ct | RoC | Cyprus | Cypriot | Born in Cyprus | 1997 | Greek |
| 2711 | UCy | Ct | RoC | Cyprus | Cypriot | Born in Cyprus | 1997 | Greek |
| 2712 | UCy | Ct | RoC | Cyprus | Cypriot | 0 | 1997 | Greek |
| 2713 | UCy | nCt | RoC | Other | English | To study | 2017 | Y |
| 2714 | UCy | Ct | RoC | Cyprus | Cypriot | 0 | 0 | Greek |
| 2715 | UCy | nCt | RoC | Other | English | To study | 2017 | Y |
| 2716 | UCy | Ct | RoC | Cyprus | Cypriot | 0 | 1997 | Greek |
| 2717 | UCy | Ct | RoC | Cyprus | Cypriot | Born in Cyprus | 1997 | Cypriot Greek |
| 2718 | UCy | Ct | RoC | Cyprus | Cypriot | 0 | 0 | Cypriot Greek |
| 2719 | UCy | Ct | RoC | Cyprus | Cypriot | Born in Cyprus | 0 | Cypriot Greek |
| 3124 | EMU | nCt | TRNC | 0 | Cypriot | To study | 2013 | X+X |
| 3142 | EMU | nCt | TRNC | Other | English | To study | 2016 | English |
| 3141 | EMU | nCt | TRNC | Other | English | To study | 2017 | English |
| 3133 | EMU | Ct | TRNC | Cyprus | Cypriot | Born in Cyprus | 1997 | Turkish |

Table 3.3 (continued)

| No | University, Interview | Ties | Part | Place of Birth | Nationality | Why in Cyprus | Time in Cyprus | Native Language(s) |
|---|---|---|---|---|---|---|---|---|
| 3102 | EMU | nCt | TRNC | Other | English | To study | 2012 | Turkish |
| 3132 | EMU | nCt | TRNC | Other | English | To study | 2016 | Y |
| 393 | EMU | nCt | TRNC | Other | English | To study | 2016 | Y |
| 392 | EMU | nCt | TRNC | Other | English | To study | 2016 | Y |
| 391 | EMU | nCt | TRNC | English | English | To study | 2015 | Y |
| 3112 | EMU | Ct | TRNC | Cyprus | Cypriot | Born in Cyprus | 1997 | Turkish |
| 3113 | EMU | Ct | TRNC | Cyprus | English | Born in Cyprus | 1997 | Turkish |
| 3101 | EMU | Ct | TRNC | English | Cypriot | Other | 1997 | English+X |
| 3121 | EMU | nCt | TRNC | Other | Cypriot | To study | 2014 | Turkish |
| 3111 | EMU | Ct | TRNC | Cyprus | Cypriot | Other | 2005 | English |
| 3131 | EMU | Ct | TRNC | Cyprus | Cypriot | Born in Cyprus | 1998 | English+X |
| 3143 | EMU | nCt | TRNC | Other | English | To study | 2016 | English |
| 3144 | EMU | Ct | TRNC | Cyprus | Cypriot | Born in Cyprus | 1991 | Turkish |
| 3122 | EMU | nCt | TRNC | Other | English | To study | 2014 | X+X+X |
| 3114 | EMU | Ct | TRNC | English | Other | Other | 2007 | English |
| 3134 | EMU | Ct | TRNC | English | Cypriot | Born in Cyprus | 2006 | English |
| 3135 | EMU | nCt | TRNC | Other | English | 0 | 2016 | Turkish |
| 3136 | EMU | nCt | TRNC | Other | English | To study | 2015 | Y |
| 3137 | EMU | nCt | TRNC | Other | English | To study | 2016 | Y |
| 3138 | EMU | nCt | TRNC | Other | English | To study | 2016 | Turkish |
| 3139 | EMU | nCt | TRNC | Other | English | Other | 2016 | Y |
| 31310 | EMU | nCt | TRNC | Other | English | Other | 2016 | English+X |
| 31311 | EMU | nCt | TRNC | Other | English | To study | 2016 | English |

**Table 3.3** (continued)

| No | University, Interview | Ties | Part | Place of Birth | Nationality | Why in Cyprus | Time in Cyprus | Native Language(s) |
|---|---|---|---|---|---|---|---|---|
| 31312 | EMU | nCt | TRNC | Other | English | To study | 2016 | Y |
| 3115 | EMU, excluded | nCt | TRNC | Other | English | Other | 2015 | Turkish |
| 394 | EMU, yes | nCt | TRNC | Other | English | To study | 2016 | Y |
| 3116 | EMU, yes | Ct | TRNC | Cyprus | Cypriot | Born in Cyprus | 0 | Turkish |
| 31313 | EMU, yes | nCt | TRNC | Other | English | To study | 2016 | Turkish |
| 3123 | EMU, yes | Ct | TRNC | English | Other | Other | 2007 | English |
| 395 | EMU, yes | nCt | TRNC | Other | English | To study | 2016 | Y |
| 3103 | EMU, yes | Ct | TRNC | English | Cypriot | Born in Cyprus | 1996 | Turkish |
| 3104 | EMU, yes & GAU, yes | Ct | TRNC | English | Cypriot | Other | 2010 | English+X |
| 3105 | EMU, yes | nCt | TRNC | Other | English | To study | 2015 | Y |
| 3145 | EMU, yes | Ct | TRNC | English | Cypriot | Born in Cyprus | 1994 | Turkish |
| 396 | EMU, yes | nCt | TRNC | Other | English | To study | 2016 | Y |
| 397 | EMU, yes | nCt | TRNC | Other | English | To study | 2015 | Y |
| 3146 | EMU | nCt | TRNC | Other | English | To study | 2012 | X+X |
| 3147 | EMU | Ct | TRNC | Cyprus | Cypriot | Born in Cyprus | 1993 | Turkish |
| 3148 | EMU | nCt | TRNC | Other | Cypriot | To study | 2016 | Y |
| 3149 | EMU | nCt | TRNC | Other | English | 0 | 2013 | Turkish |
| 31410 | EMU | nCt | TRNC | Other | English | To study | 2017 | Y |
| 3125 | EMU | Ct | TRNC | Cyprus | Cypriot | To study | 0 | Turkish |
| 3126 | EMU | nCt | TRNC | Other | English | To study | 2013 | Turkish |
| 3127 | EMU | nCt | TRNC | Other | English | To study | 2013 | Turkish |

**Table 3.3** (continued)

| No | University, Interview | Ties | Part | Place of Birth | Nationality | Why in Cyprus | Time in Cyprus | Native Language(s) |
|---|---|---|---|---|---|---|---|---|
| 31314 | EMU | nCt | TRNC | Other | English | To study | 2015 | Y |
| 31315 | EMU | Ct | TRNC | Cyprus | Cypriot | Born in Cyprus | 1998 | Turkish |
| 31316 | EMU | nCt | TRNC | Other | English | To study | 2016 | Turkish |
| 31317 | EMU | Ct | TRNC | Cyprus | Cypriot | Born in Cyprus | 1998 | Turkish |
| 31318 | EMU | nCt | TRNC | Other | English | To study | 2016 | Turkish |
| 31319 | EMU | nCt | TRNC | Other | English | To study | 2016 | Y |
| 31320 | EMU | nCt | TRNC | Other | English | 0 | 2016 | Turkish |
| 31321 | EMU | nCt | TRNC | English | Cypriot | To study | 2016 | English |
| 31322 | EMU | Ct | TRNC | Cyprus | Cypriot | Born in Cyprus | 1996 | Turkish |
| 31323 | EMU | Ct | TRNC | English | Cypriot | 0 | 0 | Turkish |
| 31324 | EMU | Ct | TRNC | Other | Cypriot | Born in Cyprus | 1998 | Turkish |
| 31325 | EMU | Ct | TRNC | Cyprus | Cypriot | 0 | 0 | English+X |
| 3117 | EMU | nCt | TRNC | Other | English | To study | 2015 | Y |
| 3118 | EMU | Ct | TRNC | Cyprus | Cypriot | Born in Cyprus | 1997 | Turkish |
| 3119 | EMU | nCt | TRNC | Other | English | To study | 2015 | Turkish |
| 31110 | EMU | nCt | TRNC | Other | English | To study | 2014 | Turkish |
| 31111 | EMU | nCt | TRNC | Other | English | To study | 2015 | Turkish |
| 31112 | EMU | nCt | TRNC | Other | English | To study | 2015 | Turkish |
| 31113 | EMU | nCt | TRNC | Other | English | To study | 2014 | Turkish |
| 31114 | EMU | nCt | TRNC | English | English | To study | 2015 | English |
| 31115 | EMU | nCt | TRNC | Other | English | To study | 2014 | Turkish |
| 31116 | EMU | nCt | TRNC | Other | English | Other | 2015 | Turkish |

Table 3.3 (continued)

| No | University, Interview | Ties | Part | Place of Birth | Nationality | Why in Cyprus | Time in Cyprus | Native Language(s) |
|---|---|---|---|---|---|---|---|---|
| 31117 | EMU | nCt | TRNC | Other | English | To study | 2015 | Y |
| 3106 | EMU | nCt | TRNC | Other | English | Other | 2013 | English+X |
| 3107 | EMU | nCt | TRNC | Other | English | To study | 2015 | Y |
| 3108 | EMU | Ct | TRNC | Cyprus | Cypriot | Born in Cyprus | 1995 | Turkish |
| 3109 | EMU | nCt | TRNC | Other | English | To study | 2014 | Y |
| 31010 | EMU | nCt | TRNC | Other | English | Other | 2013 | Y |
| 31011 | EMU | Ct | TRNC | English | Cypriot | Born in Cyprus | 1996 | English+X |
| 31012 | EMU | nCt | TRNC | English | Other | To study | 2012 | Turkish |
| 31013 | EMU | Ct | TRNC | English | Cypriot | Other | 2005 | English+X |
| 31014 | EMU | Ct | TRNC | Cyprus | Cypriot | 0 | 0 | Turkish |
| 31015 | EMU | nCt | TRNC | Other | English | To study | 2013 | Y |
| 31016 | EMU | nCt | TRNC | Other | English | To study | 2013 | Y |
| 398 | EMU | Ct | TRNC | Cyprus | Cypriot | Born in Cyprus | 1993 | Turkish |
| 399 | EMU | nCt | TRNC | Other | English | To study | 2016 | Y |
| 3910 | EMU | nCt | TRNC | Other | English | To study | 2012 | X+X |
| 3911 | EMU | nCt | TRNC | Other | English | To study | 2015 | Y |
| 3912 | EMU | nCt | TRNC | Other | English | To study | 2015 | Y |
| 3913 | EMU | Ct | TRNC | English | Cypriot | To study | 2006 | English |
| 3914 | EMU | nCt | TRNC | Other | English | To study | 2015 | Y |
| 3915 | EMU | nCt | TRNC | Other | English | To study | 2015 | Y |
| 3916 | EMU | nCt | TRNC | Other | English | To study | 2017 | Y |
| 3917 | EMU | Ct | TRNC | Cyprus | Cypriot | Born in Cyprus | 1991 | Turkish |

Table 3.3 (continued)

| No | University, Interview | Ties | Part | Place of Birth | Nationality | Why in Cyprus | Time in Cyprus | Native Language(s) |
|---|---|---|---|---|---|---|---|---|
| 3918 | EMU | nCt | TRNC | Other | English | To study | 2015 | Y |
| 3919 | EMU | nCt | TRNC | Other | English | To study | 2016 | X+X |
| 3920 | EMU | nCt | TRNC | Other | 0 | To study | 2016 | Y |
| 3201 | EMU, yes | nCt | TRNC | English | English | To study | 2014 | English+X |
| 411 | GAU, yes | nCt | TRNC | English | English | To study | 2017 | X+X |

Eighty-two participants in this study are students of UCLan Cyprus. All were in their first semester of various study programs, attending program-independent language classes at the time of their participation in October 2016. Seventy-four students (90.2 percent) were identified as Ct- and eight (9.8 percent) as nCt-students, while 4.9 percent state having moved to Cyprus to pursue their HE. Of UCLan Cyprus students, 63.4 percent are male, 36.6 percent female, and 78 percent were born in Cyprus. The majority of the UCLan Cyprus participants (79.2 percent) were born in the years 1996 to 1998, while their mean age is 19.87 (SD 2.88). Half of the participants at UCLan Cyprus identify as native speakers of only Greek or Cypriot Greek, with 3.7 percent as native speakers of only Turkish and 9.8 percent as native speakers of English and another language (see Appendix 2.1). Ten Ct-students and two nCt-students volunteered to participate in follow-up interviews.

At UCy, twenty-six students of the Department of English Studies offered to partake—twenty-one Ct- and five nCt-students (80.8 percent and 19.2 percent, respectively). All participants were students of the Department of English Studies: 84.6 percent female and 15.4 percent male. Of the twenty-six participants, 84.6 percent were born in Cyprus and 92.3 percent identify as native speakers of Greek or Cypriot Greek only. No participant identifies as a native speaker of English. The participants were born between 1990 and 1997, with 42.3 percent born in 1997. The sample's mean age is 20.16 with a standard deviation of 1.63 years (see Appendix 2.1). Four students in this participant sample agreed to partake in a subsequent interview, all of them Ct-students.

Ninety-six students in this sample are students at EMU—thirty students are identified as Ct- (31.3 percent) and sixty-six are nCt-students (68.8 percent). Thirteen of these participated in individual interviews, five of which were Ct- and eight nCt-students. All participants were students of a bachelor's or master's degree in English Language Teaching (ELT), divided into 65.6 percent female and 34.4 percent male students. While 18.8 percent of the students were born in Cyprus, 53.1 percent state having come to Cyprus to study. The majority of the participants (59.2 percent) were born in 1994 or later, with a mean age of 22.19 years (SD 3.98). While 40.6 percent of the participants at EMU identify as native speakers of only Turkish, 20.1 percent identify as native speakers of English or English and another language (see Appendix 2.1).

One of the local undergraduate students at EMU later attended GAU for her master's degree and offered to share a comparison of her experiences from an informed perspective. She has not been counted twice in the general frequency analysis but will be included in the following for completeness. At GAU, the author was introduced to nCt-students by the Ct-student, of which one student, who did her bachelor's degree at GAU, agreed to be interviewed. The sample, therefore, consists of two female students of ELT, both of whom agreed to an extensive follow-up interview. The students were twenty-three and thirty-three years of age at the time of their participation and both were born in a country that uses English as (one of) the official language(s). However, only one identifies as a native speaker of English. While the Ct-student came to Cyprus for family reasons, the nCt-student moved to Cyprus to pursue her HE journey.

### 3.6.3 Research Suppositions

The following suppositions are motivated by the author's experiences and impressions during her visits to Cyprus. Using them as a scaffold allows for capturing and operationalizing topics and concepts that recurred during conversations and interactions with the participants to unveil the value of English in Cyprus's HE landscapes. The suppositions provide a frame to explore and contextualize the heterogeneous, rich, and complex encounters that are part of Cyprus's HE. Furthermore, this framework enables a discussion of the received information and existing trends across the participants' narratives, while acknowledging and appreciating their individual life trajectories, biographies, and experiences. The suppositions are phrased in such a way as to represent the most common threads that surfaced during the conduction of the study.

1. For its users, the value of the English language lies in its communicative potential. Native speaker standards and its cultural embeddedness are less important.
2. Universities in Cyprus use the value of the English language primarily to attract fee-paying nCt-students.
3. Students invest in the English language because it represents immediate or future upward social mobility.
4. The value of the English language outweighs nCt-students' concerns about the local contexts it is offered in. The students' abstraction of English-as-a-marketable-attribute from its context is openly utilized by the universities.

### 3.6.4 Study design

The present study aims at developing a comprehensive and inclusive description of the value of the English language in Cyprus's HE while putting local and international students at its center. Since assessing the value of English requires an in-depth and nuanced investigation of complex dynamics, this study constitutes a combination of quantitative and qualitative research—biographical and sociolinguistic questionnaires and voluntary semi-structured qualitative interviews (see Appendices 1.1, 1.2, 2.2, and 2.3 for some of the questions)—while focusing on the qualitative analysis of the data. To assess the value of English comprehensively, the students' life trajectories, motives, experiences, and backgrounds must be considered and integrated. Furthermore, the prevailing social processes and organization must be understood and incorporated, which requires the consideration of their partakers' individuality as well as their firm foundation within their complex situatedness and experiences (Mason 2002: 65). Conducting qualitative interviews enabled the consideration of these factors. The insight and findings provided during these interviews are embedded into the larger context of Cyprus's HE, to enrich and contextualize the data sample and to understand their respective relevance. The quantifiable contextual information has been collected using sociolinguistic questionnaires.

The study was executed in two parts. First, the prepared questionnaires were distributed by the author in in-class settings at EMU, UCLan Cyprus, and UCy in

October 2016 and March 2017; only the nCt-student at GAU, who participated in October 2018, received the questionnaire via email. Participants, who agreed to be interviewed, were contacted to arrange for an individual or a group appointment. Second, twenty-eight semi-structured interviews with thirty participants were scheduled and conducted (Section 3.6.4.2). All twenty-eight interviews were executed by the author—twenty-five in a one-on-one setting (one student was interviewed twice) and three with the author interviewing two students at the same time. While sixteen interviews were conducted in person, twelve were conducted remotely, using voice-over-IP services to accommodate the participants' requests. The first data collection session served to provide a more general overview of the diversity of the participants and the range of their language use and attitudes employing questionnaires, while the second aimed at further exploring the participants' experiences and in developing a more nuanced picture of their individual valuation of English in the specific context of Cyprus's HE. The two parts were always conducted in chronological order and in separate meetings. Commencing with the quantitative part of the study offered the opportunity to revisit potentially insightful answers during the interviews and to customize some of the interview questions in order to uncover the dynamics of the assignment and an acceptance of the value of English in greater detail. Furthermore, executing the first part of the study in class was found to assist in approaching potential interviewees; first interacting with the researcher in a familiar and in-group setting has increased the students' motivation to meet again and partake in an interview in which their trust, honesty, and motivation have been essential. The institutional setting of this first encounter was expected to also support the legitimacy of the study in the eyes of the participants. However, concerning the qualitative interviews, the remotely conducted ones were experienced as especially open and somewhat liberated interactions. While the formal university-related setting might have supported the study's legitimacy, distancing from the locally imposed restrictions and social hierarchy, as well as revoking the author's direct connection to the attended university, increased the participants' openness. The semi-structuredness of the interviews ensures the inclusion of the participants' language use and biography in every interview while offering a satisfying degree of flexibility to allow for a comprehensive understanding of the participants' individual experiences and beliefs. Furthermore, this degree of flexibility helped create a relaxed and trusting atmosphere during the conversations, in which the students felt comfortable and at ease to share these personal opinions and experiences.

In addition to the information provided by the participants, the webpages of the involved universities were revisited after the second research visit to Cyprus in March 2017. Since the universities' webpages represent "the institution[s'] 'global face'" (Jenkins 2014: 81), their composition and content matter were assumed to be approved by the respective university's management level and therefore view the content matter as reliable research data. The presented information about scholarship requirements, tuition fees, and the various study programs' languages of instruction has been focused on specifically. Furthermore, following Jenkins's (2014) approach in including (language) policy-related pages, "About X" pages, "mission statements," and "anything relating specifically to language requirements" (81) have been included. The universities' webpages were also used to contextualize the participants' statements, if necessary. After having introduced the general procedure of the study, a more detailed description of its two parts in order of their execution will be provided.

### *3.6.4.1 Questionnaire*

Sociolinguistic and ethnographic questionnaires have been developed to collect information about the participants' biographies, their language use, and attitudes, as well as their reasons for choosing the respective university and their linguistic and social experience as students in Cyprus (see Appendices 1.1, 2.2, and 2.3 for some of the questions). The collected information was used to provide a more comprehensive picture of the individual student and his/her social and linguistic biography as well as to explore general tendencies within the student body.

The first three parts of the questionnaire are variations of Buschfeld's (2013) Cyprus-focusing adaption of Künstler, Mendis, and Mukherjee's (2009) questionnaire to investigate Sri Lankan English. While the wide range of contexts of use, which is addressed in both studies, has been maintained, the individual items have been altered to fit the specific contexts of HE in both parts of the island. The prepared questionnaire contains metric, categorical, and ordinal variables. Due to the different nature of the variables, a unique coding system for the descriptive quantification of the participant sample at hand has been developed. While metric variables remained in their natural form (e.g., the number of years the participants have spent in Cyprus or their year of birth), categorical variables were grouped and coded based on the multiplicity of provided answers, that is, the variable *sex* has been coded

"1" (male) and "2" (female), and the variable *native language* has been coded "1" to "9" reflecting various individual languages and combinations of two or more languages. Missing values have always been coded "0." Ordinal variables (Likert scales) were translated into a rising numerical sequence from "1" to "5," again using "0" for missing values. Although the author has decided to use Likert-scale data to gain quantifiable data whose elicitation does not exceed the participants' patience and motivation, she refrains from a potentially problematic statistic evaluation (cf. De Winter and Dodou 2010 for a discussion) in offering a quantified description of the data sample (see Section 3.7). The interview data, however, has been analyzed from a qualitative perspective.

### *3.6.4.2 Qualitative Interviews*

Aiming to "achieve depth and roundedness of understanding" (Mason 2002: 65) in an interface area of personal experiences with complex and changing dynamics, the methodological choice of centering individual students is based on the constructedness of critical realism. This study follows the ontological understanding of people's knowledge, experiences, and views as meaningful and as existing independently of the human mind, while epistemologically constructed in social interactions and, therefore, situated and subjective (cf. Levers 2013; see also Bergin, Wells, and Owen 2010; Crotty 1998). Consequently, personal and interactive qualitative interviews—which are "in-depth, semi-structured or loosely structured forms of interview[s]" aiming at "generating qualitative data" (Mason 2002: 62)—constitute the second part of this study.

Preparing the elicitation of qualitative and meaningful data, Mason's (2002: 74) guidelines for qualitative interviewers were adapted as well as Tagliamonte's (2006: 39–47) techniques and Labov's (1982, 1984) goals of sociolinguistic interviews selectively included. Although Labovian sociolinguistic interviews were not conducted, the author similarly depended on the creation of a relaxed, benevolent, and trusting atmosphere to elicit "narratives of personal experiences" (Labov 1984: 32) and on achieving "rapport," a stage in which interviewee and interviewer "no longer worry about offending each other or making mistakes in asking or answering questions [and interviewees] offer personal information" (Spradley [1979] 2002: 47). The synopsis of these approaches resulted in the following guidelines of qualitative interviews:

1. Be interested: To create a trusting atmosphere and a supportive environment for the interviewee to offer cooperation in, the interviewer has to reflect an authentic interest in the social and private persona of the interviewee. This might be realized by "respond[ing] to new issues" or "following the subject's main interest and idea wherever they go" (Tagliamonte 2006: 39).
2. Be considerate: Although the purpose of the interview is the collection of research data, the interviewer must be "sensitive to the interviewees, to their needs and rights, in accordance with [his/her] ethical position and moral practice" (Mason 2002: 74). Qualitative interviewing allows for a fair and full "representation of the interviewees' perspectives" (ibid: 66), which should always be considered in the interviewer's epistemology and research practices.
3. Participate: Qualitative interviews are "conversation[s] with a purpose" (Burgess 1984: 102), which require at least two participants to be active (Holstein and Gubrium 1995: 4; see also Edley and Litosseliti 2010: 160). The focus of the interviewer should not be on collecting data but rather on being present in the moment of the social interaction. In this case, the interviewer can "help the flow of the interview interaction," for instance, by referring back to the "interviewee's' circumstances, experiences and so on" that have already been established (Mason 2002: 74). Furthermore, the interviewer can "volunteer experiences" (Tagliamonte 2006: 39) or "take an insider's point of view" (Tagliamonte 2006: 47; see also Labov 1982: 34) to relate to the interviewee and show personal investment, which also facilitates the rapport process (Spradley [1979] 2002: 45). This might very well contradict Labov's (1984: 34) and Tagliamonte's (2006) advice to "ask short questions" (47).
4. Stay focused while allowing for guidance: Although the interviewer should follow Tagliamonte's (2006) advice to "let the informant talk" (46), unlike in sociolinguistic interviews, extensive off-topic narrations are not productive. The interviewer must achieve "an appropriate focus on issues and topics relevant to [the phenomenon in question]" (Mason 2002: 74). However, if the interviewer agrees to "be the learner" (Tagliamonte 2006: 47; see also Labov 1984: 40–1), the interviewee might feel more comfortable in filling the position of the "expert," which potentially results in an assimilation of the perceived power difference and a more liberated conversation. The interviewer needs to

be flexible and to "be able to 'think on [his/her] feet' in the interview itself. [The interviewer has] to do this quickly, effectively, coherently and in ways which are consistent with [the research purpose]" (Mason 2002: 67).

These guidelines enabled a conversation about certain topics while allowing for the interviewee's guidance and the interviewer's flexibility to follow up on information provided during the interview or in the questionnaires. The interviews have been semi-structured, based on interview options (cf. Appendix 1.2). While the wording of these options might have been changed, following Tagliamonte's (2006: 46–7; see Labov 1984: 33) advice of adjusting the formality of the language to the interview situation, the interviews were always initiated by using questions that invite the participant(s) to talk. Asking the participants to talk about themselves and their childhood experiences encouraged their cooperation and reduced tension. Depending on the individual interview, the emerging relationship between the interviewer and the interviewee(s), and the respective experience shared, the author decided how to proceed—"thinking on her feet." In engaging on the content and social level, the social positions of interviewer and interviewee were assimilated, and potential inhibition in the interviewees to share their honest experiences, opinions, and beliefs was avoided.

All interviews were recorded, which all interviewees had given their permission to. Two interviews were excluded from the analysis due to communication difficulties based on either language or technical obstacles. The remaining twenty-six interviews included two interviews with the same interviewee, which were separated by one year, and three interviews including two interviewees each. Consequently, statements by twenty-eight students were included in the analysis of the qualitative interviews. The generation of all transcriptions included at least three people to increase objectivity and accuracy. The transcription of the interviews was based on MacWhinney's (2000) Codes for the Human Analysis of Transcripts (CHAT), as this is a commonly used and accepted format. Since the present study focuses on the content level of the interviews rather than on linguistic variation or pragmatic strategies, the code was simplified and adapted to the needs of this research (cf. Appendix 1.3). The excerpts that are cited in this book were revised for reader friendliness only to the extent of shortening accumulations of utterances of reflection (i.e., ehm, eh, uhm) or active listening (i.e., mhm, right, okay) and of including punctuation markers.

## 3.7 Descriptive Analysis

While this study requires a strong qualitative focus, an analysis of the answers provided in the participants' questionnaires offers a helpful overview of the composition of the participant sample, their language use, and language attitudes. Furthermore, a quantification of the answers provided in the sociolinguistic questionnaires might signal potential (dis)similarities, tendencies, and prioritizations within or across student groups. While a statistical analysis of the elicited data would have been possible, its results would not be convincing, due to the wide range of group size and the diversity in the composition of the groups (cf. Section 3.6.2). Instead, frequencies that offer an explicable and reliable overview of the sample and can reveal possible tendencies within it are presented for relevant parts of the data.

Despite the diversity of the students' biographies and experiences, they are all united in their choice to pursue their HE in Cyprus. Interestingly, more participants stated that they were in Cyprus to study (29.3 percent) than that they were on the island because of having been born there (25.9 percent). Concerning their English language use, almost all participants had English as their medium of instruction and use the language when communicating with their friends and academic staff at their respective universities. Furthermore, the majority of participants agree to like the English language, and 72.2 percent feel that knowing English is important in their private lives (see Appendix 2.3).

A "top-box" approach is used in this study to summarize the participants' information and language use attitudes, that is, summarizing the two top boxes as showing "agreement" and the two lowest as signaling "disagreement." In so doing, it is found that 57.6 percent feel that English is a tool to communicate with, and its users do not have to be familiar with British or American. Furthermore, a large majority of participants agree that knowing and speaking English is advantageous and important in various contexts and agree that it is sufficient for global communication (Table 3.4). Concerning the participants' reasons for choosing the respective university for their HE, only 6.8 percent stated to have picked it because of the use of the English language. Most students name the university's reputation (20.5 percent) or a recommendation (21.5 percent) as their reason; only 6.3 percent pick their university because of its location. Furthermore, only 30.7 percent of all students in this study claim to be planning to stay in Cyprus after their graduation; 38 percent do not want to stay and

Table 3.4 Language Attitudes of All Participants (in Percentage, Rounded)

| All Participants | I Strongly Agree | I Agree | Indifferent | I Disagree | I Strongly Disagree |
| --- | --- | --- | --- | --- | --- |
| I think knowledge of English is important | 84.9 | 13.7 | 0.5 | 0 | 1 |
| Speaking English is an advantage | 78.5 | 19 | 1 | 0.5 | 1 |
| English offers advantages in seeking good job opportunities | 78.5 | 18.5 | 1 | 0 | 2 |
| Without the knowledge of English, I could not get a job | 28.3 | 23.9 | 25.9 | 17.6 | 3.4 |
| I prefer using another language whenever possible | 17.6 | 37.1 | 35.6 | 5.9 | 3.4 |
| When living in Cyprus speaking English and Greek/Turkish is important | 65.9 | 30.2 | 1 | 2 | 1 |
| Speaking English suffices to live and communicate anywhere | 56.6 | 32.2 | 4.4 | 2.9 | 2.4 |
| I like speaking English | 64.9 | 25.9 | 6.8 | 0 | 1.5 |
| English is a communicative tool and users don't need to be aware of British/American culture | 31.7 | 25.9 | 22 | 12.7 | 5.4 |

23.4 percent are undecided (see Appendix 2.3). For a clearer understanding of the students' attitudes toward the English language, their use, and valuation of it, the participants will be grouped by the university they attend and their ties to Cyprus.

At UCLan Cyprus, the English language is used as the official medium of instruction and administration. Of the Ct-students, which are 90.2 percent of the participants at UCLan Cyprus, 43.3 percent state that English is or has been a language of instruction in education, while most name their primary language of education to be (Cypriot) Greek (59.5 percent). While the majority of Ct-students use the language to communicate with faculty members, 45.9 percent use the language when communicating with their friends at the university. Furthermore, 35.1 percent of the participants name English as the only or as one of the languages they use most often. Concerning these students' attitudes toward the English language, the majority feels that knowing English is important in their private lives (71.6 percent; see Appendix 2.4). Furthermore, a large majority believes that English is advantageous and important for their employability, while 52.7 percent think they would not get

**Table 3.5** Language Attitudes UCLan Cyprus (in Percentage, Rounded)

| UCLan Cyprus | I Strongly Agree | | I Agree | | Indifferent | | I Disagree | | I Strongly Disagree | |
|---|---|---|---|---|---|---|---|---|---|---|
| | Ct | nCt | Ct | nCt | Ct | nCt | Ct | nCt | Ct | nCt |
| English offers advantages in seeking good job opportunities | 67.7 | 37.5 | 27 | 50 | 2.7 | 0 | 0 | 0 | 2.7 | 12.5 |
| Without the knowledge of English, I could not get a job | 31.1 | 25 | 21.6 | 25 | 35.1 | 12.5 | 6.8 | 37.5 | 4.1 | 0 |
| I strongly identify with my home culture and language | 29.7 | 25 | 37.8 | 25 | 23 | 37.5 | 1.4 | 0 | 2.7 | 12.5 |
| English is a communicative tool and users don't need to be aware of British/American culture | 31.1 | 12.5 | 27 | 50 | 20.3 | 12.5 | 10.8 | 25 | 4.1 | 0 |

an occupation without this knowledge. While 67.5 percent claim to strongly identify with their respective native language and culture, 58.1 percent of the Ct-students at the British UCLan Cyprus feel that English is a tool to communicate with, and that its users do not have to be familiar with British or American culture (see Table 3.5). When asked why they had picked UCLan Cyprus for their HE, 23 percent named its reputation, 16.2 percent a recommendation, 12.2 percent the English language, and 10.8 percent the university's location as being the decisive factor. While 41.9 percent of the Ct-students claim to be planning to stay in Cyprus after their graduation, 20.3 percent do not want to stay and 24.3 percent are undecided (see Appendix 2.4).

A total of 9.8 percent of the eighty-two UCLan students are identified as nCt-students. While 25 percent of these students plan to stay in Cyprus after their graduation, 37.5 percent state to have moved to Cyprus to study. All of them have been taught in English and 62.5 percent name English as having been the/a primary language of instruction. Furthermore, all nCt-students use English to talk to faculty members, 75 percent use it exclusively when talking to friends at the university, and 50 percent of the participants believe English is the only or one of the languages they use most. When asked about their attitudes toward the English language, 50 percent feel that knowing English is important in their private lives (ibid.). Furthermore, a large majority believes that English is advantageous and important for their employability, while again 50 percent think they would not become employed without this knowledge. While half of these participants state to strongly identify with their respective native language and culture, 62.5 percent of the nCt-students at UCLan Cyprus feel that English is a tool to communicate with and that its users do not have to be familiar with British or American culture (Table 3.5). Half of the nCt-students at UCLan Cyprus gave more than one reason for their choosing the university; 12.5 percent named the English language and a recommendation, respectively (see Appendix 2.4). EMU students show a clearer tendency when naming the reasons for their choice.

This study includes ninety-six EMU students, of which 31.3 percent are identified as Ct-students. While 63.3 percent of the Ct-students at EMU claim to have been born in Cyprus as their reason for living on the island, 49.9 percent state English is or has been the language of instruction in their previous education. English is also used by most Ct-students for communication with faculty members at EMU (83.3 percent) and by all Ct-students to converse with their friends in university contexts. English is, furthermore, the only or one of

Table 3.6 Language Attitudes EMU (in Percentage, Rounded)

| EMU | I strongly Agree | | I Agree | | Indifferent | | I Disagree | | I Strongly Disagree | |
|---|---|---|---|---|---|---|---|---|---|---|
| | Ct | nCt | Ct | nCt | Ct | nCt | Ct | nCt | Ct | nCt |
| English offers advantages in seeking good job opportunities | 67.7 | 37.5 | 27 | 50 | 2.7 | 0 | 0 | 0 | 2.7 | 12.5 |
| Without the knowledge of English, I could not get a job | 31.1 | 25 | 21.6 | 25 | 35.1 | 12.5 | 6.8 | 37.5 | 4.1 | 0 |
| I strongly identify with my home culture and language | 29.7 | 25 | 37.8 | 25 | 23 | 37.5 | 1.4 | 0 | 2.7 | 12.5 |
| English is a communicative tool and users don't need to be aware of British/American culture | 31.1 | 12.5 | 27 | 50 | 20.3 | 12.5 | 10.8 | 25 | 3.1 | 0 |

the languages 56.7 percent of this group uses most often on an everyday basis. At EMU, 76.7 percent of the Ct-students feel that knowing English is important in their private lives (see Appendix 2.5). While all agree on the importance and advantage of English on the job market, 53.3 percent believe they could not get a job without this knowledge. While 80 percent agree on strongly identifying with their respective native language and culture, 60 percent of the Ct-students at EMU feel that English is a tool to communicate with and that its users do not have to be familiar with British or American culture (Table 3.6). One-third of the Ct-students chose EMU for their HE because of its reputation, 13.3 percent followed a recommendation, and for 16.7 percent its location was decisive. The use of the English language was not given as a reason in this subgroup. At the time of the study, 53.3 percent claim to be planning to stay in Cyprus after their graduation; 33.3 percent do not want to stay and 13.3 percent are undecided (see Appendix 2.5). This situation is different concerning nCt-students.

Of the sixty-six nCt-students at EMU, 74.2 percent came to Cyprus for their HE and only 12.2 percent are planning to stay after their graduation. Only 4.5 percent have not been taught in English and 42.4 percent name English as having been the/a primary language of instruction in their previous education. English is also used by a large majority of nCt-students for communication with faculty members at EMU (89.4 percent) and by most nCt-students to converse with their friends in university contexts. English is, furthermore, the only or one of the languages 69.7 percent of this group uses most often on a daily basis (see ibid.). Concerning their attitudes toward the English language, for 71.2 percent of the nCt-students at EMU knowing English is important in their private lives. Furthermore, almost all students believe that English is advantageous and important for their employability, while 48.4 percent even think they would not become employed without this knowledge (ibid., Table 3.6). While more than half of these participants (63.7 percent) claim to strongly identify with their respective native language and culture, 59.1 percent of the nCt-students at EMU feel that English is a communicative tool, and that its users do not have to be familiar with British or American culture (ibid.). More than one-third of the nCt-students at EMU claim to have followed a recommendation when choosing EMU for their HE; 7.6 percent named its reputation and 6.1 percent the English language as decisive factors (see Appendix 2.5). The English language was not mentioned as a reason for UCy students' university choice, as will be shown in the following.

**Table 3.7** Language Attitudes UCy (in Percentage, Rounded)

| UCy | I strongly Agree | | I Agree | | Indifferent | | I Disagree | | I Strongly Disagree | |
|---|---|---|---|---|---|---|---|---|---|---|
| | Ct | nCt | Ct | nCt | Ct | nCt | Ct | nCt | Ct | nCt |
| English offers advantages in seeking good job opportunities | 85.7 | 60 | 14.3 | 40 | 0 | 0 | 0 | 0 | 0 | 0 |
| Without the knowledge of English, I could not get a job | 28.6 | 20 | 28.6 | 40 | 14.3 | 20 | 28.6 | 20 | 0 | 0 |
| I strongly identify with my home culture and language | 23.8 | 0 | 38.1 | 60 | 33.3 | 40 | 4.8 | 0 | 0 | 0 |
| English is a communicative tool and users don't need to be aware of British/American culture | 28.6 | 0 | 28.6 | 20 | 19 | 40 | 14.3 | 20 | 9.5 | 20 |

Of the twenty-six UCy students in this study, 80.8 percent are Ct-students. While 66.7 percent of this subgroup did not give a reason, the remaining third named having been born on the island as their reason for living in Cyprus. While the language of their previous instruction was mainly Greek, all Ct-students at UCy were taught in English, among other languages, at the time of the study. Furthermore, English is used by Ct-students for communication with faculty members (42.8 percent) and when speaking with their friends in university contexts. English is, however, the only or one of the primarily used languages for only 14.3 percent of this group. For 81 percent of the Ct-students at UCy, knowing English is important in their private lives (see Appendix 2.6). While all of them agree on the importance and advantage of English on the job market, 57.2 percent believe they could be employed without this knowledge. While 61.9 percent agree to strongly identify with their predominantly Cypriot Greek native language and culture, 57.2 percent of the Ct-students agree that English is a tool of communication and that its users do not have to be familiar with British or American culture (Table 3.7). Almost half (47.6 percent) of the Ct-students chose UCy for their HE because of its reputation, while 33.3 percent gave more than one reason and 4.8 percent followed a recommendation. The use of the English language was not given as a reason in this subgroup. This group is, furthermore, most united in their future plans; 71.4 percent of Ct-students of UCy do not want to stay in Cyprus after their graduation; 19 percent want to stay and 9.5 percent are undecided (see Appendix 2.6). This situation is more open concerning UCy's nCt-students.

In this study, 19.2 percent of the UCy students are identified as nCt-students. Eighty percent of these students came to Cyprus to pursue their HE and 20 percent are planning to stay after their graduation; 20 percent do not want to stay in Cyprus and 40 percent are undecided. While English is part of their current education, 20 percent name English as the language of their previous education. The English language is also used by all nCt-students for communication with their friends and by most nCt-students to converse with faculty members (60 percent). English is, however, the only or one of the languages that 20 percent of these students use during the majority of their daily routines. nCt-students at UCy generally show positive attitudes toward the English language. For 60 percent of these students, knowing English is important in their private lives (see Appendix 2.6). Furthermore, all students believe that English is advantageous and important for their employability, while 60 percent believe that their future occupation will depend on their knowledge of English. While 60 percent of these participants claim to strongly identify with their respective native language and culture, only 20 percent agree that English is a communicative tool and that its users do not have to be familiar with British or American culture (Table 3.7). When asked about their reasons for choosing UCy for their HE, 60 percent of its nCt-students claim to have followed a recommendation and 40 percent gave more than one reason (see Appendix 2.6). While the English language was not mentioned as a reason for UCy students' university choice, it is of special importance for the GAU students in this study.

At GAU, the author had the opportunity to talk at length with two students, one Ct-student, who had been a student at EMU before enrolling at GAU, and one nCt-student. While the Ct-student moved to Cyprus for family reasons and chose GAU because of its convenient location, the nCt-student came to Cyprus to pursue her HE and chose GAU primarily because of its name and because her sister was already a student at this university. Both students state that they are planning to stay in Cyprus after their graduation. Furthermore, for both students, English has been and is the primary language of education. They claim that they always use English when talking to GAU faculty and their friends in university contexts. While the nCt-student uses only English during the majority of her daily communications, the Ct-student uses English and Turkish. Both students believe they have near-native proficiency in English in all four language skills.

Both the Ct- and the nCt-student show very positive attitudes toward the English language and use the language extensively in their private lives. Both students identify strongly with their respective home language and culture. While only the Ct-student is a British citizen, both disagree with the understanding of English only as a communicative tool and believe that its users need to be familiar with British or American culture. Furthermore, they strongly believe that they could not get a job without their knowledge of English and that English is advantageous for a person's employability in general.

## 3.8 Summary

In the first part of this chapter, the historical, linguistic, and economic background information necessary to understand the newly emerged market of HE in Cyprus have been presented. Cyprus's history of settlements and external ruling has been introduced, followed by its struggle for independence and the social and political difficulties that have resulted from it. The concatenation of actions that led to the Turkish invasion and the division of the island have been illuminated, as well as the island's status quo. The current and historical linguistic situation in both parts—the RoC and the TRNC—has been described, showing the relevance the English language used to have in Cyprus and to what extent it still does. Furthermore, the role and prestige of English in both parts of Cyprus have been compared to show the language's power—a power that is no longer purely colonial but influenced by the rise of neoliberalism. In the second part of the chapter, the methodological framework of this study has been introduced. The four involved research sites and the reasons for choosing them have been presented; in order to create a picture of the role and value of English in Cyprus's HE, which is as complete as possible, a wide range of differently organized universities were included. Due to their different foci, affiliations, and policies, these universities attract different groups of prospective students that all add to the understanding of the value of English as a globally used language. They serve as examples for the rise of the market of HE in Cyprus and illuminate how different facets of the English language can be combined and used for a successful commodification of English and HE. Cyprus exemplarily exploits the "Britishness" and the internationality of the English language. Furthermore, as an EU member, it presents itself just "foreign-enough" and "familiar-enough" to the relevant groups of people. It, therefore, appears accessible and attractive enough to be invested in, for instance, by fee-paying international students.

English in Cyprus is not only used as a cultural and social good; instead, it is mainly exploited as an attribute of Cyprus's most requested product—university education.

The English language is used quite differently at the two universities in the RoC; while it is the official language at UCLan Cyprus, its use is mainly limited to international (teaching) collaborations and the English department at UCy. While it is attractive for nCt-students, the large majority of the participants at UCLan Cyprus are Ct-students. The university's connection to the UK and its remaining prestige in Cyprus makes it especially attractive for local students who are interested in a British degree but cannot afford to or do not want to leave the island. UCy, in contrast, is the first public university of Cyprus and is located in the southern part of the divided capital Nicosia. UCy represents a more "traditional" picture of a university that does not (yet) focus on its profitability and is attended by a majority of Ct-students. In the TRNC, both included universities are organized economically; while EMU bills the lowest tuition fees for Cypriots and the highest for students from "third nations," GAU proceeds in reverse order. This hierarchization might represent different policies in attracting prospective students, although both rely on nCt-students for their economic survival. Furthermore, both universities rely on and advertise their use of English as one medium of instruction and offer in-house language support for all students who do not meet the comparably low English language entrance criteria. While EMU, furthermore, promotes its internationality and wide range of offered programs, GAU relies on its name (Girne *American* University) to attract prospective students. Ct- and nCt-students with a wide range of different backgrounds, experiences, and intentions participated in the study to add to the understanding and conceptualization of the role and value of English in Cyprus's HE. In approaching the value of English, four suppositions have been formulated. The methodological underpinnings of this approach—consisting of semi-structured interviews and sociolinguistic questionnaires—are introduced and relevant findings from a descriptive analysis of the questionnaire data on the participants' language use and attitudes are presented. These findings show a discrepancy between the language use and attitudes of students in the TRNC and the RoC. This may hint at a stronger marketization of the language and higher mobility of students in the former part. In Chapter 4, the information provided by the participants during their interviews will be analyzed qualitatively to create a comprehensive understanding of the students' perspective on the value of English in Cyprus's HE.

# 4

# The Value of English in Cyprus's Higher Education

## 4.1 Introduction

Assessing the value of English allows for a reflection of the complex sociopolitical and multilingual situation in Cyprus. The value of English is a flexible and inclusive framework that can be applied to an altering speaker group with multiple and varying linguistic repertoires, bringing together a kaleidoscope of cultural and social backgrounds and ambivalent relations toward the English language and its historical implications to a small island. Furthermore, the potential detachment of higher education (HE) from these local contexts and participant groups can be incorporated by demonstrating the ultimately shared objectives for using the English language to be economic advantages. This study is not only the first application of the three-layered framework of the value of English but also the first comprehensive investigation of the role and value of English in Cyprus's HE, which explores both parts of the island. This combination of framework and local contexts highlights the framework's flexibility and potential to offer a more fine-grained understanding of the heterogeneity of the participants' objectives and the complexity of the functions and roles the English language fulfills in Cyprus's HE landscape. This chapter begins with portraits of three not Cyprus-tied (nCt-) and one Cyprus-tied (Ct-) students, before presenting findings on the four research suppositions based on qualitative interviews conducted with Ct- and nCt-students at four universities in Cyprus.

## 4.2 The Value of English: Student Portraits

This study aims at centering the individual student. To comprehensively reflect the diversity and complexity of the individual students' biographies, experiences, and perceived repercussions of the commodified role of English, it takes the language users' perspectives. The trusting atmosphere that is needed for a comprehensive understanding of the individual student's perspective on and experiences with English and in Cyprus's HE could only have been established during personal and honest conversations. During these conversations, the reasons for the use of English by students and universities were examined, showing that the underlying rational—the common denominator—is the internationally shared value of the language and the accompanied upward social mobility. For students in Cyprus, an important aspect of the value of the language is its communicative potential that reflects the number of speakers sharing the language and adding to its communicative reach—its international usefulness (de Swaan 2001). While sharing a language potentially unites people—and might make them equals—not speaking (or choosing not to speak) a language might lead to the exclusion from a certain social group. This exclusion is known as social othering. The suppositions reflected upon in this study have been developed as synopses of the participants' understanding of the value of the English language. Based on their observations and experiences it became apparent that students and universities value the language differently.

> *Supposition 1*: For its users, the value of English lies in its communicative potential. Native speaker standards and its cultural embeddedness are less important.
> 
> *Supposition 2*: Universities in Cyprus use the value of English primarily to attract fee-paying nCt-students.

The functions of English in Cyprus's HE are diverse; it is, for example, used as the medium of instruction or publication. During the conversations with students in both parts of Cyprus, however, an imbalance between the purposes for its use surfaced. While universities in Cyprus tend to primarily use the English language for their financial benefits, students see it as a means of upward social mobility—a tool needed to climb the social ladder in national or international contexts. The students' perspective on this imbalance is shown in the following portraits, depicting the effect of English on each of them, as well as their assessment of its value and their perception of the language's relevance in each of their lives. The first three portraits also demonstrate the gatekeeping potential of the English language in Cyprus's HE across speaker groups and universities. Furthermore, the portraits exemplify the diversity of students as well as their common denominator: their investment in the English language, hoping for a better future. During their conversation with the author, these nCt-students, each with different life trajectories and previous experience, shared to not have *chosen* Cyprus; they had chosen English-medium HE that just happened to be offered in Cyprus. Whether they were interested in where they were going or not, and whether they followed personal recommendations or online advertisements, all of them saw their education as being the most important factor, while its location, the local people, and languages were viewed as subordinate to this.

## 4.2.1 Portrait 1: Jim

Jim (name changed) is an nCt-student at UCLan Cyprus and was nineteen years old at the time of his participation. He was born in Panama, the home country of his mother, and raised in Libya, the home country of his father. He describes himself as a bilingual speaker of Spanish and Arabic and a proficient speaker of English. His parents do not share a language and met in the UK, which is why English was used as the home language. However, he states that he prefers to speak Spanish with his mother and to speak Arabic with his friends and in public in Libya. He presents a very positive attitude toward the English language—he even calls it his preferred language—and was very decisive about wanting to enroll in a study program that uses English as the medium of instruction (EMI) (Excerpt 1a). He explains that he uses English in all his conversations in Cyprus and speaks in his other languages only when speaking with his family. He represents the perspective of a newly arrived student, having been in Cyprus for three weeks at the time of his participation, and can offer his first insight and impressions.

Jim describes the reasons he has chosen UCLan Cyprus for his university education as rather rational. He states that he wanted to study in Canada but did not receive the necessary visa to do so. He was sure about wanting his tertiary education to be in English and outside Libya, so he investigated other universities in Europe. Because of his friends' recommendations and the lack of alternatives, he decided to enroll at UCLan Cyprus (Excerpt 1b). He knows that living costs in Cyprus are lower than in other European countries and that English and Greek are important languages, therewith excluding the TRNC and the Turkish language and its varieties from his account of the island. Being used to living in Tripoli, the capital city of Libya, Jim does not yet feel at home on the small island. However, he appreciates the fact that English is widely used in Cyprus's urban and rural areas alike.

For Jim, English is "the language of business and it's used worldwide and it's very important to have knowledge" (Excerpt 1a). He further states that, to be successful, it is no longer sufficient to have a university degree. Instead, "you wanna try to get the best education that you can get" (ibid.). This "best education," for him, appears to be connected to "Inner Circle" countries, given that he wanted to study in Canada, does study at a British university, and hopes to continue his education at an American university. Jim reasons that, for Ct-students, a UCLan (UK) degree might be helpful for their future employment and explains that those students, therefore, transfer from other Cypriot universities to UCLan Cyprus. This might not leave many open spots for nCt-students, which, as he claims, are already lesser in number than he had expected (Excerpt 1c). However, Jim appears to be unhappy with his current situation in Cyprus and plans to stay for no longer than one year. He plans to move to Panama to study at the branch campus of Florida State University there, enrolling in another "dislocated" campus of an "Inner Circle" country university. He expresses that a US or Canadian degree might be more useful to him than a European degree and that, considering his bad luck during his application for a study visa in Canada, attaining it in Panama appears to be a reasonable choice. Again, financial reasons appear to be an important factor for his choice, as he does not want to pay the tuition fee required for an education at a university in the United States, which he claims is almost four times the tuition fee he would have to pay in Panama (Excerpt 1d). Jim also expresses that he did not have the wish to learn the local language or to further settle in Cyprus, as it has merely been the best and most reasonable alternative he had had, rather than being his first choice. He, therefore, did not research the background of Cyprus during his preparations or make any attempt to improve his situation by, for example, socializing with local peers.

Jim has been chosen as an example for students who come to Cyprus for an internationally valid degree and for whom English represents opportunities. For these students, investments in nonacademic local contexts and languages are secondary, as Cyprus functions as a stepping-stone to "better" locations and future success. Jim exemplifies the customer "student," who invests in the English language and the opportunities it can provide through HE, while often remaining indifferent to the specific context this HE is provided in. These students are willing to partake in the commodification of HE to enable their immediate or future upward mobility.

*Supposition 3*: Students invest in the English language because it represents immediate or future upward social mobility.

To gain this upward social mobility, students are willing to invest resources, such as time and money, and to not question, or even actively disregard, the circumstances and the context they invest these resources in. The following two portraits were chosen as examples of students who observe the unawareness of their fellow students (Sue) and of students who coincidently but trustingly and ultimately indifferently move to Cyprus for their EMI HE (John).

### 4.2.2 Portrait 2: Sue

Sue (name changed) is a female student from Kenya and was in her early thirties at the time of her participation. She is a student at Girne American University (GAU) in the TRNC, who came to Cyprus following her sister. Although Sue was not fully aware of all the implications of her study program at GAU in the TRNC, she was quite well informed, due to the honest and trustworthy descriptions of her sister. Before she arrived in Cyprus approximately one and a half years before the interview, she had worked as a freelancing journalist and was then working as a student assistant. Sue is a bilingual speaker of Swahili and Kimeru and claims near-native competence in English. She reports having a positive attitude toward the English language and the information provided by her concerning her language use suggests that she uses English predominantly in private and public contexts while in Cyprus, adding Swahili for family and friends at home. She has learned some Turkish while in the TRNC, claiming that it is essential for communication in public off-campus contexts (Excerpt 2a). Sue states that Cyprus had been her and her sister's "last option" (Excerpt 2b) and that they had wanted to study in the UK but could not due to financial reasons. She further states that the infrequent use of English is not only limited to locals in the public domain. Students would, furthermore, use their native languages outside the classroom and refrain from using English. In the classroom, teachers and students would use Turkish, as the majority of students are often local and, therefore, Turkish speaking (Excerpt 2c). To justify her observations, she refers to the limited English language abilities and "the culture of the people" (Excerpt 2d), stating that people would not use English in cases where they could use another language to achieve their goal. She confirms earlier information about the threshold of the entrance English language test to be 60 percent and adds that this is not an internationally recognized language proficiency test, like TOEFL, but a university-internal test.

Sue is involved with the admission of students at GAU and is very reflective and thoughtful about the precarious situation nCt-students might find themselves in. She claims to have chosen GAU because "of the name American" (Excerpt 2c) since she assumed this would refer to the language use as well as the academic profile of the university. She, for example, became aware that her degree might not be valid outside the TRNC and Turkey only after her arrival. She states that this is rather common, because "education agents" in the students' origin countries, who link prospective students and Cypriot universities, have the policy of offering selective information, creating a convenient picture of their respective offer (Excerpt 2e). She would recommend the TRNC for HE purposes but would prefer students to be educated about the reality to expect, so there will be less disappointment and capitulation (Excerpt 2f). Furthermore, from her perspective, the TRNC does not necessarily welcome nCt-students, due to a development in which students come to Cyprus for a safe environment or for employment rather than to study (Excerpt 2g).

While Sue was aware of much of the geopolitical situation of the TRNC before her arrival, and is, therefore, able to observe and reflect on how it affects other people, other students are not that well prepared. The following portrait serves as an example of a student who was not as fortunate as Sue and came to Cyprus less prepared.

### 4.2.3 Portrait 3: John

The third portrait introduces John, a male EMU student from Nigeria who was in his mid-twenties at the time of his participation. He is a bilingual speaker of English and Yoruba (Excerpt 3a) and shows a very positive attitude toward the English language, clearly choosing its use and the university's reputation over its location. The information he provided about his language use indicates that he uses Yoruba slightly more often when communicating with his family than English but that he uses English for most nonfamily communication. Although he is very knowledgeable and thoughtful concerning traditional classifications of English and their implications, he does not seem to be fully aware of the linguistic and social circumstances Cyprus currently finds itself in. He mentions Turkish and English as the languages that play a role in Cyprus, thereby excluding the Republic of Cyprus (RoC) and its Greek-speaking community completely. He moved to Northern Cyprus to study at EMU, following a friend's recommendation, and admits that he was under the impression that he was moving to and studying in Turkey until he had to change planes in Istanbul, Turkey, to continue his trip to the TRNC (Excerpt 3b). He had chosen EMU for its international setting, which is rooted in its use of the English language. However, he remained unaware of the social, economic, or political surroundings he had moved to and, only after moving to Cyprus, found out that the TRNC is not a member of the EU and that communication in English is not as easy as he had expected. He uses the example of communicating with Turkish shop owners in the city of Famagusta to explain that being able to speak English, in his experience, does not necessarily lead to successful communication in the TRNC (Excerpt 3c). John also feels that social conversations in departments other than in the English Language Teaching Department are preferably conducted in Turkish, although EMU requires an "adequate" proficiency in English as part of its admission criteria. From his perspective, the English language is, consequently, used to differing extents on-campus and far less off-campus.

John grew up in Nigeria, a country in which English is the official language, and declares himself a native speaker of English and Yoruba. He describes himself as a native speaker of English and is also recognized by the university as such. Therefore, he was not required to partake in an introductory assessment test of his English language abilities. Still, in the course of the conversation, he differentiates between different kinds of native speakers. This seems to be an unintentional differentiation, as he clearly articulates that correctness is not key to being a successful and rightful user of the English language and that the concept and hegemony of the native speaker is, in his opinion, not valid. Although stating that "English is not based on a particular standard ... especially in a global setting, it's basically for communication" (Excerpt 3d), he also differentiates between "real" natives and himself as an English user from the Outer Circle, as he refers to the English language by name and to Yoruba as "the native language" (Excerpt 3a). John describes English in Nigeria as being a unifying language because it displays the shared identity of multiethnic Nigeria. In Cyprus, English appears to be a separating language for him when he interacts with other Nigerians (Excerpts 3e and 3f). His different perceptions and uses of the English language reflect the language's capacity to function as a reflection of the speaker's identity or to disconnect from its cultural and social attributes and function as a neutral asset. In Cyprus, however, John feels limited in his freedom to express himself in English, due to the lower level of proficiency of most of his interlocutors (Excerpt 3d). He, furthermore, recounts an incident in one of his classes when he was told his accent was too strong and that he should talk more slowly for his fellow students to understand what he was presenting. He says that he was happy to alter his language use so that it meets his interlocutors' needs and facilitates mutual understanding (Excerpt 3f) but that at the same time he feels his language skills remain unexhausted.

John is an example of a very proficient speaker of English who moved to the TRNC for educational reasons only. He left his family in Nigeria while remaining in close contact with them. He is a well-educated young man who is aware of the potential of English-medium education and its international use. He made a rational choice to get exactly this kind of education abroad. As in the case of Jim, the exact location of his targeted educational institution was apparently secondary for his decision; instead, he focused on recommendation and reputation. John is aware of the influence a language has on its speaker's identity and understands that the English language does not necessarily have the same impact on his fellow students as their native languages have (Excerpt 3g). Academically speaking, he tries to eliminate the concept of the native speakers' ownership and authority over the English language but has not yet internalized this change of concept. He still uses social othering to differentiate between different speakers and organizes them in a hierarchical order. However, he clearly describes his changed attitude toward the English language after coming to the TRNC. He perceived English as a uniting language with a slightly formal connotation in Nigeria. In the TRNC, he perceives English as a neutral asset that is used to communicate and which is, for most users, separate from their identities.

The portraits of John and Sue exemplify another common denominator among nCt-students in Cyprus's HE—their clear focus on investing in the English language and the consequential subordination of the specific location and context in which they do so. This disregard is exploited by universities.

> *Supposition 4*: The value of the English language outweighs nCt-students' concerns about the local contexts it is offered in. The students' abstraction of English-as-a-marketable-attribute from its context is utilized by the universities.

The native speaker ideology realized in valuing English as a Native Language (ENL) higher than other uses of the English language is also followed by Ct-students. The following portrait shows the perspective of a Ct-student in the TRNC.

### 4.2.4 Portrait 4: Laura

Laura (name changed) is a student at EMU, who was born and raised in the UK. She has both a Cypriot and a British passport, is a bilingual speaker of

English and Cypriot Turkish, and was in her early twenties at the time of her participation. Laura and her family lived in the UK until she was fifteen years old and then moved to Cyprus for family reasons. Her father is Cypriot and a speaker of Cypriot Turkish, English, and Cypriot Greek. Laura's mother is of Turkish nationality and speaks Modern Turkish only. Turkish, therefore, has always been the family's home language. Laura states that she uses Turkish more often than English in nonacademic conversations, for reasons including her various conversation partners' lack of proficiency in English or the community's lack of appreciation toward her use of English (Excerpt 4a). She is very aware of the political, social, and linguistic situation in Cyprus and has a clear opinion on the possibility and the necessary circumstances for the reunification of Cyprus. She speaks very reflectively about Turkish immigrants and the various generations of Cypriots in both parts, assessing potential areas of tension between Turkish immigrants and Turkish Cypriots or between Turkish Cypriots and Greek Cypriots, from both angles. She is well informed on the groups' historical, political, and social entanglements concerning the separation and potential reunification of Cyprus and is an outspoken supporter of this reunification herself. Furthermore, she feels very strongly about the importance of education, which is why she aims at attending UCLan Cyprus for her graduate degree. Her openness and knowledge were two of the various reasons for interviewing her again approximately one and a half years after the first interview (cf. Section 5.1).

Laura was a student at the ELT department during her first participation in this study. She offers detailed information on the department's position and value within EMU, clearly separating it from the other departments. She expresses the feeling of sociability and solidarity among ELT students and with their lecturers. More importantly for her, she experiences being seen as a human being within the ELT department, rather than a source of money, which is, according to her statement, how the university sees its students (Excerpt 4b). She describes how student fees, in general, increase each year and that their exact amount depended on the individual student's nationality. According to Laura, moreover, EMU has a hierarchy of scholarships that are offered automatically to attract students (Excerpt 4c).

Nationality is an important factor for EMU students, as the university differentiates between Cypriot, Turkish, and "third-nations" students; the first group pays the lowest and the third group the highest student fees (cf. Tuition fees for newly registered students n.d.). Furthermore, it influences which classes a student is required to take. Laura states that Cypriot students, in contrast to "third nations" students, have to take Turkish language classes, which appears to have been the main reason for her to have enrolled with her British passport (Excerpt 4c). International students apparently do not have to attend Turkish language classes and, therefore, can avoid learning Turkish entirely. This reflects the accepted disconnectedness of nCt-students from their Northern Cypriot surroundings as well as the partitioning of the market "education." English is used as a tool here, which just offers enough connectedness between the students and their environment to be successful in completing their university degree, rather than the opportunity to connect culturally and socially with local people (Excerpt 4e). However, it might also reflect the enforcement of the political bond between Cyprus and Turkey on a linguistic level. English, therefore, appears to not be the only language that is being used as part of the local economic and political agenda. The nationality of the students appears to also be a relevant factor for the job market. Laura has experienced "racial problems" during the assignment of a student assistant position when nationality was used as a reason for not assigning the position to multiple students (Excerpt 4b). Since this argument was used against Cypriots as well as international students, their stance cannot be specified. However, it becomes clear that EMU staff appears to be aware of the importance of the students' nationality.

Laura, in contrast to the social stratification she observes at EMU, supports multiculturalism and is very supportive of Cyprus's connection to the EU. She wishes for future children in Cyprus to receive an EU education, which is also one of her main reasons to support the reunification of Cyprus (Excerpt 4e). She would expect a reunified Cyprus to resemble England "where everyone uses English for communication, yet everyone at home has a native language" (Excerpt 4f). Evidently, she assigns the role of a lingua franca, a unifying language, to English and expects it to function alongside the different groups' native languages. An overview of the role and value of English from the nCt- and Ct-students' perspectives will be elaborated on in the following.

## 4.3 Layers of Value in HE: Assessing the Research Suppositions

As in many other countries, the English language is used diversely and reflects various relationships in Cyprus; among other functions, it is the native language of the island's former ruler, the majority of ex-pat Cypriots, and multiple Cypriots who have returned or remained in Cyprus. English is the language of tourism and international diplomacy, trade and exchange, and, lately, it is the language of international HE. In this last use alone, English functions (1) as the means of communication between a constantly changing group of speakers with differing linguistic repertoires, (2) as an advertising tool by profit-oriented universities that aim to attract students so as to increase their income, (3) as the representation of an improvement of these speakers' future perspectives and possibilities, and (4) as an impersonal attribute of its speakers they constantly invest in and which is, therefore, commodified to capacity both in and outside Cyprus.

The following presents how different speaker groups in both parts of Cyprus assess these functions based on the globally shared value of the English language. Furthermore, the Cyprus-specific and global implications of the value of English and its consequential economic utilization will be discussed, showing the neoliberalization of HE. In doing so, the consideration of "value" as being essential for a comprehensive conceptualization of the current use of English and to create an in-depth understanding of the complex trajectories involved, both in local and global contexts, is supported. To provide a full picture of all four suppositions, the quantified information (cf. Section 3.7) will be incorporated with an in-depth qualitative assessment of the conducted interviews, starting with the students' perspective and the aspect of the English language they value most.

### 4.3.1 Supposition 1: Communicative Potential

> For its users, the value of the English language lies in its communicative potential. Native speaker standards and its cultural embeddedness are less important.

This supposition, and therefore the assumption that the communicative value of English is higher or more dominant for students in Cyprus's HE than the language's ideological value, can be strengthened. Only 13.7 percent of all participants identify as native speakers of English (Table 3.3), while 47.8 percent of the students state to use English during the majority of their days and 57.6 percent support the statement that "English is a communicative tool and users don't need to be aware of British/American culture" (Table 3.4). However, differences in the value constellations have been found between the Ct-students and their nCt-peers during the assessment of this first supposition. For nCt-students the value of English is primarily communicative, appreciating the language's communicative potential and often valuing the language independently of its cultural embeddedness (e.g., Excerpts 3d and 1e). For Ct-students the most dominant value of English is also communicative; however, the ideological value of English in its connection to the UK and its education is admixed (Excerpts 5a and 6a). The ideological value of English for Ct-students at UCLan Cyprus appears to be indirect, as these students value the language and the university mostly because of its connection to the UK (Excerpts 7a and 8a). For some Ct-students in the TRNC the ideological value of English, however, is direct, as they are self-identified native speakers and, therefore, also identify with the language itself (Excerpts 4g and 5b). NCt-students, especially in the TRNC, appear to conceptualize English as a global language rather than as a language that is necessarily tied to its native contexts of use, clearly highlighting the language's communicative value. Only a minority of nCt-students disagree with the claim that "English is a communicative tool and [that] users don't need to be aware of British/American culture" (Tables 3.5–3.7; cf. Section 3.7). Although a certain degree of influence by the university's Britishness on nCt-students at UCLan Cyprus is expected, they still value this connection to the language's native contexts and potential cultural embeddedness less than its communicative potential (Excerpt 1a).

The ideological value of English for Ct-students—their affinity and the respective emphasis of their valuation of (British) English—appears to be a trace of colonialism—a result of the maintained prestige of the language and the sustained close ties to the UK (see Buschfeld 2013; Karatsareas 2018; McEntee-Atalianis, and Pouloukas 2001; Sciriha 1996; cf. Sections 3.2.1, 3.3.1, and 3.5). The use and identification with the English language do not necessarily differ from other, more typical postcolonial contexts; for most of the interviewed students, there is a personal connection to the UK, for example, as the student's birthplace or the residence of a branch of his or her family, which is transferred onto the language (Excerpts 4h and 9a). The language, consequently, is not valued independently of the UK. Instead, it is always understood as a connection to the former colonizer—as the personal bond Cypriots maintain, and as "linguistic and cultural capital" (Tsiplakou 2009: 78). The language is still valued based on the historical power of the UK over Cyprus, the bidirectional migration, and the resulting irrevocable relation between the two peoples (Kappler in Hadjioannou et al. 2011; Karatsareas 2018). Although 96.1 percent of the students in Cyprus agree that "when living in Cyprus speaking English and [Greek or Turkish, respectively] is important" (Table 3.4), the experienced reality of the colonial repercussions is noticeably different in the respective parts of Cyprus. While Ct-students, especially in the TRNC, experience the context dependence of the local value of English in Cyprus (de Swaan 2001; Piller 2016; Excerpt 4a) and the language is often important for them on- and off-campus (Table 3.7), the majority of their peers in the RoC do not identify as native speakers and feel that the English language is of minor importance for their private lives off-campus (Tables 4.5 and 4.6; cf. Section 3.7). Furthermore, the public attitude toward the English language in the RoC is described as mostly positive by Ct-students, while in the TRNC this is not necessarily the case (Buschfeld 2013; Kappler in Hadjioannou et al. 2011; Karatsareas 2018; McEntee-Atalianis and Pouloukas 2001; Sciriha 1996; Tum, Kunt, and Kunt 2016; cf. Sections 3.3.1 and 3.5, Excerpt 4a). One reason for the decreased prestige of the English language in the TRNC might be that the majority of its inhabitants are either Turkish settlers or their descendants who do not share the colonial experience and thus an affinity to the UK in the same way as their Turkish Cypriot neighbors do (Excerpt 4i). Furthermore, while Cypriots in both parts share a general gravitation to the UK, Ct-students in the TRNC, mostly Turkish Cypriots, have expressed stronger feelings toward the UK (e.g., Excerpt 9b). This is expected to be a counterreaction caused by Turkey's diplomatic mediation between the TRNC and the UK or any other country, highlighting the TRNC's dependencies on its "big brother." Furthermore, the strong fixation on the value of English and the close connection to the UK by Turkish Cypriot Ct-students in the TRNC might have been caused by the economic and social difference between the TRNC and the RoC. For Turkish Cypriots, who are allowed to cross Cyprus's inner border, the historical connection to the UK might be one way for them to enhance their less-privileged situation. However, English, for Cypriots, is not exclusively associated with the UK but rather with the hope of a solution to the Cyprus problem (Kappler in Hadjioannou et al. 2011: 536; McEntee-Atalianis and Pouloukas 2001).

In addition to the Ct-students' personal ties to the UK and the resulting valuation of its language and culture, which have been observed in the TRNC slightly more than in the RoC, for Ct-students, the English language constitutes hope—the hope of Cyprus's reunification. While most Cypriots in both parts are in favor of reunification, they do emphasize the complexity of the situation and the discrepancy between the two parties' respective demands and concessions, especially concerning the Turkish settlers. However, they agree in expecting the English language to be used as a, whether preliminary or permanent, lingua franca if there is reunification. Furthermore, Ct-students agree that English should only be used in addition to the local languages rather than as their substitution, highlighting the communicative value of English and the ideological value of the local languages (e.g., Excerpts 4j and 10a). This is more than a mere repetition of the language situation under the British rule (Annual Colonial Reports 1937: 4; cf. Section 3.2.1); it is a reflection of two

Cyprus-specific circumstances: the majority of both Cypriot parties respects the other group's individuality and otherness by including their language, and both parties uniformly feel like confident speakers of English, independent of the age group (e.g., Buschfeld 2013 on Greek Cypriots). In addition, this reflects the students' transfer of their assessment of value from a personal to a societal level, while keeping the primary value communicative rather than ideological.

Moreover, while older Cypriots might be confident speakers of English due to the remaining linguistic consequences of its colonization, the confidence of younger Cypriots might be caused by English having officially been adjudged increasing value within the Cypriot school systems (Kappler in Hadjioannou et al. 2011: 542; Tsiplakou 2009: 83; cf. Section 3.3.2, Excerpt 5c). Consequently, English holds communicative value for Ct-students, who are aware of the language's international use and communicative potential, independent of their extensive personal connection to the language and its promise of a unified Cyprus. However, this valuation of the English language does not expand on a societal level—to Cyprus public domains or outside the classroom. Consequently, English remains a private language for these students who use it at home and it does not play a role outside the educational context for the others (Piller 2016). NCt-students, in contrast to their Ct-peers, do not have a choice when it comes to using English outside the classroom. Instead, they have to rely on it for everyday communication in a non-native context. For these students, the communicative value of the language is its most valuable asset, although this value might not be shared by locals on a societal level.

De Swaan (2001: 6) argues that there is no language that is more central than English—he calls it hypercentral—because there is no language shared by more speakers than English (cf. Section 2.3.1.1). Especially for nCt-students in Cyprus, the language's value is primarily communicative, building on its hypercentrality—its extensive communicative potential. As English is used on a global level like no other language, it is located at the very center of any language system or the very apex of any hierarchy. This global use results in a constant increase of speakers and, consequently, a constant increase of the language's communicative potential and value (de Swaan 2001: 6; cf. Section 2.3.1.1). For nCt-students, who often have to use the language on a daily basis and for every conversation they intend to have, English is valued as a global language rather than as the language of the former colonial power, and its value lies both in its usefulness and in the unparalleled scale of its being shared. As a result of this sharedness and the growing number of current and future speakers, English is "rapidly losing its national cultural base" (Dörnyei, Csizér, and Németh 2006: 9), resulting in a stabilization of its communicative value on a global level. The value of English on a global level is (almost) independent of the location and context of its use. It is, therefore, in contrast to its value on a societal level, not Cyprus-specific. Still, and at first sight surprisingly, nCt-students choose to invest in the English language in Cyprus's HE.

The, admittedly, simplified reason for this is: nCt-students invest in the English language in Cyprus's HE because studying in Cyprus is their gateway to the Global North. Cyprus is peripheral; it is at the periphery of Europe, at the periphery of "traditional" English use due to its colonial past, and at the periphery of the Global North (see Section 4.3.4 on the fact that the TRNC is even more peripheral, as it does not grant access to Europe or the Global North). English enables mobility—social (cf. Sections 2.3.2 and 4.3.3) as well as geographical mobility (cf. Section 2.4.1)—and is, therefore, chosen as a worthwhile investment. Cyprus represents the first stop on nCt-students' way to their desired destination (Excerpt 11a). This mobility is enabled by the communicative potential of English and the language's globally shared communicative value. However, it is also a reason for less powerful languages to not be learned (Excerpt 3h). Nonetheless, Cyprus is often not the desired destination of nCt-students—they rather aim at a destination that is central, or at least more central, in the Global North (Excerpt 1b). NCt-students in the TRNC, in particular, have no wish to stay in Cyprus after completing their education; only 12.2 percent of the nCt-students at EMU expressed their wish to stay, while 25 percent of nCt-students at UCLan Cyprus and 20 percent at UCy in the RoC did so (Appendices 2.4–2.6). This incline of students' affinity between the RoC and the TRNC is depicted also by the students' social status and, consequently, options (Excerpt 12a; cf. Block 2015: 3; Savage et al. 2013: 223; cf. Sections 2.3.2 and 4.3.3). NCt-students who are aware of the geopolitical situation of Cyprus are often in the privileged position of being granted a visa and can therefore choose to pursue their HE in the RoC.

For privileged nCt-students, the English language has not been entirely reduced to its pragmatic function. Although for them the communicative value of English is higher than its ideological value in Cyprus, nCt-students, who identify as native speakers, position themselves above other speakers because they find themselves in a "non-native" context of use within Cyprus's HE (Excerpt 3d). This stratification of speakers constitutes a reproduction of colonial power relations and the belief in the traditional ownership of English by its native speakers (Widdowson 1994; see, for a critical discussion of this ideology, e.g., Baker 2015; Cook 1999; Davies 2003; Pennycook 2012; cf. Section 1.2.1). Within this ideology, the "native speaker" is perceived as more powerful than other speakers and their respective variety of English is valued higher than other realizations (Bonfiglio 2013: 29; Woolard 1998: 7; cf. Section 1.2.1). Consequently, ENL is the goal of any language learner and the only acceptable and valued option (Strang 1970 for the differentiation and, e.g., McArthur 1998: 43; Schneider 2007: 12, 2011: 30 for its implementation), allowing for the exclusion and devaluation of English speakers who do not reach this goal. This exclusion and devaluation are realized through social othering (Holliday 2006: 385; Vichiensing 2018; cf. Section 2.2.2). This social othering is practiced in multiple social formations in the context of Cyprus HE; nCt-students engage in it to separate themselves from, in their interpretation, less proficient speakers (Excerpt 3d), local inhabitants use it to separate themselves from nCt-students (e.g., Excerpts 12a and 13a), and local Turkey-bound inhabitants do so to devalue those Turkish Cypriots who identify with the language more than with Turkey itself (Excerpt 4a).

The presented findings represent the duality of the value of English in Cyprus—unlike any other language, the English language commonly holds a high communicative value as the most important globally shared lingua franca, while at the same time, it holds ideological value in representing Cyprus's history and its people's biographies and family trees. The value of the English language in Cyprus is assessed on all three levels—as a globally shared language (e.g., Crystal 2003; de Swaan 2001; Piller 2016; Seidlhofer 2011) and as the island's colonial heritage influencing its status on a societal (e.g., Buschfeld 2013; McEntee-Atalianis and Pouloukas 2001; Sciriha 1996) and personal level (cf. Aronin 2016; Bonfiglio 2013; Ferris, Peck, and Banda 2014; Omoniyi 2006; Woolard 1998). While the value of English in the latter contexts is rooted in the use of the language and might be transferred to just any language, the valuation of English as a global language is English-specific and the language's value is created by objectifying it and using English-as-a-marketable-attribute without implications on the users' identities (Heller and Duchêne 2016; Park and Wee 2012; cf. Sections 1.4.2 and 1.4.4). Cyprus combines the three layers of the value of English—its ideological, communicative, and economic value—in its HE landscape, catering for Ct as well as for nCt-students. The economic value of the English language, furthermore, functions as the ultimate motivation for the language's use in Cyprus's HE; the universities' implementation and transformation of this value of English are assessed in the following.

## 4.3.2 Supposition 2: Attracting nCt-Students

> Universities in Cyprus use the value of the English language primarily to attract fee-paying nCt-students.

For universities in Cyprus, the value of English is primarily economic in nature, as their use of EMI functions as their capital and currency—the mere inclusion of English as one medium of instruction might grant them access to a top position in university rankings and among the most valued groups of institutions (Lasagabaster 2015; Wilkinson 2013). Furthermore, universities exchange this use in order to receive another desired component of HE, namely fee-paying students (Lasagabaster 2015). Although this is commonly true, it has been found that the groups of targeted fee-paying students differ in each part of the island; while the universities in the TRNC target nCt-students, universities in the RoC do not necessarily do the same.

Following Foskett's (2012: 44–5) categorization of universities, the four research sites each appear to belong to a different category. Beginning with an assessment of the universities in the TRNC, EMU is internationally committed and represents an internationally aware university, that is, having an international profile that is focused on the globally interconnected nature of society and HE (e.g., EMU Web Office n.d.-a). In contrast, GAU fits into the category of imperialist universities, located in its local domain. Foskett (2012) characterizes imperialist universities as aiming at recruiting international students while preserving their local internal structure rather than advocating international culture and cooperation in research or publishing (e.g., GAU 2019f, 2019h). The university pursues an economic objective and aims mainly at international students. The university's webpages provide information for prospective students who are not from Cyprus, like information about Girne, international admission, and housing options, in prominent positions. Furthermore, and most interestingly, GAU maintains "regional offices." These are seventy-five contact persons or organizations, which are all in the Global South and which are presented with contact details and visitors' addresses. These agencies appear to be part of the university's economic orientation, used as direct contact between prospective students and GAU, and part of the university's economic objective; however, further details on them are not offered (cf. GAU 2019k). In addition to GAU's "regional offices," external for-profit agencies and businesses benefit from GAU. Although unnecessary for the enrollment and admission process, these external agencies pretend to be go-betweens, promising international students facilitated access to GAU and high-quality education.

While they accept Ct- and nCt-students, EMU and GAU appear to focus on attracting nCt-students. They use the English language, among other functions, as their (main) medium of instruction, on-campus and media communication, as well as for publishing (Excerpt 2h; cf. EMU I-REP n.d.; EMU Web Office n.d.-a; GAU 2019a). Both universities, however, appear to focus mainly on their teaching function rather than on research or international collaborations, which centers their actions on the acquisition of students. A clear focus on attracting nCt-students rather than Ct-students is suggested by the composition of the participant samples of this study, which consists of 68.8 percent nCt-students at EMU (cf. Section 3.3). Both universities have initiated scholarships exclusively for international students and appear to focus predominantly on nCt-students in generating the most possible financial profit. This goal is reached in different ways: EMU differentiates between Cypriot, Turkish, and "third nations" students—the first group paying the lowest and the third group the highest student fees (cf. Tuition fees for newly registered students n.d.). However, students from the same family might receive a discount of up to 75 percent in addition to a "large portion of ... international students [being] on 50% and 25% scholarships" (EMU Web Office n.d.-e). GAU attracts international students, so nCt-students and Ct-students who are not solely of TRNC nationality, by offering "an unconditional 50% tuition fee scholarship, valid throughout the duration of study" (GAU 2019b), in addition to three scholarships, all students can apply for—the scholarships for "High Honour," "Work Team," and "Sports" (ibid.). Consequently, while GAU tries to attract as many nCt-students as possible through lower fees, EMU charges them higher fees than Cypriot students. This discrepancy most often remains even after the "third nations" students, who can be of any nationality except Cypriot and Turkish, have been granted a scholarship or some other fee reduction (see Holborow 2013: 233 on non-EU students).

Both universities in the TRNC coincide in their approach of how to legitimize their students while benefiting from them at the same time—they maintain language schools. EMU and GAU list a number of standardized, and often expensive, language certificates that students can present in proving their English language skills. However, they do also accept students without proof of their language abilities and have them enroll in and pay for classes in these language schools. Both universities establish a comparably low entrance examination threshold of 60 percent for most of their undergraduate classes (cf. EMU n.d.-b: English Medium Programs; EMU n.d.-c: Table 1; GAU 2019g). Students who do not meet this threshold must attend language classes in the university-led language schools. The number of classes that have to be attended—and paid for—in these language schools depend on the applicants' English language skills. Furthermore, they might have to be completed before commencing the desired study program or at least parallel to it, which potentially prolongs the students' residence in Cyprus. However, they are always charged for this in addition to the requested tuition fee (EMU n.d.-b: English Medium Programs; EMU Web Office n.d.-f; GAU 2019g).

Nowadays, universities, especially private ones, do not necessarily have a choice in their implementation of the English language, as they have to generate their expenses completely without or with very limited support of government funding (Holborow 2013: 233; see also Ferguson 2007; Lasagabaster 2015; van der Walt 2013; cf. Section 1.4.3). The investigated universities in the TRNC do not concentrate on research or international collaboration but rather on teaching and serving students. As a consequence, they need to generate their profit through these students' tuition fees rather than from external research or project funding. In van der Walt's (2013: 3) terms, these universities aim at globalization—at the commodification of their HE offer—rather than international exchange and collaboration. In turn, to be interesting for students generally but all the more so for nonlocal ones like nCt-students, the universities need to be perceived as international and globally engaged, which is reflected by their implementation of the English language (Lasagabaster 2015; van der Walt 2013; cf. Section 1.4.3). Because of the common belief that English reflects internationality, EMU and GAU do not have a choice but must include English as the main medium of instruction in their portfolio; this valorizes their offer to prospective nCt-students (ibid.), which they advertise extensively, both online and through overseas agencies (cf. Section 4.3.4).

Although the local value of English is context-dependent and differs in every country, its global value is shared (cf. Sections 2.3.1.1 and 3.3.1.2). This shared value (de Swaan 2001), reflected in the willingness of people to invest time and money in its acquisition and to move to another country to receive a certificate that includes the confirmation of their competence in the English language, is what the market of HE in Cyprus is built on. Because numerous people in various places agree that English has value and is desirable as something to "have," its incorporation into the offer of universities in the TRNC, as well as in the RoC and just any other country, is utilitarian and also profitable (ibid., cf. Section 2.3.1.1). Although the value of English might be lower in the students' home societies than it is on a global level, they choose to invest in the latter when coming to Cyprus (Piller 2016 on local value; cf.

Section 2.3.1.2). The two universities in the RoC have been found to set their foci on a different group of students who, in turn, often invest in the local value of English.

Concerning the two universities in the RoC, UCy, and UCLan Cyprus, the provided data shows that, although accepting nCt- and Ct-students, these universities are primarily focused on and are attractive for Ct-students. Although UCy is involved in international partnerships and networks (cf. UCy n.d.-f) and takes part in the Erasmus+ Program to enable student and staff mobility within Europe, the limitations in pursuing "an internationalization agenda 'at home'" (Foskett 2012: 45) lead to its categorization as an internationally aware university developing to become an internationally engaged university. UCy uses the Greek language as its main language of instruction and EMI is implemented primarily in the Department of English Studies and in classes that are cooperatively taught by multiple universities (UCy n.d.-i). The English language, therefore, is not used universally enough to make UCy attractive for non-Greek-speaking and nCt-students. Furthermore, it is free of charge for all EU students (ibid.), resulting in and making sure that the university does not focus on its financial profit but rather on international research and the transfer of knowledge. While UCy neither uses English to attract students nor to focus on nCt-students, UCLan Cyprus does use the language to attract Ct-students.

UCLan Cyprus uses the English language as the exclusive medium of instruction and the main medium of on-campus communication. Furthermore, it is profit-oriented and charges tuition fees, while offering scholarships for local and international students. Although it promotes that "studying at UCLan Cyprus is almost 50% less compared to any other British University" (UCLan Cyprus 2017c), the university offers merit-based scholarships, as well as scholarships for related students, that is, siblings and alumni, which can be granted to both Cypriot and non-Cypriot students (ibid.). However, only Cypriot students receive "large families bursaries," which increase with each additional child of a family enrolling at UCLan Cyprus (UCLan Cyprus 2017d). As a British university, it is a priori attractive to most groups of students due to the remains of the UK's historical power and its centrality in the Global North (Phillipson 1992, 2009; cf. Section 1.2.1). However, the university's language and scholarship requirements, as well as the composition of the respective participant sample (90.2 percent Ct-students; cf. Section 3.6.3), imply that the university is mainly interested in attracting Cypriot or Ct-students. Cypriot students might even be labeled as "international" from the university's perspective based on the university's British home and structure. Due to this transfer of British education to Cyprus, UCLan Cyprus could be categorized as an imperialist university in a foreign domain (Foskett 2012). Rather than the economic value of English or its international recognition, this Britishness is, moreover, the reason for UCLan Cyprus's implementation of the English language. Similarly, the scholarship and language requirements, which are quite similar to those of the universities in the TRNC, are not the primary reasons for Ct-students to choose UCLan Cyprus for their HE. These students aim for "premium British higher education and quality standards" (UCLan n.d.) without having to relocate to the UK and spend the respectively high tuition fees. This valuation of British education is not limited to the RoC but is shared by Ct-students in the TRNC (Excerpt 4j). The ideological value of English and the remedy of the superiority and power of the British Empire are reflected in the successful implementation of UCLan Cyprus in Cyprus. It is built on the colonial traces of the island but is not linked to the disadvantages of this period of heteronomy (cf. Section 3.2.1) and the following civil turmoil (cf. Section 3.2.2).

These findings show that the above-explored universities need to be divided into three categories: the local University of Cyprus, which is mainly concerned with Cyprus and its population and development; the British UCLan Cyprus, which offers a prestigious and affordable alternative especially for Ct-students who, for example, cannot move to the UK for their HE; and the universities in the TRNC that appear to follow a structure that can maintain itself only by accepting more paying students than the local population can offer. The latter universities, therefore, have to attract international students to survive. In the TRNC, one university exists for approximately 18,600 inhabitants (cf. Section 3.4), with the universities consequently being forced to target nCt-students (cf. Section 1.4.3); the most promising prerequisite in convincing nCt-students to move to Cyprus and enroll at the respective university is the use of EMI, which they valued highly due to its upward social and economic mobility potential (Lasagabaster 2015: 265; cf. Section 4.3.3). In offering EMI programs, the universities use English-as-a-marketable-attribute to valorize their offer and thereby make use of the economic value of the language, which is, in turn, based on and reproduced by its global use. Not only this economic value of the language is reproduced and consolidated by the language's global use, its gatekeeping function to specific social groups and classes—its potential to facilitate or initiate its user's upward social mobility—is another factor rooted in the global recognition of English.

### 4.3.3 Supposition 3: Upward Social Mobility

> Students invest in the English language because it represents immediate or future upward social mobility.

The global value of English is based on its shared use (de Swaan 2001). While the language might have diverse personal meaning, function, and value for each individual speaker, it has shared public connotations of internationality and world-openness—both essential for a successful global citizen. Overall, students in this study agree that English functions as a prerequisite to success. About 97 percent of the students in this study agree that "English offers advantages in seeking good job opportunities," while 52.2 percent agree that "without the knowledge of English, [they] could not get a job" (Table 3.4). English is perceived as an asset of the students' human capital (Holborow 2015) and, hence, as the gatekeeper of success and a marker of social structures. The analysis of the interview data has shown that, for its speakers, the English language represents future opportunities or positions and the belonging to certain groups (Bourdieu 1977). This aspect of the value of the language—its function as the catalyst of upward social mobility—can be realized and observed on different axes: English (1) can lead to negative or positive social mobility, realized as inclusion in or exclusion of individual speakers or speaker groups from social groupings, and (2) is the direct or indirect marker of social positioning, which is the starting point of any future upward mobility. The ability to speak English is usually positive in a global context, as it includes the speaker and enables communication and upward social mobility. However, it might be a negative factor in a local context, resulting in downward social mobility and social othering. Furthermore, competence in English can be a marker of the users' social position (Bourdieu 1991: 67; Heller and Duchêne 2016; O'Regan 2016; Piller 2016; cf. Section 2.3.2)—the more privileged a person is or has been raised, the more likely s/he speaks English. However, for their future attainment or upward social mobility, students in Cyprus invest further in the English language, making it their "language of possibilities."

While downward social mobility might occur on local scales (Excerpts 4a and 4i), in globalized contexts, it is upward social mobility that is promised by of the English language (e.g., Phillipson 2009; Park and Wee 2012; cf. Section 2.3.2; Excerpts 1a and 11a). English initiates upward social mobility whenever it is required or added to a person's skill set and downward social mobility in cases where it is not in accordance with these requirements—might these be the use or nonuse of English in specific contexts. This understanding of English as a marker of social stratification and initializer of social mobility through education appears to be the basis of the Ct-students' and nCt-students' investment in the English language in Cyprus's HE. While the language does not always lead to upward social mobility for Ct-students (Excerpts 4a and 4i), English almost certainly promises social as well as geographical mobility and improvement for nCt-students, like moving from the Global South toward the Global North (Leung 2017: 2714; Parreñas 2001; cf. Sections 2.3.2 and 2.4.1). For nCt-students, especially in the TRNC, HE is the first step on their way to the Global North, which, in their understanding, represents a social and economic enhancement of their current positions—upward social mobility. For some nCt-students, this advancement is achieved by moving to Cyprus (Excerpt 2g); for others, Cyprus is just one step on their way (Excerpts 1d and 11a).

For nCt students, Cyprus is a country of proximity and represents almost what these students target; the RoC belongs almost to the Outer Circle of English and is almost the nCt-students' ticket to the UK—at least prior to BREXIT—however, the RoC is their ticket to programs like Erasmus+ and Inner-European mobility; the TRNC is almost Europe, almost part of the Global North, and, therefore, only almost their ticket for the desired better future. All these "possibilities" are initiated by the use of the English language, which in turn creates a smokescreen of potential and promise, ignoring the local friction between geography and politics. This smokescreen is effective for nCt-students but unmasked by Ct-students, as they can discern the potential and promise of the English language in Cyprus realistically and based on their local familiarity (Excerpt 4g).

Bourdieu (1991) points out that language is always indexical of social structures—a reflection of its user and receiver as well as of the social conditions of its use. For Ct-students in both parts of Cyprus, English functions as the catalyst of the prevailing social structure and stratification and its use nurtures their continuation. However, the resulting repercussions differ and are based on the social and political differences between the two parts of the island. While Ct-students at UCLan Cyprus act and move within an environment, informed by the remaining value of English as the language of its former colonial ruler (Excerpts 6a, 7a, and 9b), Ct-students in the TRNC do so within a society divided between world-openness and the wish for inclusion, on the one hand, and nationalism and loyal subordination to its "big brother" Turkey, on the other (Excerpts 4e, 4j, 5c, and 14a). Ct-students at UCLan Cyprus invest in the ideological value that is built on a subconscious rationalization of the language's hegemony, historically rooted in the colonial power of the British Empire (see Phillipson 1992, 2009; Wortham 2001; cf. Sections 1.2.1 and 3.2.1). Belonging to the group of English users—which might be entered through various options, like language proficiency or a British degree—is accompanied by privileges of a globally dominant social group. These "unearned benefits" (Piller 2016: 208) reflect the users' upward mobility—their introduction into a higher social class (Block 2015; Iversen, Krishna, and Sen 2017; Jöns, Heffernan, and Meusburger 2017; cf. Section 2.3.2). Ct-students at UCLan Cyprus predominantly target their advancement within the local social structures, as only 20.3 percent state their wish to leave Cyprus after their graduation (Appendix 2.4). Because the Ct-students at UCy were students of English Studies, the English language is a part of their study subject, rather than a medium of instruction for a non-language-related content. For them, it is an investment in their international social and geographical mobility, rather than an asset on the local job market and within the local social structures. In the RoC, the Ct-students' investment in the English language primarily leads to local or global upward social mobility (Excerpt 1c). For Ct-students in the TRNC, however, this might also lead to downward social mobility, due to the division of the society and the two groups' differing attitudes toward the English language and the UK (see Leung 2017 concerning academic mobility; Legewie and Bohmann 2018 concerning gender (in)equality; Ponzo 2018 concerning socioeconomic mobility; cf. Excerpts 4a, 4e, and 14a).

The reasons for and the effect of Ct-students' investment in the English language are more diverse in the TRNC. These students might be located on a continuum, based on their affiliation and appreciation of the UK; some Ct-students maintain close ties to the migrated Turkish Cypriot communities in the UK and often identify as native or near-native speakers of English (Excerpts 4a, 4f, 5b, and 14a), while others feel more affiliated to Turkey and its current economic and political influence on the island (Excerpt 4k). The students' location on this continuum influences the reasons for their investment in English as well as the effect of it within the local social hierarchy. For them, English might represent either a global language or a language of colonial heritage and social division between Turkish Cypriots and Turks (Excerpts 4i and 4j). Depending on their socially affiliated group(s) and the concept the English language represents for this local group(s), Ct-students in the TRNC experience a discrepancy of the ideological, communicative, and economic value of English within the local and any international or global context. Because Ct-students are familiar with this discrepancy and the limitations to the language's value in the local TRNC society, they choose to invest in English for their future potential advancement within the international community. In local contexts, English might be used as a tool of social othering and downward social mobility, either by excluding nCt-students who cannot speak the local language or by marginalizing local bilingual speakers of English and Cypriot Turkish (Excerpts 2i, 4i, and 4j). Its high communicative value is purposely neglected for nationalist reasons—to show that it is not the language that is valued highest in the local social structures (see Bourdieu 1991; Piller 2015; Woolard 1998; Wortham 2001 on the interrelation of language and social structures). Although nCt-students and Ct-students, who identify with the English language in an environment that does not value the language and gravitates toward Northern Cypriot nationalism, experience social exclusion because of having invested in the language, they continue to invest, in the hope of a future reward in another environment or social group (e.g., Excerpts 4a, 11a, and 12a).

While nationalism is also experienced in the RoC, it is, reportedly, about Greece and Turkey—and not about Cyprus itself (Excerpt 10b)—and, therefore, ideologically less connected to and provoked by the use of English. As outside of HE, English does not necessarily initiate or facilitate social mobility, for Ct-students in the RoC it is perceived as a means of mostly future advancement (Excerpts 1c and 10c) but current unification of people with different linguistic repertoires (Excerpts 8b and 15a). Local stakeholders within the HE market, however, do rely on the language; 71.6 percent of the Ct-students at UCLan, 76.7 percent at EMU, and 81 percent at UCy state that English is an important language in their private lives (see Appendices 2.4–2.6).

These findings offer some insights into the negative impact of the high value of English and its extensive commodification (e.g., Heller and Duchêne 2016; McGill 2013; Park and Wee 2012; cf. Section 1.4.2). Its gaining importance for the global economy leads to the urge of some people to show their detachment and independence from it—their devaluation. Although this is only an ideological rejection, as most of the locals still benefit from the economic value of English (see Bourdieu 1991; cf. Section 2.3.1), that is, the money it brings to the TRNC through nCt-students, it is a further indication of the multilayeredness of the language's value. Some nCt-students even move blindly to Cyprus for the simple wish to invest in their futures. These students choose to believe the information provided, for example, by recruiting agencies and to believe in the opportunities an EMI education in Cyprus offers (Excerpts 2e, 3b, and 11a). Local Ct-students who are members of privileged social classes and who do not have to rely entirely on their education for their future perspectives and success can take a perspective that is less influenced by emotions and credulity. These students, especially in the TRNC, suffer from the local reality, the extensive loyalty and idealization of Turkey, and the accompanied partitioning of the TRNC from the global community (Excerpts 4e and 14a). Students who can even depart from the island might choose to escape this reality (cf. Section 5.1). The universities in the TRNC are completely aware of the differences between their potential students and their respective needs and wishes. In their effort to recruit enough students, they aim at catering to their individual needs; they offer, among other things, language classes for less proficient English speakers, scholarships for students from less well-off backgrounds, and "all-inclusive" care, which includes, for example, accommodation, transfer from the airport, and a supermarket on campus, for students who do not wish to immerse themselves in the local environment (see, e.g., EMU n.d.-b, n.d.-c, n.d.-d; EMU Web Office n.d.-b, n.d.-e, n.d.-f; GAU 2019b, 2019l). However, all these efforts are only effective because they are made in addition to offering EMI education.

The analysis has shown that the English language leads to upward social mobility, especially in international contexts and in local RoC contexts. However, it might result in social marginalization in local TRNC contexts. Therefore, for nCt- and Ct-students in the RoC, their investment in the English language is expected to be worthwhile—they invest in the internationally shared economic value of English-as-a-marketable-attribute and are likely to be rewarded with opportunities their non-English-using competitors do not have access to, both in local and global contexts. For nCt- and Ct-students in the TRNC, the investment is expected to pay off in international contexts rather than local ones, due to the discrepancy between the local and the global value of the language and its effects on social mobility. While Ct-students are mostly aware of the reservations against the language and its users, nCt-students are often encouraged to ignore such concerns to be part of the "Cypriot Dream"—the use of Cyprus as a stepping-stone for their desired attainment, which is realized through English. The extent of the nCt-students' willingness to invest in English and to ignore any rising concern is discussed in the following.

### 4.3.4 Supposition 4: English-as-a-Marketable-Attribute

> The value of the English language outweighs nCt-students' concerns about the local contexts it is offered in. The students' abstraction of English-as-a-marketable-attribute from its context is openly utilized by the universities.

Within Cyprus's HE, the English language's commodification is accepted by students and universities alike. Its abstraction from a social practice is facilitated by the neoliberal shift "from primarily use value to exchange value in addition to use value" (Block 2019: 123; Evans 2014; cf. Section 1.4.2) and is based on the conceptualization of language as an autonomous system or entity (Heller and Duchêne 2016; Park and Wee 2012; cf. Section 1.4.2). Because language, in this episteme, exists in itself and prior to use, the English language can be and is used as a valorizing attribute (see Heller 2010; cf. Section 1.4.4). All universities except for UCy use English to valorize their study programs and, consequently, to increase their programs' economic value; the use of English promotes an almost-connection to Europe at GAU, a connection to the UK and its native English context at UCLan Cyprus, and is a reflection of internationality at EMU (cf. Excerpts 2f, 7a, and 11a). In addition to the universities' use of the language to valorize their programs and to attract prospective students (Section 4.3.2), they also use it as an obstacle for their students to overcome and, potentially, as a skill to master. This often happens without any accountability for the implementation of specific thresholds toward their students. GAU, for example, is described as a "degree factory" and as using the English language for its economic value only—to the extent of using other languages than English for teaching or additional explanations (cf. Excerpts 2c and 4g). Following Laura's elaborations in her second interview, the university appears to objectify and decontextualize the language (see, e.g., Heller 2010; Park and Wee 2012); the seemingly common practice of deliberately issuing certificates that confirm the use of English as the exclusive medium of instruction, while the actual teaching is often in Turkish, corroborates the use of English-as-a-marketable-attribute. By apparently issuing certificates in EMI study programs without ensuring the adequacy of its students' English language skills, GAU confirms the students' language proficiency and enables them to announce they "have" English, despite their potential incompetence in using it. English, in this context, is no longer to be used but an exchangeable and detachable asset. This transformation of the English language into an abstract attribute is also observable in the participants' choices.

In the HE market of Cyprus, Ct- and nCt-students function as stakeholders exchanging capital (see Holborow 2013; Lasagabaster 2015 on the role of students in neoliberal universities; cf. Section 1.4.3)—they invest private resources, that is, their time, money, their physical location, and their living conditions, in exchange for HE. This HE is perceived to be good, as it is offered in English and, in return, functions as an additional asset of the students. Students who "have" the asset of English are potentially valued higher by future employers than those who do not have it, returning their initial investment by access to high-paying positions (Excerpts 1a and 1c; cf. Sections 2.3.2 and 2.3.1). This trusting belief in the value of English and the benefits of its inclusion into a person's linguistic repertoire is founded in neoliberal ideologies (Gray, O'Regan, and Wallace 2018; Holborow 2012; Shin and Park 2016; cf. Section 2.4.4) and functions as a prerequisite of any successful commodification (Heller 2010; Heller and Duchêne 2016; Park and Wee 2012; cf. Section 2.4.5). The acceptance of English and education as commodities is, of course, welcomed by the universities and is also reflected in their structures; students are conceptualized as consumers and universities as providers (Holborow 2013: 234; Excerpt 4b). Education functions to produce "subjects with the knowledge and dispositions which are appropriate for servicing the economy" (Gray, O'Regan, and Wallace 2018: 475; see Foucault 2008; Holborow 2015; Shin and Park 2016 for the concept and role of the individual under neoliberalism; cf. Section 1.4.1) and to serve the economy, students feel and are encouraged to have the attribute "English."

Ct-students at UCLan Cyprus and EMU report using the English language as an instrument with which to gain social and geographical mobility and future opportunities (Excerpts 5a and 16a), and they, therefore, use the interrelation of the language's communicative and economic value across unified global markets and social structures (see Bourdieu 1991 on the transfer of value and Ferguson 2007; Murray 2016 on mobility based in English; cf. Sections 1.4.3, 2.3.1, and 4.3.3). Ct-students at all of the included universities are aware of the possibilities and limitations of their respective choices; their perspective on the potential offered by English-as-a-marketable-attribute is less global but based on their familiarity with the local context and their awareness of the economic substructure and orientation of the university (e.g., Excerpts 5a and 17a). Apart from the student at GAU, most Ct-students do not explicitly feel that they are part of the economic endeavor of the universities, although they do know of and accept the economic nature of the institutions (see Holborow 2013 on neoliberal universities). They also do not predominantly abstract the language but use English as part of their linguistic resources and sometimes even identify with it (Excerpt 4b). Ct-students, consequently, confirm the universities' abstract use of the English language, while not automatically following suit. They are aware of the local circumstances of their education and are, therefore, less vulnerable than nCt-students.

Some nCt-students are not aware of the circumstances awaiting them; they might have been informed incomprehensively or even incorrectly (Excerpt 3b; Cyprus: Students duped by good life 2019), while others are just not interested in anything but the desired degree itself (ibid.; Excerpt 1a). NCt-students often choose Cyprus for their HE based on secondhand information; they might be recruited by third-party agencies or receive their information via university webpages or rankings (cf. Section 4.3.2). These students trustingly believe the provided information and tend to not verify it (cf. Excerpts 2e and 3b). Consequently, they might be disappointed or even overwhelmed and unprepared when they realize the unexpected shortcomings of their choice (Excerpt 2f). Other nCt-students are aware of the local reality of Cyprus and its universities; they receive firsthand information, for example, from family members who had gone to study in Cyprus before (Excerpt 2j). Despite these differences, all nCt-students share the motivation to go to Cyprus for their HE because of the globally shared and transferable value of English. The universities, in turn, instrumentalize and objectify the language and its gatekeeping function to the students' ultimately desired goals to various degrees to create profit (cf. 4.3.2). Due to this commodification in Cyprus's HE landscape, linguistic proficiency does not necessarily "mediate social participation" (Piller 2016: 2)—English is rather used as an attribute of a person or entity. This objectification causes the use of English to be perceived as "context-free" and versatile, increasing the economic value of the language, while making any identification with it optional. The prevalent acceptance of and compliance to the objectification and accompanied value of English raises the language to function as a gatekeeper to desired assets, social positions, and goods for nCt-students. NCt-students invest in English to pursue long-term goals, like the improvement of their future employability or access to another location, like the UK or Europe (e.g., Excerpts 1a, 1d, 2b, and 11a). Their goals are well known by the universities, which further use them to modify and personalize their offers for each specific student group.

The universities aim their advertisement at each student group's specific goals and desires. In so doing, they attract especially those nCt-students who do not have reliable informants, like a family member, as additional sources of information. While, as described above, nCt-students want to believe in the benefits of HE in Cyprus, they also describe an obvious strategy of providing only partial or even misleading information by some universities in the TRNC and most recruiting agencies (Excerpt 2e; GAU 2019k; Section 4.3.2). These agencies rely on the prospective students' described credulity and limited access to firsthand information before their arrival, which represents an unethical sales strategy, at the very least (cf. ibid.). In this practice, nCt-students remain unaware of the reality behind the advertised use of the English language, that is, its limited use and instrumentalization, while they conceptualize the language as an asset of themselves to invest in for economic purposes. Furthermore, any discrepancies or concern about the validity of the information provided are biased, because the nCt-students see the language's neoliberal valuation as a commodified attribute of a global citizen (Block 2018b: 578; Bourdieu 1991; Holborow 2013, 2015; Shin and Park 2016; cf. Sections 2.4.1 and 2.4.4) and want to belong to this group.

While the value of English is multilayered—English might be valued as a part of the speaker's identity and cultural good or as a communicative tool—it is fundamentally economic (see Bourdieu 1986, 1991). NCt-students in Cyprus appear to abstract the English language from its use as a communicative tool and social practice (Excerpt 11a) and use English as capital that has acquired its own layer of value and functions as a source "of power and prestige in [its] own right" (Heller 1994: 7). This value, in turn, valorizes the speaker in various globally shared markets (cf. Section 1.4.4). The identification with the language, therefore, is optional, causing English to be classroom-based (Excerpt 2a) only and part of the nCt-students' *Dominant Language Constellations* (cf. Aronin 2016; Section 2.2.2) only for the time of their studies. However, the neoliberal value of English-as-a-marketable-attribute appears to not necessarily be in complementary distribution with its traditional valuation as the language of the British Empire, as exemplified at UCLan Cyprus.

The neoliberal marketization of the English language is a major part of the island's economies (cf. Section 3.4), which is supported by extensive advertising. UCLan Cyprus mainly relies on the maintained prestige and appreciation of the UK as the island's former colonizer in Cyprus and adds only the financial advantage of the location and its lower tuition fees and living cost, compared to the UK, to this convincing argument (cf. Section 4.3.2). The universities in the TRNC, however, add to their, in some cases, aggressive advertisements, collaborations with recruiting agencies to increase their reach and potential profit, and false claims in online advertising (e.g., Goldenchips Educational Services International 2019; Study in North Cyprus 2017) depict the ultimate neoliberal instrumentalization of the English language in this context. These strategies aim at enticing people who are unaware of the reality of the TRNC, to pack their bags and leave for any of the advertised universities in the TRNC, in the hope that this might lead to better job prospects and a better future (e.g., Excerpt 2j). Misleading or incomplete information about the study program, the accruing liabilities, the facilities, or the island in general result in nCt-students finding themselves in precarious circumstances, unable to reach their goals or even to live self-sufficiently (cf. Bilge 2018; Investigation into killing Nigerian students 2018; Kastamonu 2014; Mashininga 2018; Rakoczy 2017; Student murder was drug related n.d.). In Cyprus, the conceptualization of English-as-a-marketable-attribute, therefore, reproduces and maintains the present social inequalities through HE.

## 4.4 Summary

This chapter has offered a supposition-based presentation of the finding gathered in the first investigation of the value of English in Cyprus's HE. The flexibility of the framework allowed for its application in Cyprus's HE without losing the heterogeneity and fruitful insight from the multitude of partakers—represented by the student portraits at the beginning of the chapter. In the course of the assessment of the multilayered value of English, it has been shown that the ideological value of English is predominantly rooted in the colonial history of the island and, therefore, only tertiary to nCt-students in both parts of the island. Furthermore, the variability with the universities' agendas and objectives has been presented—a fact that had been expected based on the multitude of universities that call Cyprus their home. While the included universities in the RoC were more attractive for Ct-students, the universities in the TRNC showed a clear focus on nCt-students and, consequently, pursued more open advertisement and recruiting strategies. Especially nCt-students in the TRNC aim at utilizing their EMI-HE for their future social advancement in non-Cypriot contexts, while local students appear to locate their future predominantly on the island. English, however, has shown to be a tool for both groups, which has the potential to initiate or facilitate this endeavor. As a result of this focus on the globally shared valuation of the English language, fraudulent practices appear to have surfaced that represent the ultimate commodification of HE and students. Unfortunately, especially nCt-students in the TRNC appear to often be not aware of these practices and might find themselves in unfortunate or even precarious situations after moving to (North) Cyprus. Which implications the here-presented finding might have on further assessing and (de)constructing the value of English will be discussed in the next chapter.

## Excerpts

### NCt-Student at UCLan Cyprus (Jim) (B) and Interviewer (A)

### Excerpt 1a

A: ... Did you want to pick a course of study that uses English? #00:16:04-5#

B: Yeah that was really important. #00:16:05-5#

A: so that is in English? That was very important independent of the country you went to so even in Spain if you could have gotten in would you have chosen a course of study that is English? #00:16:18-4#

B: Yeah for as in English, yeah definitely. #00:16:20-5#

A: Why? #00:16:20-9#

B: Because you know it's the language of business and it's used worldwide and it's very important to have knowledge? #00:16:29-8#

A: Ok so you think that your diploma here, your degree as having in a course of study that is English medium of instruction is giving you the chance or more chances to get jobs somewhere? #00:16:45-8#

B: Yeah because ehm I think many people, they have diplomas and degrees and doesn't mean that they will be successful so you wanna try to get the best education that you can get. #00:16:56-7#

### Excerpt 1b

B: Eh well at first I was planning to go to Canada. ... I was really excited but eh at the end I couldn't get the Visa. #00:01:48-3#

A: Oh no ... #00:01:48-3#

...

B: Yeah, so eh then I looked at other eh countries in Europe like Italy, Spain but because of my grades I couldn't get the places that I wanted. ... So then eh I've had [/] had some friends who are in Cyprus here for one year. Some, they were in the North and some here in Nicosia. #00:02:15-0#

A: Ok. #00:02:16-4#

B: So ehm they said that I know it's ok you know start cos' my idea it's start somewhere. And maybe, you know, transfer or move on. #00:02:25-3#

## Excerpt 1c

B: Yeah, I've noticed that there aren't too many international students here. #00:25:29-7#

...

B: Yeah but I also think having too many universities is not a good [/] is not a good idea because like you said is a small country, small market so competition is a gonna be a lot harder so. #00:26:38-9#

A: right so that's also why so many people form outside come to Cyprus to study? #00:26:43-8#

B: Yeah even eh some they said they transfer from chance form a public university and they come here to UCLan. #00:26:51-3#

A: to UCLan? Yeah, it's special you've got an [/] an UK degree in the end. #00:26:57-9#

B: Yeah that's more attractive to employee, yeah. #00:27:01-0#

## Excerpt 1d

B: 'Cos ehm [//] because I wanna [/] I wanna like try you know the university in Panama because it's a lot cheaper. #00:30:28-0#

A: Ok yeah. #00:30:28-0#

B: and also have the chance to transfer I think after two years you can go to Florida. #00:30:35-6#

...

B: Yeah and also for the same grade for the tuition [in] Panama we have to pay [//] in America let's say it's 30 000 [USD] per year [in] Panama it's 8[000 USD]. #00:30:51-3#

## Excerpt 1e

A: ... what do you like about Cyprus? #00:04:48-7#

B: Ehm, I think eh people are friendly and most of them speak English. ... So like in other countries in Germany or France, it's quite difficult to communicate. #00:05:02-0#

## NCt-Student GAU (Sue) (B) and Interviewer (A)

### Excerpt 2a

B: I think cause the environment does not support English use, because after class you will go to [/] to the shop and you need to [/] to speak in Turkish, or something, so then you [/] you will not be able to practice your English. #00:11:45-1#

### Excerpt 2b

B: Ahm, we had options. Cyprus was like our maybe our last option? (laughs) #00:02:02-9#

A: Okay? (laughs). What other options were you thinking about? #00:02:08-5#

B: … especially the UK because that's what I wanted to go, you need to have some money on your accounts like to show you can support yourself during your study. But here we … you don't have to show your bank records, so that was easy, even you can make a fast installment. #00:02:33-7#

…

B: and everything can work out with time, so we picked this one because it's [/] it's affordable. #00:02:40-3#

A: Right. Okay, so like your first choice was native English speaking or UK because of another reason? #00:02:48-5#

B: Yeah, yeah, because of [/] of English and eh opportunities to work after school. #00:02:55-1#

### Excerpt 2c

A: … Why did you choose Girne American University? #00:04:29-4#

B: … Well, because of the [/] of the name American, I guess [?]. … In a Turkish uhm [//] Turkish-speaking country … you're thinking probably, because it's American, then the [/] the academic is also American and then they expect more English-speaking staff and students, yeah so basically that is what I was looking for and yeah. #00:05:02-2#

A: And what … (laughs). And what did it turn out to be? Is it like you expected it? #00:05:09-1#

B: Not 100 per cent what I expected (laughs) really because even in classroom teachers and students use Turkish. #00:05:15-4#

…

A: Okay (laughs). Okay, so but teaching, the actual teaching, does it happen in English or is that Turkish too? #00:05:37-3#

B: No, if it's an English ehm [//] English-based program, they teaching in English but sometimes students ask Turk or maybe the teachers … the teacher explains in English and then she stops and explains also in Turkish. #00:05:58-9#

A: Right. #00:06:00-1#

B: Sometimes they get too involved, they forget there's some English-speaking students in classroom. It can go on for like five minutes and at the end of the lessons we should be going back to English. #00:06:12-1#

…

A: So, from your experience, there are more Cypriot Turkish or Turkish students in class than international ones? #00:06:30-9#

B: mhm, yes, yes, well international [//] it depends on the program really, because say for example business may be getting more international students or probably half-half international and local, but other programs are more [//] they have more locals than international, like my program … We have more students from Turkey and Cypriot studying here. #00:07:00-7#

# Excerpt 2d

B: And … even [/] even international students, because though we go to class and learn some English, but when they go out of class they speak French, if they are from Cameroon, Africa, from Congo, or they will speak their native languages outside of classroom learning, because it's just class-based. And sometimes when they [/] they finish uhm English foundation and they're coming out to enroll for the program they passed, wanted to study, you try to talk to them and you realize, … they couldn't express themselves as much. #00:10:01-9#

…

B: Well, maybe it's because of the acquisition [?] or maybe it's because of the culture of the people, and [/] and also because of the group [/] group thinking mentality, so for example if [/] if African students come and get together and they want to feel bonded, they would rather speak their native language than English. … #00:11:10-4#

## Excerpt 2e

B: Yeah, it's really difficult, because most international students if you ask them why they came to Cyprus it's because of affordability and maybe not because of the location per se. … Because here on the island there is the question of if you leave is your degree valid out there? Because the land is not look nice especially with these Turkish side, so we're not very sure what you are doing is the right thing, that's why after school you have to have your documents uhm valid [//] verified by the Turkish education something something … #00:25:52-0#

A: Right. #00:25:53-7#

B: … I would [recommend Cyprus] but I would also give them all the information that there is, because when we were coming we did not have the [/] the right information. … Yeah, so many students really come on the island but so many of them also leave after one semester, after one year, because the information that we're given before we come is not the correct information. #00:26:21-9#

A: Who gave you the information? #00:26:25-6#

B: Uhm, or maybe we don't ask the right questions because, well one we have agents, before you come here there's some education agents either in Africa or probably in Cyprus who are helping you to some courses, your documents to come and study, so they give you information, the information that you need to come here. #00:26:45-8#

A: Ah, okay. #00:26:46-4#

B: ... just the right information for them, so that you can actually come here. ... But when you come then you realise these, that question of ... is your degree valid, is it valid, and also the fact that [/] that country is not English-speaking, well from the map and from how it is said you would think because they're next [//] near Europe you'd think they speak English, but then you come and realise they don't. #00:27:08-1#

## Excerpt 2f

B: So it's [/] it's really sad when you see these things happening. So, probably they had enough information of exactly how it is, so that you're not shocked, because what really makes people want to turn back home is [/] is they expect Cyprus to be [/] to be like going to Europe, you know? ... These development, these technology, all that thing [//] all those things, but when they come here they realise it's [//] where you come from is actually way, way, way better. Kenia is actually more developed than Cyprus. #00:52:29-9#

## Excerpt 2g

B: ... they don't want to leave ... Cyprus because one it's safe, two it's much better than where you come from. ... So, you don't want to go and you're hoping maybe if you stayed here long enough you might find a way to go outside of here and possibly to better places. #00:44:49-2#

...

B: And now they are also regulating the number of people coming in, they might not say it but at Ercan there are so many students especially from Bangladesh uhm that have been turned away, because especially students from the Asian Bangladesh, Pakistani, most of them don't come to study because of the situation in their country, it's not like they're in war, but they need [/] they need money. #00:45:50-9#

### Excerpt 2h

B: … especially say [//] for example lecturers and uhm, the staff members that work in office they [//] yes they speak English, but I feel others some secretaries also do not know English, but they're trying to change this because those [//] some stuff members who do not know English and Turkish have been replaced by those who can, so they're trying. Slowly they're trying to ensure that every person who is involved with students on a day-to-day basis, they are speaking two [//] the two languages. #00:24:25-3#

### Excerpt 2i

B: … most students from Africa not treated in a [//] I wouldn't say, well in a good way, say for example you're going to [/] to um restaurant or maybe a club at night, … African students would tend to be treated in a suspicious manner. … Arabs or people with a lighter skin are given more privileged treatment and a special treatment than Africans, because maybe they think Africans will cause chaos, so even though they are inside you will see maybe there's some bouncers placed strategically just in case somebody is going to do somethings. … And some bars and um at night they don't allow Africans sometimes. #00:40:33-8#

### Excerpt 2j

A: But you knew what to expect, right? Because of your sister? #00:54:12-5#

B: Yeah, fortunately, she told me almost everything so … But I have two cousins who came here as well and I told them everything, but sometimes people maybe they want also experience, to learn from their own experience. They're two [/] two gentlemen and I tell them "this is what you will find if you're coming" and well like will you find a job? "Yes, you can find a job but it's not white-collar job, you can work … in a restaurants, in bars, in shops, that kind of jobs you can find, but any other kind of job, you have to learn the local language" and they were happy they said "yeah, we can do everything." So they came very happy, but two months down the line they were sad, they wanted to pack their bags and go home and they did! #00:55:10-1#

## NCt-Student EMU (John) (B) and Interviewer (A)

### Excerpt 3a

B: Actually when I was growing up I learned English and my native language is Yoruba, together. So it's like, I'm a bilingual speaker. … At home, we used the native languages, while in the school we used the foreign language, which is the official language of the country, English. #00:01:49-0#

### Excerpt 3b

A: Ok, good. How did it come that you study in Cyprus? … #00:02:45-3#
B: Actually it was through the recommendation of a friend back there in Nigeria. I was in school … and I wanted to study outside the country. And he gave me suggestion of top schools in Turkey and I applied, I just browsed through some of the schools and I saw that EMU is one of the most reputable schools, and so I applied and I was given the admission xxx. #00:03:08-9#
A: … Before you came to Cyprus, did you know it was divided? #00:03:35-9#
B: Actually, before leaving my country I thought I was going to Turkey. #00:03:41-4#
A: Ah, ok (laughs). #00:03:44-0#
B: It was when I got here that I realized that I'm coming from a diff XXX (breaking up) which is not Turkey and which is another country (breaking up) so I never knew anything about North Cyprus, the information was just that I am coming to Turkey. It was when I got to Istanbul Airport that I realized that. #00:04:04-6#

### Excerpt 3c

A: Ok, when you go to Famagusta to shops are you able to communicate in Turkish there? Or is that when you stick to English for sure? #00:08:47-6#

B: I speak to them in English, and I use some Turkish vocabulary so they can understand me a bit. #00:08:55-8#

A: Ok, well shop owners' English doesn't seem to be that good, right, in Famagusta? #00:09:01-6#

B: Oh, not at all. It's worst, you don't believe it, but sometimes it affects the way you even try to communicate. You have to, sometimes after speaking you just wonder how am I speaking this way? It's like your English is going out the other side. … You mix the sentences together, you put Turkish words and just to get them to understand. #00:09:29-3#

## Excerpt 3d

B: I think it doesn't really matter the language you use, in as much as the other person can understand you. That is ok. So, in as much as, in the way you speak English, it's comprehensible. … And looking at the concept that English is not based on a particular standard is basic [//] especially in a global setting, it's basically for communication. So, in as much as communicative competences are set in, and the interlocutors understand each other, that is the most important thing. #00:34:55-3#

…

A: Are there [//] like besides that you are getting more conscious of ehm your interlocutors' language abilities, is there any other advantage or disadvantage that you feel that occurs when talking to non-native speakers? With a range of proficiency? #00:35:31-3#

B: Actually, the forced advantage is that, it tells you to master how to speak to people with different fluency. And like before, I just speak, without the consciousness of the fact that probably they don't understand me. But this time around I have to speak with the consciousness of, "OK they don't understand me, let me try to bring down my fluency." … #00:36:09-9#

## Excerpt 3e

B: … because from Nigeria when you speak, you don't need to worry if others understand. You know that they understand. … But in this setting you have to be conscious of the fact that they might not really get what you're saying, you just have to come down to their level. So it gives me the ability to do that. #00:10:26-5#

A: ... Is this something you learned in Cyprus only? #00:10:46-2#

B: It's something I learned in Cyprus only, yeah. #00:10:49-0#

A: Ok. Okay, Ehm, do you think that people ehm perceive you differently depending on the language you speak? ... #00:11:12-6#

B: Actually sometimes, I discussed this also with some of my friends, whenever I am speak in Yoruba ... I feel informal, rather. Whenever I'm speaking English I feel more formal. ... Especially in North Cyprus, but back there in Nigeria when I'm speaking English or Yoruba, it doesn't matter. But in Cyprus imagine you are speaking to somebody ... in a foreign language, and you're speaking in English. It's like you are creating a barrier between the two of you. ... So whenever I'm speaking Yoruba in North Cyprus I feel OK with friends. But when I go to speak in English, I feel I am speaking a formal language. #00:11:49-5#

## Excerpt 3f

B: ... For example when I started in the department, there was a time I went for a presentation. And after everything I was told that "you need to calm down, you are too fast." ... So, with that knowledge, speaking another accent but I decided to just reduce my fluency, you know, in order for them to understand. Not probably because I'm conscious of the accent or not. #00:21:46-9#

A: Ok. So you would rather speak more slowly than pronouncing words differently to make sure your fellow students understand? #00:21:56-5#

B: Yeah, in as much as I speak slowly. They understand better. Pronouncing words differently doesn't really make any difference. #00:22:04-9#

...

B: ... When I speak with a Turkish person, I try to [//] I tend to speak with the accent of English. ... When I speak to a Nigerian, I speak normally. And when I speak with somebody, probably from the US or the UK, I tend to also speak the same way. ... So, it's not really that it's affected me, just my flexibility, I'm very flexible about all these things. … It is something that I learned more probably in Cyprus. In Nigeria I never care about things like that because what ever way you speak everybody understands you so I say it another time before cause is not really about the communication, it's just about unity. The ability to go to another region and speak to them and come together as brothers. #00:23:33-5#

## Excerpt 3g

B: Yeah, so many areas of my life where I can't work with English alone, in [//] even in different departments in the school, most of the instructors speak in their native languages, in Turkish. … And you know in the end you have to have friends from this place. You have to learn their language. Most of them, yeah, they don't really have this fluency about with English. I've already been very close with English-speaking students because I prefer speaking their languages. But to really know them better, you need to learn their language. #00:13:25-4#

## Excerpt 3h

B: Ehm, I would have loved to learn Turkish, but looking at the concept that Turkish is just limited to Turkey and North Cyprus, I'm not really interested in it. #00:31:32-7#

## Ct-Student at EMU/GAU (Laura) (B) and Interviewer (A)

## Excerpt 4a

B: … but in my village [English] it's used as a joke. #00:33:21-1#
A: By the, by your …? #00:33:25-1#

B: Locals, locals, like I can't speak any English, like if someone comes over, my mum says "only Turkish please." People feel offended when I speak English in the village. #00:33:33-1#

A: Be ... [//] Why? #00:33:35-6#

B: Because they don't know any. ... like sometimes, you know when someone's bilingual? ... Sometimes you forget words in the other language. ... So, sometimes when I'm speaking Turkish [//] because I speak Cypriot Turkish and there's also formal Turkish, so I don't really know that much formal Turkish but sometimes I forget the words, like, I blank out, and I turn to my sister, who is more fluent in Cypriot Turkish, ... and I turn to her in English and I ask her what it is, so everyone thinks I'm like trying to say "hey look, I'm from London, I have the perfect English!" But I'm actually just trying to find the words to explain to them. #00:34:27-7#

## Excerpt 4b

B: ... Our class, our teachers and everything, we're like a community. ... Our teachers love us, we love them, and we have this whole sad feeling that we're leaving. That's how special it is. #00:13:30-2#

...

B: Ehm, when it comes to EMU, I said this before. I love my ELT department, I always put it aside, but I don't like how EMU [//] they have this system that's like they see the student as money. Every year the financial fees raise. I understand it's a private university and they need money. But there is some kind of racial problems as well, for instance. My [//] and they lie a lot. My friend went and asked "can I be a research assistant?" and they said to her, "you're Cypriot, we only accept people from Turkey." Yeah. My friend from Turkey went and asked, and they said to her, "We only accept Cypriots." And then, an international student went and said, "We only accept Cypriots." So, they're like, these whole lying, racial problems, I guess. #00:14:38-7#

## Excerpt 4c

A: ... Uhm, do you have a scholarship or something like that? ... #00:22:23-5#

B: Actually, no because I registered with a British passport, but if you're Cypriot you automatically get 50% off. … And I get a scholarship because I'm high honor. I only get 25%. If I wasn't high honor, I wouldn't get a scholarship. #00:22:41-5#

A: Ah, ok. So why did you register with your British passport? #00:22:46-5#

B: … if you're Cypriot, you have to see Turkish lessons, like really hard Turkish lessons, and my Turkish wasn't competent enough for that. I mean think about it, I get A's in ELT, and suddenly if I fail a Turkish course. … I mean, it is more money, cause it's dollars for me, but I tried [//] for instance, Cypriots pay 5000 TL for one year, no sorry, one term, I think. … I pay one term, 10,000 TL if I don't get a scholarship. Because I get a scholarship, I pay around 7000 TL. #00:23:31-2#

## Excerpt 4d

B: Yeah, in Girne. It's exactly the same [as at EMU], honestly. That's why, uhm, it's even worse. At least in Famagusta the shop keepers try to learn English. In here, no one learns English. … So everyone is literally calling me to write messages or translate. Yeah, 'cause I'm the only English teacher in the whole village who speaks formal English.

…

B: What [international students] do is they have, at school they have canteens, so they usually shop from there or eat there, they don't really go off to Kyrenia without a Turkish speaker and it breaks my heart, because they really want to explore. … Like, people who are studying other English things. I mean there's, in Kyrenia there's more people who come from London, Australia, they actually moved to Kyrenia. Turkish Cypriots who speak Turkish and English, they help them out. #00:28:36-8#

…

A: But they have it from other departments, like the people in my department are mainly from Turkey, they just came because GAU gives people scholarships, you know trying to get money. GAU is more money-based. Everything is about money. … #00:29:26-3#

## Excerpt 4e

A: So would you prefer Cyprus to be reunified? #00:15:40-0#

B: Yes, I want it. Because in a sense, not for me right now, but for future children, I want them to get an EU education. … I want their abilities to grow. #00:15:54-5#

…

B: I know a lot of things happened in the past between the Greeks and the Turks. And I have family members who don't even want to talk about that war. But they said to us, if you guys are gonna be happy, and the children's future is gonna happen, then we want this unification. But some people just have a narrow mind, we can't change them. #00:17:26-1#

## Excerpt 4f

B: We think English will be the medium of communication [in a united Cyprus], because English is as you know the lingua franca as well of the world, and even on the Greek side, the Turkish Cypriot side, English is mandatory in schools, so every student knows it. I think English will be used as the medium. I mean there will be people who know Turkish Cypriot, Greek Cypriot. It'll be just like England, where everyone uses English for communication, yet everyone at home has a native language. #00:31:11-5#

## Excerpt 4g

B: Yeah, I mean I used to think my classmates didn't know English in EMU. … But they are perfect compared to GAU. (laughs). Honestly. #00:09:55-1#

A: You as a native speaker, you always have like, you know, the difference between you and the other classmates who are not natives, but … #00:10:02-8#

B: Of course, but, like, I used to say that it's not about native, ok we are native, we have good use of English, but there were native students who didn't know English, I mean their grammar, the spelling, … #00:10:20-3#

A: But they would pass classes? #00:10:22-9#

…

B: Oh yeah, I mean, they just give them money and everyone passes. I mean GAU is known for "you pay the university, you get your diploma." #00:10:40-8#

## Excerpt 4h

A: Ok, so why did you come to Cyprus? #00:05:01-4#

B: England was starting to become a dangerous place, the area I lived in, to raise children. And my grandfather [//] he was old, … So we moved here to have a better future. And I'm not [//] I don't regret it at all. … #00:05:29-5#

## Excerpt 4i

B: So, it's like [locals] have a fear of speaking with a native speaker. … I felt guilty for using English! Even with my friends. I would type English to them and they'd me Turkish even though they're ELT students and they have really good English. #01:13:07-1#

…

A: mhm, do you have a feeling that they are more accessible [//] people are more accessible if you use Turkish, also your generation? #01:13:22-7#

B: yeah, yes exactly, yes. … I feel like they're reserved against English, especially if you are a native speaker. So, most of the time I feel like I'm ashamed because I'm a native speaker. #01:13:51-6#

## Excerpt 4j

A: …, are [locals] more willing to maybe learn [English]? #00:52:51-6#

B: Yes, to get money. (laughs) To get money they are. I mean, if they don't have English they can't work anymore, they can't [//] I mean all the tourists that come, even if you're like a barman, you need to ask them ingredients. They want to now. Before when we told them "Hey, let's teach you some English," they'd be like "I don't need it!" But now they come back. #00:53:14-6#

A: But are they also interested in the cultural aspect of the language? #00:53:25-0#

B: Not really. That [//] they're not really interested. ... #00:53:36-4#

...

A: So, so motivating, XXX. But I guess, I think English is the key for peace as well, because we need a third language. Like, I know some Greek Cypriot words but I'm not fluent. But we need a communication tool between each other. If there is peace. I mean honestly if God wills it and I have children, I want my child [/] I want my child to study at UCLan. Why should my child go all the way to England when she can get a much cheaper education, better education, stuff like that? But my child can't study in UCLan right now and that's what breaks my heart. #00:54:48-6#

## Excerpt 4k

B: I can honestly tell you that [Turks] do not want it. Because they have a theory that if we get the reunification, we will kick out the mainland Turks out of the country. And also, because there's this whole saying that Cypriots don't like mainland Turks, it's like this whole going around thing, that they're scared that we're gonna kick them out. ... And plus, if we become unified, our currency will be Euro, not Lira, and they can't afford to stay here if it's Euro. So, they're completely against it. I mean, if you talk to any mainland Turk, they will start saying mean things that even is not true, just to get people to change their minds. #00:20:36-2#

A: Mm, ok. But, well Cypriots and Turks get along ok, right? Or is there still this kind of feud in general? #00:20:49-5#

B: I mean, it depends on the area. ... I mean, I have mainland Turks in my family, my cousin married a mainland Turk, and he's the most cultural, most intelligent man I've met in my life, I mean, I could worship him. But there are mainland Turks that come [//] and they have this whole narrow view, and they end up fighting with the Cyp & [//] like, for instance, they don't, like mainland Turks, usually they have a hijab, and they say to Cypriots that we're sinners because we don't have hijabs. Like, there are some narrow-minded ones, and they come in numbers, and the cultural ones come in less numbers, which causes fights. #00:21:29-7#

## Excerpt 4l

B: Well actually now in job requirements, they say you have to know English. So even if you're forty years old [//] so I had a couple of fourty-year-olds come up to me, say "can you teach us like English for estate agents or I'll get fired." #00:44:28-6#

A: Okay, so they do have the job already and need to re-educate themselves basically in English. #00:44:36-0#

B: Yeah, that's the like tragic point is like, in [//] when they were younger they never got the education. The fact that the educational system is still the same all these years is a tragedy and they got a job, but now. Because Cyprus is becoming more international, you know? We got people coming from all over the world, moving here because it's a peaceful area, great place to raise kids … #00:45:18-0#

## Excerpt 4m

B: No, just like quick English specific purpose courses. I actually started it this year, no one's ever done it in Kyrenia. I'm the first person ever to come up with the idea here, because of EMU. They taught me ESP. And they were like "I'm gonna get kicked out my job, can you just give me a two-month course, just teach me some English words about my job, that's it." So they don't have any context behind it. #00:56:19-4#

A: Okay, so it's just a tool. #00:56:21-4#

B: Yeah, they use it as a tool. #00:56:23-8#

## Excerpt 4n

B: People who don't have English they have an English degree, but when they go to apply for a job they get accepted, because it says this person has an English degree! But that's why they can't speak English in their job. And that's why we have English language teachers who don't speak English! That's what I just don't understand. #01:10:30-0#

## Ct-Student at EMU (B) and Interviewer (A)

### Excerpt 5a

A: …, so why did you pick EMU in the first place? #00:12:35-2#
B: Well, EMU wasn't my first option … but the other school I had to go was in England, and ehm, I had to go and prepare papers and things like that … but, I didn't want to go, then I changed my mind … because it was going to be expensive. #00:12:53-5#

### Excerpt 5b

A: Bilingual. So, you also native in Turkish. #00:04:17-9#
B: but I started my education, yeah, life in English … I feel more comfortable [using English]. #00:04:31-9#

### Excerpt 5c

B: Well, Greek used to play huge role in Cyprus. But now that they're separated, people don't know Greek no longer, English plays a bigger role because I think the governments and people are all introducing this English language importance at school. Like state schools, the one I went to, by the time I got to high school, the government changed and they decided that they had an ICGCSE section, that's where I continued my education. And the books come from England to take ICGCSEs and we followed that curriculum, and there are private institutions which give private English lessons. … so English had become really important, and everybody except from the people in administration, like people everywhere are sending their children to get English education. But not Greek education (laughs), it's all in English. #00:36:35-9#

### Ct-Student at UCLan Cyprus (B) and Interviewer (A)

### Excerpt 6a

A: So, are you planning to stay in Cyprus after you finish your studies? #00:03:48-1#

...

B: Not sure, but maybe for Master's I'll go to England and maybe for [//] through Erasmus I'll go. #00:03:59-0#

### Ct-Student at UCLan Cyprus (B) and Interviewer (A)

### Excerpt 7a

A: So why did you pick this university? I just read that in Cyprus you have so many universities. #00:00:59-9#

...

B: It's the only English [//] not an English, a British-certified university. … I do believe, that is, [//] I'm not saying the Cypriot certificates are any bad, but British are more recognized and accepted all over the world. #00:01:27-7#

### Ct-Student at UCLan Cyprus (B) and Interviewer (A)

### Excerpt 8a

A: Why did you come here? #00:05:12-0#
B: Well actually, I don't know. I always wanted to live on my own. So UCLan was a chance an opportunity [to studying for] six months in the UK so that is what matters for me. #00:05:33-9#

### Excerpt 8b

B: When I have to ask something in the bus station or … in a supermarket where [//] which in person is eh not from Cyprus. … So you have to communicate in English. #00:02:37-6#

## Ct-Student at EMU (B) and Interviewer (A)

### Excerpt 9a

B: Oh. Usually I'm using my native language, Turkish. Cause I'm at home [//] cause my brother, he must speak English that's why. Normally with my mom I speak English, and usually on Saturday I'm going to my grandparents' home and I have to speak English as well cause my grandmum is English. #00:06:46-0#

### Excerpt 9b

A: So you were thinking about going abroad? … Where did you want to go? #00:04:04-7#
B: I want to go, ehm, England, for my Master. But we will see. #00:04:17-5#

## Ct-Student at UCy (B) and Interviewer (A)

### Excerpt 10a

B: In the Turkish Cypriot community, from what I've heard, there are a lot of Turkish Cypriots who are bilingual in Greek. In, eh, the Greek Cypriot community though, That would be very very rare. … [In general,] I'd like us to communicate, ehm, in Greek and Turkish but for now, since we don't speak [//] most of us, at least Greek Cypriots, don't speak Turkish and a lot of Turkish Cypriots don't speak Greek. I think we could use English for now. #00:15:20-2#
A: Okay so English would be something like a lingua franca, medium of communication? #00:15:26-1#
B: It already is for bicommunal, ehm, event and bicommunal organizations and things like that. #00:15:32#

### Excerpt 10b

B: But in Cyprus, when someone someone's nationalist they care about Greece or Turkey not [/] not about Cyprus. #00:12:16-5#

## Excerpt 10c

B: I'm definitely going to abroad for masters. I haven't decided where yet though. … I'm thinking of the US and Canada as well. # 00:07:51-1#

## NCt-Student at EMU (B) and Interviewer (A)

### Excerpt 11a

B: to be perfectly honest, I came here to study, just for study, … I came here to uh astord[?] the journey of uh you know, education, because it is really difficult for me to go to European countries, and my purpose is going, as I mentioned before, going to some European countries, especially Germany. #00:05:21-1#

…

A: and why did you pick Cyprus to go to study? #00:05:46-8#
B: Because eh the 50 percent scholarship is available for me … and eh it was the only way I can leave my country and begin my study in an international university. #00:06:01-7#
A: Okay, so you picked not Cyprus but EMU. #00:06:05-9#

…

B: yes, just EMU, because as far as I know, this is the best university in this area. #00:06:25-4#

## NCt-Student at EMU

### Excerpt 12a

One more thing I wanted to add, ehm, not all of them, but you have let's say, some Turkish people who know English but refuse to use it … cause I remember I needed to do something, I needed help to fix my university email and everyone told me "go talk to this guy," I go and I talk to this guy, and he is like "I don't speak English, go find someone else." "You're talking to me in English, and it's not broken, its fluent, what?" like I've seen it also more than once. #00:19:58-6#

## NCt-Student at EMU (B) and Interviewer (A)

### Excerpt 13a

B: I think maybe Turkish speakers are much better in English than Cypriot ones, uhm, because to be honest I've had [//] I have Turkish friends and Cypriot ones, but I always feel that the ones who came from Turkey are much able to actually talk and communicate and like, explain things much more clearly. #00:08:49-3#

A: OK, ehm, do you also go to the city center? What you can call center, sometimes? Are you able to buy things there, go to a cafe, communicate with people there? #00:09:02-5#

B: Yes, yes, uhm, but communicate not that much, because whenever sometimes I wanna approach someone to ask for example about directions or about anything, they're like English jock [?], so, and sometimes I get this feeling that they know English but they don't want to talk in English. Because they have this kind of fear that it won't be perfect, you know what I mean? #00:09:27-2#

## Ct-Student at EMU

### Excerpt 14a

We will sleep in our windows open our doors open now. There's too much bad people come from Turkey. So most of [//] if you talk to a Turkish Cypriot they will say that we don't want Turkey people come in. Hello, my friend's from Turkey. I like them too but there was bad people sent to us [//] too much from Turkey. … if they say "I'm from Cyprus." "OK, come in." But they say "my country is better." "We saved you in 1974." Like that things. Most of them, say, "I hate them." Exactly. Because he wasn't saving us. His grandfather was saving us and we would welcome all of them. They get him [//] getting jobs from here. The government gives them houses, money, everything and just saying that we saved you. If that wasn't Turkey we would be all weak. So let me be clear. Turkish Cypriots are in no less than Turks. #00:13:39#

### NCt-Student at UCLan Cyprus

### Excerpt 15a

… sometimes I was go to church with [friends]. They have some church activity [and] they were invite me so I come. I think is eh good way to know different people like that so I will come. [And] is English. Eh … British English. So I think the sound is very beautiful so I always go. #00:12:55-9#

### Ct-Student at UCLan Cyprus

### Excerpt 16a

Yes, for sport science if you don't know English there is a disadvantage for you because eh the English is an international language okay? And the eh [/] the people when they came to a gym then maybe 60% are speaking English eh okay? #00:04:11-6#

### Ct-Student at UCLan Cyprus

### Excerpt 17a

Uhm, I think it brings more European sense in a way. When I'm here, I don't really think I'm in Cyprus. It's very different, but it's also because I'm not from this city. I'm from Larnaca. So, it's completely different that what I grew up in. So, I don't know, I like this feeling of European, so. #00:08:47-4#

# 5

# English in a Globalized World

## 5.1 Introduction: Laura Revisited

In the previous chapters, the value of English in Cyprus's HE landscape has been conceptualized and assessed from the students' and universities' perspectives. It seems that the value of English (almost) always represents a combination of the different value layers with context- and speaker-dependent prominence and importance. For some, the economic value of English is most intriguing to invest in learning or using the English language; for others, the ideological value of English is essential especially if they identify as native speakers of the language or feel a sense of loyalty to its cultural base. This chapter will offer a passage from the individual student's experiences with the English language (and) in Cyprus's higher education (HE) to an assessment of the effects of the current understanding and utilization of the value of English on global and local social structures. It ends with an outlook at understanding the value of English as a tool of empowerment for individual speakers—a tool that does not consolidate social inequalities but initiates their dissolution.

## 5.1 Laura Revisited

During her first participation in this study, Laura has been an undergraduate student at Eastern Mediterranean University (EMU) in the Turkish Republic of Northern Cyprus (TRNC). She was planning to do her graduate studies at University of Central Lancashire Cyprus (UCLan Cyprus) in Pyla, Republic of Cyprus (RoC), to refresh her English language skills and obtain a British certificate. She was worried about her future in Cyprus and would have liked to be prepared in case she had to leave the country and find employment abroad. She was a politically well-informed global citizen who made sure to stay informed through various independent sources. She stated that she double-checked the Cypriot news by using the BBC or other international news services because she felt a certain bias in local coverage. In general, she was very supportive of Cyprus's connection to the EU, especially concerning the educational opportunities it might offer, which, at the same time, was one of her main reasons to support the reunification of the island. She hoped for Cyprus to become a place "where everyone uses English for communication, yet everyone at home has a native language" (Excerpt 4f) after its reunification. She assigns the role of a public language (Piller 2016) to English and stresses its unifying potential when English is used in addition to the different groups' native languages.

One and a half years later, Laura agreed to partake in another interview and offered a comparison of her experience of being a student at EMU and at UCLan Cyprus and living in the TRNC and the RoC. Unfortunately, life had not proceeded as planned: She had been accepted at UCLan Cyprus and had moved to the RoC, when, as she accounts, she was expelled for what seem to be political reasons. As a result, she moved back to her home village and did a master's degree at GAU. The comparison of her experience there with those she encountered at EMU is characterized by inferiority in both the quality of the content and the medium of instruction. Laura's assessment of the language abilities is rather biased, since she identifies as a native speaker and has been trained to teach, and, therefore, evaluates the English language proficiency of others from this position. She reports experiencing negative attitudes toward herself as a native English speaker and justifies this, partially, by the locals' lack of proficiency.

> Locals, locals, like I can't speak any English. Like, if someone comes over, my mum says "only Turkish please." People feel offended when I speak English in the village. … Because they don't know any. (Excerpt 4a)

This attitude appears to change only when it comes to economic profit.

**Interviewer:** Is that [cultural mixing and growing immigration] something that promotes English with locals, too? So, are they more willing to maybe learn it?

**Laura:** Yes, to get money. (laughs) To get money they are. I mean, if they don't have English they can't work anymore, they can't, I mean all the tourists that come, even if you're like a barman, you need to make the drink, you need to ask them ingredients.

|  | Them [//] they want to now. Before when we told them "Hey, let's teach you some English," they'd be like "I don't need it!" But now they come back. |
|---|---|
| **Interviewer:** | But are they also interested in the cultural aspect of the language? |
| **Laura:** | Not really. That [//] they're not really interested. (Excerpt 4j) |

Laura perceives the growing demand in speaking English as a job requirement as detached from the long-standing goal of communicative competence, stating that "now in job requirements, they say you have to know English. … I had a couple of forty-year-olds come up to me, say 'can you teach us like English for estate agents or I'll get fired' " (Excerpt 4l). It seems that for local Cypriots, the English language is no longer necessarily seen as a part of the speaker's identity:

| **Laura:** | So, they don't have any context behind [learning English]. |
|---|---|
| **Interviewer:** | Okay, so it's just a tool. |
| **Laura:** | Yeah, they use it as a tool. (Excerpt 4m) |

Part of this development appears to be the disposability and purchasability of degrees (Excerpt 4g), which leads to a reduction in quality and social inequality. Laura states that

> people who don't have English they have an English degree, but when they go to apply for a job they get accepted, because it says this person has an English degree! But that's why they can't speak English in their job. And that's why we have English language teachers who don't speak English! (Excerpt 4n)

Laura is a very reflective young woman, who experienced HE in the TRNC at two universities. Although she takes a native speaker perspective when advocating the importance of the English language in the TRNC's education system, she supports its communicative potential and, especially when regarding the reunification of the island, its uniting potential. Her childhood and education abroad have enabled her to assess the TRNC—and Cyprus as a whole—from an open-minded and metropolitan position. The so-emerged privileges and liberty allow her to compare the social structure and inequalities in Cyprus to other societies and to take action to improve her situation if need be; approximately one year after her second interview, Laura decided to leave Cyprus and move back to London, UK, to pursue her PhD. Laura's experiences are an example of the complex relations at work in Cyprus's HE landscape, combining local and global as well as economic and personal objectives. An overview of these objectives and their effects on social hierarchies will be presented and discussed in the following.

## 5.2 Synopsis of findings

In the previous chapter, the four suppositions have been explored from the perspective of students who study in Cyprus with and without any existing ties to the island (Cyprus-tied (Ct-) students and not Cyprus-tied (nCt-) students, respectively). The assessment showed the following:

1. Only for Ct-students the value of English is primarily in its ideological connection to the UK; nCt-students appreciate the language's globally shared communicative value more.
2. The four universities target different groups of prospective students by offering English as the medium of instruction (EMI) study programs. The universities in the RoC are more attractive for Ct-students and the universities in the (unrecognized) TRNC for nCt-students from the Global South.
3. Most students invest in the English language for their social advancement. However, they have been found to aim at different hierarchies and markets; some are interested in the local Cypriot social structure and labor market, while other groups tend to show a more international orientation. Furthermore, the analysis shows that the use of English does not always lead to upward social mobility; in some contexts, it might also lead to temporary downward social mobility of local Ct-students within their primary communities.
4. A discrepancy between the promoted and the actual use of English in the classroom and in Cyprus as well as between the expectation and the reality of life in Cyprus exists. NCt-students, however, are found to have a strong trust in the necessity of the English language, which increases their willingness to move to Cyprus for their HE, despite potential concerns and perils. Students choose to ignore certain information and warnings and still move to Cyprus.

Approaching the value of English as being divided into an ideological layer, a communicative layer, and an economic layer has shown that the use and role of English in Cyprus's HE is highly complex. In addition to its function as a first language (L1) and its communicative potential, the value of English in Cyprus's

HE is reproduced and enhanced by its use as a tool of social advancement and a marketable attribute of its users. These utilizations both reflect a shift toward centering the economic value when assessing the English language.

## 5.3 The Value of English in Cyprus's HE

The English language is essential to the global neoliberalization of HE and the emergence of new markets around it. While one of the reasons for the continuity of its extensive use in the twenty-first century might be the fact that English is already spoken by a great number of people, another reason is the extensive economic value of the language (see Graeber 2001 for a definition of "economic value"). The value of English in any given context can traditionally be ascribed to its conceptualization as a system or as a communicative practice (e.g., Heller 2010; Saraceni 2015). However, with increasing neoliberalization, the economic value of English becomes increasingly prominent and centered on. While the economic value of English often emerges from the ideological and communicative value of the language, it can also be detached from these layers, that is, when English is used as a marketable attribute of a commodity or user. The economic value of the English language is built on and reproduced by the countless for-profit organizations, diplomatic associations, and services that use the language for financial gain and global reach and that depend extensively on the English language. Because of the undisputed dominance of English in these contexts, the increasing internationalization, globalization, and human mobility are facilitated and accelerated by the language. While a certain openness and convention to use and include "English" to anything that aims at internationality is commonly shared, the exact implementation, intensity, and specific use of the language vary widely and often depend on economic needs. English might function as the backbone of the respective undertaking, for example, in international business, or simply as an alternative communication tool, for example, within a global and multilingual company. However, "English" might also be just a box to check without actually implementing it; it might create only the impression of internationality. Based on the range of this variation, the global value of English appears to be primarily economic and lies in its conceptualization as an attribute of entities, people, and concepts. The economic value, which enables the conceptualization of English-as-a-marketable-attribute, is one layer of the value of English and has been found to become more important in international settings than the use of English as a native language or as a social practice of communication. English-as-a-marketable-attribute can be conceptualized based on three main concepts that are utilized in HE contexts in Cyprus and beyond: (1) students do not necessarily have to be competent in English to profit from it; (2) English is objectified and instrumentalized by institutions, businesses, agencies, and students for the sole purpose of future or immediate financial and/or social gain; and (3) the English language is idealized and accepted as a prerequisite of students' future attainment and thereby enables illegal activity, crime, and social injustice in both the center and periphery of HE (cf. Section 5.4).

In this book, the value of English has been theorized as consisting of three layers. The importance and prominence of each of its layers vary as they depend on multiple conditions, including the specific context of use, the aim of its use, and the involved users. The most restricted but also most clearly defined layer is the ideological value, represented by the conceptualization of English as a system. This aspect of the English language is especially valuable in traditionally Anglophone and postcolonial contexts (cf. Görlach 1990; Kachru 1985, 1990, 1992; McArthur 1987, 1998, 2003; Strang 1970 on differentiating Englishes; Bauer 2002; Kortmann et al. 2004; Mesthrie and Bhatt 2008; Schneider 2007, 2011 on postcolonial contexts) as well as when concerning concepts like standardization, variation, right of use, and language ownership (cf. Ferris, Peck, and Banda 2014; Quirk 1990, Schneider 2007 on standardization and variation; Baker 2015; Cook 1999; Davies 2003; de Swaan 2001; Pennycook 2012; Widdowson 1994 on ownership and right of use, among others). While these concepts have been widely discussed, they are of limited relevance to the current use of English in Cyprus's HE. Differentiating types of Englishes or English speakers, for example, using Kachru's (1985) Three Circles model or Strang's (1970) division, would show the diversity of English users in Cyprus and its HE, respectively. However, the individual speaker's motives for choosing, staying in, or moving to Cyprus would remain unseen. A classification of English in Cyprus as a postcolonial variety or as a foreign language (see Buschfeld 2013; Tsiplakou 2009; Yazgin 2007) might increase the (assumed) variety's value and strengthen the island's connection to the power and prestige of the British Empire. However, a Cypriot variety of English is not used in the island's HE context. Due to the diverse composition of the student body in the TRNC, the use of English in the classrooms and on-campus cannot be homogenized and categorized. Students in the TRNC constitute communities of practice (Cox 2005; Eckert 2006; Lave and Wenger 1991), which share a social practice rather than develop a new standardizable variety (cf. Section 1.3.1). In the

RoC, direct references to the UK are prevalent, as students refer to having been born or having family in the UK, and a British university has been established. "Standard English" is primarily used in Cyprus's HE when it comes to language testing (cf. Section 4.3.2). A certain value is, however, offered by the concept of English as a system in Cyprus; it confirms the legitimacy of its use. Although English is used around the globe, the colonial history of Cyprus legitimizes the continuity of English on the island (see, among others, Kachru 1985, 1990, 1992; Mesthrie and Bhatt 2008; Schneider 2007, 2011 on the valuation of Englishes in postcolonial contexts). This "right of use" is, furthermore, transferred into a "right to offer" and valorizes the island's HE landscape. The island's history as a British Crown Colony, in theory, also corroborates the nCt-students' assumption of the widespread use of English off-campus. The actual use of English is based on another layer of the value of English relevant in Cyprus's HE—the value of English as a communicative practice.

While the value of English as a system is mostly shaped by language ideologies, speaker hierarchization, and the identification of linguistic features (cf. Sections 1.2.1 and 2.2.1), its actual use(fulness) is reflected by its value as a communicative practice. The communicative value of English can be assessed taking a microsocial or macrosocial perspective (see Jarvis and Pavlenko 2007; Mauranen 2012; Milroy 2002; Trudgill 1986). From a microsocial perspective, the individual speaker, his or her identification, and language choices are focused on, while from a macrosocial perspective the use of English by multiple speakers in social contexts is explored (see, e.g., Heller 2010; Saraceni 2015). The communicative value of English in Cyprus's HE lies in a combination of its users' identification with the language, its local prestige, and its communicative potential (see de Swaan 2001; Norton 2010; Piller 2016; cf. Section 1.3; Tables 3.1 and 3.2). In Cyprus's HE contexts, English users identify primarily as native speakers, as willing users, or as clever investors. Since identity options coexist and more than one identity can be performed in any given situation (Omoniyi and White 2006), Ct- and nCt-students in Cyprus often identify as more than one of the presented user types, based on the context they use the language in. All these identities are constructed and negotiated via language use in social interactions and are either imposed, assumed, or negotiable (Pavlenko and Blackledge 2004). The most prestigious identity is the assumed identity of a native speaker, which is often performed by Cypriot students who were born in the UK. Students from nontraditional native-speaking countries, such as Nigeria, have to negotiate their native speaker status among traditional native English-speaking students. The universities grant both groups the status of native speakers and exclude them from having to take an English language entrance test or from proving their language proficiency in another way. Imposed identities are often directly connected to the speakers' proficiency levels; whether, for example, Turkish or Cypriot Turkish students are more proficient willing users of English is a belief that, as it allows for many outliers in both directions, is not negotiable and not revised (Excerpts 3c, 12a, and 13a). Because "language choice and attitudes are inseparable from political arrangements, relations of power, language ideologies, and interlocutors' views of their own and others' identities" (Pavlenko and Blackledge 2004: 1), some students in Cyprus identify as clever investors in the English language. These students potentially but not necessarily also identify as willing users or native speakers of English. However, they know of the usefulness of English on the global market and thus choose to invest in the language. This investment does, in contrast to the other two speaker identities, not include the identification with the language as cultural and social capital (Bourdieu 1986). Users of English who identify as clever investors either aim at improving their skills (Heller 2010) or at gaining the assumed identity of a proficient—or proficient enough—speaker to allow for upward social mobility. Since the global value of English might differ in local contexts, upward social mobility is not always a direct result of the students' investment in English (cf. Section 4.3.3). The local value of English in Cyprus is reflected in the language's prestige.

The reason for nCt-students' temporary downward social mobility while in Cyprus is represented by the difference between the language's local and global prestige (cf. Sections 1.3 and 4.3.3; Tables 3.1 and 3.2). In both parts of Cyprus, the language is a *public but unofficial language* (Piller 2016: 16), used especially in areas like tourism, media, and education (cf. Tables 3.1 and 3.2). Consequently, it is valued higher than a *home* or *heritage language* and less than a *public and official language* (Piller 2016: 16). In the RoC, English is valued as a lingua franca in international fields and as the cultural heritage of Cyprus's ties to the UK. Using English is accepted in public and private settings. In the TRNC, the language is less valued as a cultural but as an economic good in public contexts. Due to the shared colonial history, students might assume the same value of English in both parts. However, due to their divergent political and economic development, students in the TRNC experience social othering when using English, while their peers in the RoC do not. During this study, it has become clear that, in some social groups in the TRNC, English is categorized as a *heritage language* with low value and prestige; it is understood as a reminder of the island (former) colonizer and is therefore not appreciated. Students experience social othering primarily off-campus; on-campus the language's value is higher, although the extent of its use might vary. This devaluation of English as a communicative practice is, therefore, part of the local value of English in the TRNC and only of marginal importance for the value of English in Cyprus's HE in general. This is rather based on the language's unparalleled communicative potential.

De Swaan (2001) defines the communicative potential of a language through the number of its speakers; the more speakers of a language exist, the higher is its communicative potential. English, as he argues, is the language with the most speakers and, consequently, the highest communicative potential. This high communicative potential of English increases its attractiveness for future learners or investors since English—like any other language—is not marketable like traditional exchangeable goods; it cannot be disowned and does not lose its value the more people have access to it (ibid.). The contrary causality is at work; English becomes a more valuable attribute the more people use it or "have" it. While the communicative potential primarily adds to the global value of English, it also influences the language's local value. It has been shown that students and universities in Cyprus value English and utilize its attractiveness based on its communicative potential (cf. Sections 4.3.1 and 4.3.2). They choose to learn or to offer English because it is the globally most useful language; the students' investment of adding English to their linguistic repertoires (see, e.g., Blommaert 2014) is rewarded with the highest number of potential communication partners and situations any language can offer and the universities' investment is rewarded with the biggest group of potential students—English speakers. For students and universities in Cyprus, the value of English is increased by the geographical limitlessness of the communicative potential of English—its internationality. It is used as a rational for coming to Cyprus by nCt-students (see, e.g., Brooks and Waters 2011; Findlay et al. 2012; Holloway, O'Hara, and Pimott-Wilson 2012; Leung 2017; Waters 2012 on student mobility; cf. Section 4.3.1) and as a political move and selling point for universities (see, e.g., Ferguson 2007; Foskett 2012; Jenkins 2014; Lasagabaster 2015; Murray 2016; cf. Section 4.3.2). However, the extensive use and communicative potential of English supposedly advantage its native speakers, as they do not have to invest in learning the language before benefiting from it. Frameworks like translanguaging and English as a Lingua Franca (ELF), respectively, are examples of a theoretical implementation of the communicative potential of English that constrains this supposed advantage by focusing on its use rather than ideological categorizations or arguing for the equality of English speakers. As translanguaging assumes a speaker's linguistic resources to be combined in his or her cumulative linguistic repertoire and does not differentiate between individual languages (see, e.g., Canagarajah 2013; Li

2018; Vogel and García 2017), the value of English cannot be assessed in this theorization.

The concept of ELF, in contrast, is concerned with the English language exclusively and its use by speakers of different L1s in multilingual settings (see, e.g., House 2012; Jenkins 2007; Seidlhofer 2011; Seidlhofer, Breiteneder, and Pitzl 2006; cf. Section 1.3.2). It argues for the rightfulness of non-native users of English and questions the appropriateness of applying native speaker standards when assessing their performance (see also Baker 2015; Mauranen 2012; Meierkord 2004). ELF might have potentially been useful in assessing the value of English in this study, as Cyprus's HE is not based on a traditionally native English-speaking context but includes students with a multitude of different L1s using English. However, it lacks a clear definition and it is based on elite contexts and highly proficient speakers who choose to speak English rather than having to improve their social and economic situation by using it (cf. O'Regan 2016; Park and Wee 2012; Prodromou 2008; Section 1.3.2 for a discussion of limitations). It remains unclear whether it is "a thing ... or a context of use" (Maley 2010: 27), representing a hypostatization—a self-fulfilling prophecy—which gains importance and stability by being used (O'Regan 2014: 536). Consequently, its usefulness in describing the value of English in a setting like Cyprus's market of HE is limited—a setting that combines speakers with varying proficiencies and of different social backgrounds, following various motives. Within the ELF framework, English is valued for its unifying communicative potential, while the reality of its use and its commodification is not represented. It neither explores the underlying reasons and the expected benefits of the use of English for the individual student nor its objectification and commodification by universities. Both, however, are essential to developing a comprehensive understanding of the value of the English language in Cyprus's HE. Instead, ELF reflects an idealized, romanticized, and privileged view of English as a tool of communication, representing "an ideologically conservative project due to the apparent reluctance of its advocates to critique—or even name—capitalism and its contemporary manifestation neoliberalism" (O'Regan 2014: 540). The value assigned to the English language causes the users' personal and monetary investment, for example, by creating the need to achieve a certain level of proficiency in English. This investment is not included in the binary conceptualization of language as a system or as a communicative practice. Consequently, another layer is necessary for describing the value of English in its entirety. This layer is economic in nature and the basis for the use of English-as-a-marketable-attribute.

While differentiating between English-as-a-system and English-as-a-communicative-practice used to suffice in assessing the language's value, the globally expanding neoliberal zeitgeist requires an additional layer to reflect the current composition of the value of English adequately. This layer is based on the use of English-as-a-marketable-attribute. English is no longer only valued for its communicative or ideological power or for its ability to reflect its speakers' identities; in current times, English is increasingly valued for its monetary value. This development is based on the neoliberalization of our global society and clearly surfaces, among other fields, in Cyprus's HE landscape. Neoliberalism is "one of the most sweeping and dramatic social experiments" of our times and "redefined the relationship between state, society and economy" (Ward 2012: 1; Section 1.4.1). This redefined relationship presents itself in the increasing influence of the economy on state and society, that is, in the reconceptualization of individuals as "human capital" and the economization of formerly social fields, such as education. In HE, universities and students can invest in the English language and profit from its global significance without identifying with it or being extensively competent users (see Sections 4.3.1 and 4.3.2), relying on very basic exchanges. In these cases, English can no longer be defined as a skill, since the concept of *skill* does presuppose competence and the ability to use English for communication. From a neoliberal perspective, "having" English is enough to be beneficial—it multiplies a person's or entity's possible fields of "use" and, thereby, competitiveness and value (see, e.g., Piller 2015; Shin and Park 2016). Consequently, great emphasis is put on including the language whenever possible, resulting in Ct-students in Cyprus attending EMI study programs, even though they do not plan to use their knowledge outside the local Cypriot job market (cf. Section 3.7; Appendix 2.4)—or in universities offering EMI study programs, although they do not have a faculty who is competent enough to realize them (Excerpt 4n).

The English language, in these settings, is understood as a property or object that one should "have." Since this objectification leads to a change in the language's accessibility—English is no longer reserved for some but potentially accessible to all—it enables its commodification (see Park and Wee 2012). In addition, the neoliberal value of English is no longer necessarily based on its use. This objectification and detachment from its use represent the basis of the excessive implementation of English in HE in general and in Cyprus specifically. Universities implement English mostly as a marketable attribute, often only in form of a language of teaching, so as to enhance the universities' international character and attract international students (Ferguson 2007; Jenkins 2014;

Murray 2016; cf. Sections 1.4.3, 3.6.1, and 4.3.2). Students in Cyprus invest in a commodity—a learnable skill, a sign of authenticity, or an attribute they can add to their inventory—which represents capital on the global market (Heller 2010; Heller and Duchêne 2016; see also Coupland 2003; Urciuoli 2008; cf. Section 1.4.2). English-as-a-marketable-attribute, however, is not a traditional commodity, as it is not bound to specific markets (see McGill 2013). This freedom increases the value of the language, for example, by being globally identified with high-quality education (Lasagabaster 2015). Through the reach of its value, the language's use is adapted, offering universities in non-English-speaking countries like Cyprus a part of the "market share of international students" (Lasagabaster 2015: 265). This results in a higher economic profit for universities in Cyprus, since international students often pay higher tuition fees than their local peers (Holborow 2013; cf. Section 4.3.2).

Especially nCt-students in Cyprus are understood as tradable and moveable; the universities expect to attract them—to move them to Cyprus—in exchange for implementing the English language in some form (Holborow 2013; Lasagabaster 2015; van der Walt 2013; cf. Section 4.3.2). The attraction of students by the use of English is, in turn, rooted in the common agreement that English valorizes anything or anyone it is "attached to." The neoliberalization of English allows for its economic value to become detached from its realization—to become a badge attachable to anyone or anything (cf. Section 1.4.4). This economic value is combined with the language's ideological value, whenever it valorized commodities and speakers as a sign of authenticity, while at the same time assuming that English is used as a skill. Park and Wee (2012) argue for a modification of Kachru's Three Circles model to assess the "amount" of value added by English. They claim that the more central a county is, the higher the value added by its English (cf. Section 1.4.4). This modification is a useful link between the ideological value through nativeness and the economic valorization of speakers and commodities by English. However, in cases in which Ct-students attend a university that advertises the use of EMI, knowing that the classroom language is often Turkish, they do not invest in the "right" English or in increasing their proficiency. These students invest in a marketable attribute—in capital they can exchange to gain access.

In Cyprus's HE, English-as-a-marketable-attribute represents a form of capital that can be procured by individuals and universities alike. Bourdieu (1986) defines both language and education as traditionally being cultural capital. However, in Cyprus's HE, the English language is transformed into economic capital, resulting in its transfer from the symbolic into the material economy (cf.

Bourdieu 1986; Section 2.3.1.3). Universities use the language to increase their economic profit by attracting more high-paying students (cf. Section 4.3.2), while students invest in the language to facilitate their future social mobility (cf. Section 4.3.3). Both parties are stakeholders in this economy that is built on the value of English-as-a-marketable-attribute. Therefore, both parties aim at preserving this value to ensure the continued lucrativeness of their investment. The concept of English-as-a-marketable-attribute can reflect the economic underpinnings of the neoliberal use of English. It is built on and includes the utility, objectification, and native-speaker-detachment of English conceived as a skill and as a commodity, as well as the neoliberalization of English users (see, e.g., Block 2018b; Harvey 2005; Heller 2010; Heller and Duchêne 2013, 2016; Holborow 2015; Park and Wee 2012; Shin and Park 2016; cf. Sections 1.4.1, 1.4.2, and 1.4.4). Furthermore, it is built on the assumption that an investment in the English language does not necessarily equal its use and acquisition. Instead, it is a reflection of the investor's agency of future success and status, which facilitates ill-intentioned and dehumanizing practices in less privileged contexts, especially in the Global South.

## 5.4 Assessing the Value of English: Reproducing Social Marginalization

Bourdieu found that economic capital is "at the root of all the other types of capital" (1986: 24); cultural and social capital, consequently, always has an economic layer. The same holds for the value of a language; although the value can be cultural and social, it is always accompanied by an economic value. This economic value layer constantly gains prominence and attention and is realized by the neoliberal use of English-as-a-marketable-attribute. The concept of English-as-a-marketable-attribute, furthermore, is an increasingly valuable assessment of the language as it adds value to its "bearers" on the global market (Shin and Park 2016) and is the basis of the language's development into a skill and the user's potential identification with it. However, this layer is rarely in complementary distribution with its more traditional layers of value—at least, this is rarely admitted. Therefore, the value of English needs to be assessed, using frameworks and theories that are applicable to or allow for more than one layer of value. In Cyprus's HE, the value of English is cumulative. It combines the value of English used as a communicative practice or as the language of the British with the value of English-as-a-marketable-attribute, keeping the economic aspect at its center. In Cyprus's HE, three specific characteristics of the use and advertisement of English-as-a-marketable-attribute have been found: (1) the actual use of English is not a condition for its economic value; (2) at the root of any investment in English is a potential future or immediate financial and/or social gain; and (3) the value of English is not scrutinized context dependently, which might enable illegal activity, crime, and social injustice in the center and periphery of HE.

The first characteristic is the detachment of the language's economic value from its actual use. This detachment makes Cyprus especially attractive for students who identify as clever investors and who do not plan at using the language for communicative purposes, as they can benefit from "having" English without being proficient users. They answer their societal construction as bundles of skills, human capital, or *homo economicus* (Foucault 2008; also Shin and Park 2016) with minimalism—the minimal investment in the language required. Students choose to learn English because it is useful rather than because they want to familiarize themselves with its cultural base. Depending on their desired goal, they might decide to add English to their linguistic repertoire or even their Dominant Language Constellations (DLCs), to use it or even identify with it (see, e.g., Aronin 2016; Blommaert 2014; Hall 2012), or not to do so, depending on the requirements of their desired future. Students in Cyprus are aware that in our current society, the uniqueness and complexity of the individual often become secondary to the number of attributes cumulated in the person and their usefulness for the purpose in question on the job market. Students who want to stay in Cyprus might invest in obtaining a certificate that includes English and puts them ahead of their local competitors "on paper," rather than aiming at actually enhancing their language skills. English, in these settings, is used to gain access to specific people, enterprises, or regions since it is the global language of the powerful. Access to specific assets or people does not always require the ability to use the language; it might function as one item on a list of requirements that have to be "fulfilled," although it is unlikely they will ever be needed. Universities in Cyprus use this conceptual disengagement of the language from its actual use, for example, to reduce the requirements of entrance tests to HE (cf. Section 4.3.2). In Cyprus, as it is common, low language skills do not hinder students' entrance into HE; limited skills represent another source of income for universities, as they are then taught in internal language schools. To attend these schools, students are required to pay additional fees, while the decision of the students' success—for instance, the extent of the required skills—is university-specific. The value of English-as-a-marketable-attribute in Cyprus does not center any specific use or required proficiency while allowing for English to still be beneficial for its bearers. Furthermore, English is, like all languages in neoliberalism, understood as neutral (see, e.g., Park and Wee 2012) and can be detached from its native contexts of use and cultural implications. English-as-a-marketable-attribute, consequently, developed to be used as an instrument of universities in attracting prospective students and of students to gain access to the desired promising future, which is, in turn, another property of English-as-a-marketable-attribute in Cyprus.

The second characteristic of English-as-a-marketable-attribute that has been found in Cyprus's HE is its objectification and instrumentalization by institutions, businesses, agencies, and students for the sole purpose of future or immediate financial and/or social gain. The objectification and instrumentalization of English are most exhaustive when the language is conceptualized as a marketable attribute since it can be assessed detached from its use. English-as-a-marketable-attribute is appreciated and valued for its salability and transferability; it is an attribute that can be attached to every institution or person in Cyprus's HE or any other setting. As discussed, Bourdieu (1986, 1991) describes education as institutionalized cultural capital and language as cultural capital, both of symbolic nature (cf. Sections 2.3.1.3 and 3.5). Their value, however, is converted into economic capital, which is material in nature. Consequently, English valorizes Cyprus's HE on a symbolic and material level as its economic value increases. However, the value of English is not entirely based on its representation as economic capital; it is still a form of cultural and social capital. The latter is of special importance in both Cyprus's market of HE and its local contexts.

Language is strongly linked to social structures. While from a discourse perspective, language is social capital and linguistic features represent a speaker's membership to a certain social group (see, among others, Bourdieu 1991; Labov 2006), from an economic perspective, social groups and their language use are associated with power and prestige, which is often realized economically by wealth (see, e.g., Block 2015; Kergoat 2010; cf. Section 2.3.2). To ascend within a local or global social structure and gain access to a desired social group, people use education. Education can serve as the foundation for the accumulation of other forms of capital, such as economic capital (Leung 2017: 2708; Waters 2006b). While members of the higher social classes in the Global North aim at attending the "right" institutions to become members of the "global elite" (cf. Leung 2017), for others who aim at global or local social advancement, the "right" education is mostly determined "just" by being provided in English; these people might enroll in universities in Cyprus. Students in Cyprus aim at improving their future social and economic situation by investing in English and EMI education (cf. de Swaan 2001: 25; Section 4.3.3). The universities in Cyprus respond to their students' intention by instrumentalizing English in easily accessible EMI study programs, that is, through low entrance language requirements, to increase their attractiveness (Section 4.3.2). English is primarily used as a marketable attribute of the universities, functioning as a sign of their internationality and the high quality of the offered programs (Foskett 2012; Lasagabaster 2015; cf. Section 3.6.1 for an introduction of the use of English at all four universities). This also holds for the British university UCLan Cyprus that merely adds the cultural value of its cultural embeddedness in the UK to the value of English-as-a-marketable-attribute. In the marketplace of HE, universities in Cyprus function as providers of a service, which they offer to their clients—Ct- and nCt-students (Holborow 2013; Lasagabaster 2015; cf. Section 4.3.4). This service, however, is primarily assented to because it is enacted in English, again instrumentalizing the language.

Students in Cyprus, however, often willingly accept their role as recipients of this service. Cyprus's nCt-students, in particular, are not concerned with the cultural implementations of English. Instead, they invest in its economic and social value in global settings, objectifying and instrumentalizing the language to serve as a means to their future hopes. Ct-students in the RoC, in contrast, use the language as a helpful addition to their skill set on the local job market, while their peers in the TRNC gravitate toward the UK. NCt-students in Cyprus primarily come from the Global South and choose Cyprus as the most fitting intermediary on their way to the desired social and economic position; Cyprus, to them, is affordable, accessible, and it is Europe, all of which increases their chances for social advancement (see, e.g., Excerpts 1b, 2f, and 17a; cf. Section 4.3.4). While all students' agency is upward social mobility through "having" English, there are unaware of the local social structures in Cyprus and often initiate their temporary downward social mobility by moving to the island.

Based on the geographical mobility enabled by the English language, students, especially from the Global South, come to Cyprus. These students are often of a well-respected social status in their home country, as they can afford to pursue their education abroad. In the TRNC, these students, however, face downward social mobility or social degradation (cf. Section 4.3.3). This phenomenon is already known in occupational settings, as well-educated migrants are often required to do menial work (see, e.g., Leung 2017: 2707). This also applies to nCt-students in Cyprus, who are likely to not find white-collar jobs (e.g., Excerpt 2j; Cyprus: Students duped by good life 2019; Kastamonu 2014; Rakoczy 2017; Student murder was drug related n.d.). Furthermore, their social status is lowered in other contexts too, which is based on their reliance on English as a global language of communication; while local businesses in the TRNC might try to use English to enlarge their clientele, for local inhabitants without close British ties, it has found to be important that the Turkish language is not "upstaged by English, as [it is] both strongly associated with identity and utility" (Lasagabaster 2015: 272), which is likely an effect of its strong political and economic ties to Turkey. This is reflected by their practice using social othering against non-Turkish-speaking Ct- and nCt-students (cf. Sections 4.3.1 and 4.3.3). NCt-students are often forced to use any tool their linguistic repertoire holds to enable communication off-campus. Students in the RoC tend to not experience social othering or temporary downward mobility to this extent (cf. ibid.). This might serve as an example that in Cyprus the value of English differs between fields (Bourdieu 1986, 1991). In each field, "the forms of capital beneficial to the preservation of that field" (Botsis 2018: 42) are reinforced to preserve the power of the already powerful. While English is rather prestigious in both parts of Cyprus (cf. Tables 3.1 and 3.2) and would be expected to not initiate social othering but social upward mobility, its diverging effects in both parts of Cyprus show that the economic layer of the value of English, realized by the use of English-as-a-marketable-attribute, cannot always be separated from its ideological value in social organizations. However, this negative aspect of English affects students in Cyprus only temporarily and does not reduce the global value of English and its marketability. In general, English becomes a more valuable attribute—concerning the communicative as well as the economic layer of its value—the more people "have" it. In turn, more social groups are receptive to its instrumentalization and are triggered by its conceptual inclusion, leading to the expansion and marketization of an objectified English language. Its usefulness and necessity for its bearers are increasingly less questioned. This acceptance and obedience to the value of English, however, also increases social injustice and enables the exploitation of certain people who choose to rely on English to achieve their goals.

The third characteristic of English-as-a-marketable-attribute in Cyprus's HE is the emergence of illegal activity, crime, and social injustice in the center and periphery of HE. This is based on the idealization and acceptance of the English language as a prerequisite for students' desired attainment and future "success." While the use of English-as-a-marketable-attribute reproduces and reinforces existing global and local social inequalities, it allows for the emergence of a new market of morally questionable or even illegal activities. The use of English-as-a-marketable-attribute does not only reinforce social inequalities in Cyprus on a local level, as the above-discussed social fabric between local inhabitants and nCt-students. It also reproduces existing global inequalities in Cyprus, like the social and economic stratification between the Global North and the Global South as well as postcolonial injustice (see, e.g., de Swaan 2001; Khattab and Mahmud 2018; Odeh 2010; Phillipson 1992, 2009). English-as-a-marketable-attribute of Cyprus's HE stimulates mobility. The effects of this mobility and the resulting new mix of people on the island are predominantly positive for students and universities. However, due to the somewhat unpredictable stream of migration to Cyprus and their linguistic and often geographical separation from the local population, the promotion of English-as-a-marketable-attribute also causes negative developments in the island's local social structure, like temporary downward social mobility and social othering. More permanently still is its impact on global social structures. While HE, in general, becomes increasingly inclusive, as more people have access to it, it does not increase its partakers' equality; while the dimension of a person's social and geographical mobility, as well as his or her future earning potential, used to depend on general access to HE, nowadays it is increasingly determined by their initial social status and the specific institution attended (Leung 2017; Marginson 2018). As this inclusiveness is mostly based on the use of English, "English education widens the discrepancy between the social classes" (Mohanty 2006: 269). Members of higher social status in Cyprus and in the Global North do not choose Cyprus for either their or their children's HE—they can afford to go to a more central and often Anglophone country in the Global North (see Excerpts 1d, 2b, and 5a). Local students in Cyprus either cannot afford to study abroad or do not want to. For them, English is more valuable as an attribute than as a communicative tool. The students who invest most in the economic value and social impact of English-as-a-marketable-attribute when pursuing their HE in Cyprus are nCt-students.

Students of other origins than Cyprus and Turkey are sometimes not integrated into the TRNC's society as equals and appear to experience social stratification off-campus.

> Most students from Africa [are] not treated in a [///] I wouldn't say, well in a good way, say for example you're going to [/] to ehm restaurant or maybe a club at night, you would tend [///] African students would tend to be treated

in a suspicious manner. … Arabs or people with a lighter skin are given more privileged treatment and a special treatment than Africans, because maybe they think Africans will cause chaos, so even though they are inside you will see maybe there's some bouncers placed strategically just in case somebody is going to do something. (Excerpt 2i)

Since these students came to Cyprus because of the use of English-as-a-marketable-attribute and its instrumentalization, the social inequalities they experience are also based on it. For nCt-students, Cyprus is a stepping-stone, as they can afford to study abroad but often do not (yet) have access to the originally desired country. Cyprus, for them, represents proximity and almost what these students target; the RoC belongs almost to the Outer Circle countries and is almost the nCt-students' ticket to the UK—at least before BREXIT. However, the RoC is their ticket to European exchange programs like Erasmus+ and Inner-European mobility. The TRNC, in turn, is almost Europe, almost part of the Global North, and, therefore, only almost their ticket for the desired better future. All these "possibilities" are initiated by the use of the English language, which creates a smokescreen of potential and promise, ignoring the local friction between geography and politics. This smokescreen is effective for nCt-students but unmasked by Ct-students, as they can discern the potential and promise of the English language in Cyprus realistically and based on their local familiarity. For all of its stakeholders, however, English is unavoidable in reaching their desired goal and is idealized as their ticket to their future accomplishments. Due to their firm conviction of English as the language of promise, they do not always question inconsistencies or clarify concerns before moving to Cyprus. They want to believe in the value of English and its power to provide them with a better future; this desire is sometimes stronger than their rationality, for example, when advice and warnings by friends or family members in Cyprus are not heeded (see Excerpt 2j). The potential students' firm belief in the benefits and the necessity of English is utilized by recruitment businesses and agencies that aim at getting their share of the economic value of English-as-a-marketable-attribute.

While the English language adds value to Cyprus's HE, its instrumentalization leads to a "dehumanization" of its speakers. The human aspect of education and the individual student is no longer focused on; one result of this practice is, for example, the emerging economy of fraud against prospective students of the TRNC. Especially students of lower social status and with limited financial means appear to be vulnerable to the recruitment agencies' intentional (un) choosing of information or blunt misinformation as they appear to not have the opportunity of accessing the TRNC unassisted and on their own terms. While the universities themselves advertise the low crime rates in Northern Cyprus ("Friendly and safe (no crime) environment," GAU 2019g), the number of crimes committed by students in the TRNC constantly rises (Section 3.4) and numerous cases of students, forced into criminality, surface (e.g., Bilge 2018; Investigation into killing Nigerian students 2018; Mashininga 2018; Student murder was drug related n.d.). Students who might have lost some or all of their money to agencies or middlemen are unexpectedly forced to earn money in low-paying jobs. Those who cannot make ends meet might see no alternative but to turn to crime in their new and unfamiliar environment. They are forced into prostitution or into selling drugs (ibid.). The increasing criminality of students is an example of the negative side of English-as-a-marketable-attribute. While it gives access to knowledge and enables geographical and social mobility in Cyprus's HE to an extent that would be impossible without the global use and the shared value of the language, its marketization and commodification recreate and enforce social injustice and stratification. The idealization and instrumentalization of English-as-a-marketable-attribute and its economic value potentially have led to the organized exploitation of overwhelmed and helpless young people who come to Cyprus to improve their future perspectives.

Cyprus's HE convincingly shows how the value of English is cumulative and is assembled of multiple layers; the successful implementation of UCLan Cyprus and its attractiveness for local and international students reflect the traditional value of English as a language of identification and cultural embeddedness, while the value of English as a communicative practice is based on its global usefulness and unparalleled communicative potential. This layer enables the extensive clientele of Cyprus's universities in the first place. The economic layer of the value of English-as-a-marketable-attribute, however, is the most dominant value in Cyprus's HE. It is based on the recreation of hegemonic language ideologies and enables the resurrection of linguistic imperialism in a neoliberal global society (Park 2009; Phillipson 1992, 2009); English is the language of the elite and, although the language can be equally used, it does not make everyone equal. The value of English-as-a-marketable-attribute, therefore, is also in its promise; it promises access and equality for the nonelites and is accepted as a prerequisite of social and economic advancement. However, it does not guarantee access or success and leaves some, who have chosen to invest in it, in precarious situations. The social irreconcilability of English-as-a-marketable-attribute and its negligence of the human aspect of language potentially endanger its less privileged bearers rather than advancing them. This downside of the global use of the English language requires more attention.

## 5.5 Value as a Tool of Empowerment: Reducing Social (In)justice?

The most relevant and alarming aspect of the rise of neoliberalism is its reflection and aggravation of current social structures. As Holborow points out, "With the global reach and influence of neoliberal ideology, the Marxist observation that in any era the ruling ideas are those of the ruling class rings starkly true today" (2015: 4). Neoliberalism, therefore, supports and reproduces social inequality, leading to "English education widen[ing] the discrepancy between the social classes" (Mohanty 2006: 269). "The consequences of the neoliberal abandonment of the commitment to social justice have been skyrocketing levels of inequality between individuals, communities, and nations in the late twentieth and early twenty-first centuries" (Piller 2016: 6). The reproduction and maintenance of present inequalities are realized, for example, through education. Education functions to produce "subjects with the knowledge and dispositions which are appropriate for servicing the economy" (Gray, O'Regan, and Wallace 2018: 475) and is no longer idealized as holistic and humanitarian. As a result of neoliberal structures, the global language English by no means leads to "linguistic communism" and equality—the access to it, on the contrary, "is constrained by the structure of the particular market" (Shin and Park 2016: 449). English, as an economic and political property, is "excessively valorize[d]" around the world (Shin and Park 2016: 475). The context and the extent of the access to English, however, are strictly limited by social class and the accompanied privilege. Although nowadays the use and value of English reflect privilege and social injustice, it may become a tool of social empowerment when assessed from a speaker's rather than an ideological perspective and as a reality rather than a theoretic concept.

Researchers have provided us with numerous models and concepts to define, categorize, and label the English language, each offering an improvement concerning some aspect of the language. While the use, roles, and functions of English have become increasingly complex with time, models are reductive in nature and cannot assess and describe the language comprehensively (Saraceni 2015: 54). Their focus on specific aspects of English often includes the actual use of the language only to a certain degree, choosing aspects of the observed reality that the model can, or should, account for. In so doing, models tend to reproduce existing structures without focusing on them or even assessing them. Furthermore, and due to the increasing complexity of the contexts of English use, developing an inclusive and comprehensive model of English is becoming more and more improbable with increasing globalization and interconnectedness. Consequently, rather than developing an inevitably rigid and inflexible model of HOW English is used, the assessment of WHY it is used might offer an alternative and more fruitful perspective on the reality of English use, especially for the involved speakers. While the use and implementation of English, on a global scale, tend to reproduce social inequalities and prevailing privilege, on a local scale or even personal level, it might represent a tool of empowerment and serve as a game changer. This empowerment appears to increase the least whenever the ideological value of English is appreciated or considered, as this is the level of value that can be altered the least by the speaker's choices.

While the use of English might not compensate for features that a speaker might miss to advance into another social group or to social status on a global scale, it can very well do so on a local level. Within its local markets, the choice of learning and using English might tip the scale and open doors for the speaker that otherwise would have remained closed. Speakers know what features to compensate for or to add to their repertoires of skills when aiming at mobility within their familiar local structures. Consequently, they might be able to estimate more realistically which impact their investment in English might have. In unknown global markets or local but unfamiliar markets, side effects are harder to foresee by nonlocals, which might hinder their social advancement. John, a participant in this study, might serve as an example: He is a member of a higher social class in its local community, which allows him to travel abroad to obtain his HE and even to go to "Europe." He identifies as a native speaker of English; however, on the local market of (Northern) Cyprus, this identity is not accepted; while the university grants him native speaker status and does not require him to take an assessment test when entering the study program, the local community does not value his use of English as native. This is expressed by their request for him to change the way he speaks English to cater to his fellow students—a request that would be unlikely to have been made to a "traditional" native speaker of English. While his time in the TRNC includes temporary downward social mobility, he aims at returning to his local market and social community where he is certain to experience upward social mobility because of the education he obtained in Cyprus. Consequently, the perception of his experience as being problematic—caused by increasing global neoliberalization and the commodification of HE without any care for the individual student—is, while still true, not what remains most important for him in retrospect. He, because of the privileged position he started his journey from, will likely be able to reach his goal and find a suitable and well-respected position back home. While this might relate the use of English to the individual speaker and their objectives and experiences, it continues to reflect privilege and the remaining effects of unequal starting blocks.

The English language is an unparalleled example of a language that has developed into a global lingua franca and which appears to be owned and used by anyone who chooses to—and can afford to—acquire it. English is no longer used for bare communicative purposes but often serves as a vehicle of other functions or objectives—mainly related to its global and local economic value. These functions of English are often based on neoliberalization and an increasing disconnection from any particular speaker group. In sum, the unfortunate reality remains that English is not yet a tool of empowerment but more likely to be a tool of social hierarchization and preservation of the elite and their privileges. However, being aware of these functions of English and the valuation system they cause and are caused by is a first step toward changing the global role of English and showing that English has the potential to increase social equality on a local and global scale.

## 5.6 Summary

The roles and value of English in Cyprus are manifold. The most prominent layer of value changed from being its ideological value during the island's time under British rule to being valued as a welcomed communicative practice. Nowadays, however, the most prominent and influential layer of the value of English in Cyprus is its economic value. In this chapter, the findings of the presented study have been summarized and used as a starting point to assess and discuss the effects of the value of English on social stratification. English, in its objectified utilization as a marketable attribute, is part of its users' public personae rather than their private ones, since the language is used as a tool or as a means to achieve the respective desired goals. These goals might be economic profit for the involved universities and agencies or social mobility and the associated economic improvement for students in Cyprus. However, their investment in English-as-a-marketable-attribute is rooted in the neoliberal valuation of English. This investment in the value of English is especially lucrative for people of lower social and economic status—people who aim at their social advancement or at entering the Global North—as it promises a greater relative improvement. In using English for their social advancement, stakeholders, like students and universities, realize and support the reproduction of "skyrocketing levels of inequality between individuals, communities, and nations in the late twentieth and early twenty-first centuries" (Piller 2016: 6). By investing in EMI education, they are conceptualized as "subjects with the knowledge and dispositions which are appropriate for servicing the economy" (Gray, O'Regan, and Wallace 2018: 475), since education is no longer a humanitarian good but understood as a neoliberal commodity. As a result of neoliberal structures, access to education is constrained by social position and economic means.

This access as well as the positive impact of an EMI education on the students' individual life trajectories depends on the contexts of comparison. While social advancement might be denied on global markets, some locally privileged users might achieve this goal on their local markets. Therefore, international students moving to Cyprus represents their first step for a better future and allows the former intellectual good of HE to become an economic market of fierce competition. This development has been shown to be predominantly negative as well as a repercussion of neoliberalism and the so-tinged valuation of English.

# Conclusion

*Many people are here like you. And they survive. Even me, someone lied to me, an agent, that this is America. I pay, pay, pay to come here and then what did I discover? Africa in Europe.*

Obioma (2019a: 277)

In this book, a framework to assess the value of English has been presented and applied in Cyprus's higher education (HE). In exploring the experiences, motives, investment, and life trajectories of individual students at four universities in both parts of Cyprus, the effects and ramifications of the language's value on the various stakeholders involved, that is, Cyprus-tied (Ct-) students, not Cyprus-tied (nCt-) students, and universities, have been unveiled. Uncovering the use and roles of English at the four universities—University of Central Lancashire Cyprus (UCLan Cyprus), University of Cyprus (UCy), Eastern Mediterranean University (EMU), and Girne American University (GAU)—and discerning their organizational nature, their objectives, and language policies enabled a deeper understanding of the underlying reasons for the students' choice to pursue their university education in English—and in Cyprus—and their perspective on the value of English. In so doing, the following four suppositions were used as guidelines, each assessing a different angle and part of the English language's value.

1. For its users, the value of the English language lies in its communicative potential; native speaker standards and the language's cultural embeddedness are less important.
2. Universities in Cyprus use the value of the English language primarily to attract fee-paying nCt-students.

3. Students invest in the English language because it represents immediate or future upward social mobility.
4. The value of the English language outweighs nCt-students' concerns about the local contexts it is offered in. The students' abstraction of English-as-a-marketable-attribute from its context is openly utilized by the universities.

These suppositions have provided a useful framework for the assessment of the value of English in Cyprus's HE, although certain limitations and specifications must be included. While all students value the English language for its communicative potential, its embeddedness in the British culture—one of the remains of the island's time under British rule—is still prevailing in Cyprus. This is observable especially when assessing the local population. Furthermore, Ct-students have been found to associate the English language with their hopes of a reunification of the island. Instead of aiming at rebuilding a former political and social situation of the island, these students rely on the language's communicative potential and common use as a lingua franca (see Section 4.3.1). This culturally and socially shared value of English as a communicative practice is Cyprus-specific and, therefore, differs from the global value of the communicative potential of English. The communicative value of English as a globally shared lingua franca is predominant for nCt-students and one of the main reasons for universities in Cyprus to include English as the medium of instruction (EMI) programs (see Section 4.3.2); implementing English enlarges the group of potential fee-paying students exponentially for any university. It has been found that all universities except for UCy aim at attracting students to increase their income and, in some cases, to be able to sustain and maintain themselves. While the universities in the Turkish Republic of Northern Cyprus (TRNC) focus on nCt-students, UCLan Cyprus appears to be more attractive for Ct-students, for whom a British degree would lead to upward social mobility and advantages on the local job market (ibid.). NCt-students in Cyprus and Ct-students in the TRNC invest in the English language and obtain an EMI degree to enhance their employability on the global job market and their status in any chosen social hierarchy—local or global. In doing so, both student groups accept temporary downward social mobility during their studies in the TRNC (see Section 4.3.3).

The elaborations on the first three suppositions show an emerging trend within globalized HE: the English language is increasingly valued as a communicative practice rather than in its social and cultural embeddedness. This, at first sight, positive and including aspect of a shared language, however, also leads to a shift of power, for example, in HE. While the quality of the education used to be the most determinative factor for choosing a university, the language of instruction is increasingly gaining impact on prospective students' decisions. As a result of the unparalleled spread and global value of English, the language nowadays valorizes a university's educational offer rather than just being one aspect of it. Consequently, students and universities often do not feel to have a choice in their investing in English—the attribute of "English" makes education become the "right" one and a university a "good" one (cf. Holborow 2013; Lasagabaster 2015; Section 1.4.3). While these findings appear not to be Cyprus-specific, the involved stakeholders and their sociopolitical relations are.

> Cyprus is starting gain quite the reputation for its universities. They're welcoming international students, delivering high-quality English-taught programmes in several subjects. Furthermore, many of these universities collaborate with American, U.K., and Northern European universities, creating a nurturing environment for students. (Studyportals B.V. 2019: para. 5)

Cyprus is located at the very edge of Europe with neighboring countries that are often categorized as belonging to the Global South. Furthermore, the whole island is de jure a member of the European Union, while, at the same time, the TRNC understands itself as an (independent) country and follows its own immigration policy. De facto, this means that students who might need a visa to enter the European Union can more easily enter the TRNC, which for them is Europe and part of the Global North as they are mostly unaware of the island's political division. Not knowing about these obscure geopolitical dynamics, students from the Global South choose to pursue their HE in Cyprus, often finding themselves unprepared for the local reality. The reason they leave for Cyprus in the first place, however, is the globally shared economic value of English, leading to the fourth supposition.

NCt-students seem to choose to pursue their HE in Cyprus because they seek their share of the language's global economic value. This, in turn, is met by the universities' utilization of the language and, more importantly, its utilization by fraudulent agencies that exploit prospective students (cf. Section 4.3.4). The assessment of the economic value of English is a rather new development. The value of English is traditionally assessed in its conceptualization as a system or as a communicative practice; these aspects are well researched and could be described by familiar theorizations and frameworks, like language ideologies, language ownership, English as a Lingua Franca (ELF), and identity construction (see Sections 1.2.1, 1.3.2, and 2.2.1). The advancement of neoliberalism, however, led to a redefinition of the value of English, adding an economic layer. Furthermore, in contexts like Cyprus, this economic value of English is also the most dominant one and includes an objectification of the language and its detachment from social and cultural contexts. Students are reconceptualized to function as stakeholders in HE when investing in the value of English-as-a-marketable-attribute. Its economic value is always one aspect of the composition of the value of English as it represents the language's promise of access and advancement. Due to the language's detachability from its contexts of use, this value—and the implied promise of access and advancement—is transferable, for example, to Cyprus. NCt-students in the TRNC appear to be willing to invest their time, money, and geographical mobility to profit from the globally shared economic value of English. These students are convinced of the unparalleled value of English and, therefore, choose to invest in it without being able to oversee the consequences of their decision (Section 4.3.4). They move to a place they do not properly research—or, in case they do, ignore their concerns or any given warnings—because they believe an EMI university degree to be their entrance ticket granting access, success, and their desired future, preferably in the Global North.

Essential for the assessment of the value of English is that any context, any user, or any intention behind the language's use always includes all layers of value. Consequently, economic considerations are always part of a person's or institution's decision to invest in English, although it is not always seen or admitted. The objectification of English into a marketable attribute—which can be bought, sold, attached, and detached to anything or anybody—and the implementation of the language's economic value into its description, furthermore, enables a shift in perspective within sociolinguistic research. As has been shown in this study, the use of "English" in HE has two main effects: the direct and indirect reproduction and strengthening of social hierarchies and an increasing, inconsiderate, and predatory marketization of the language as an attribute of human capital. Cyprus's HE is a transferred image of the globally prevailing social stratification, which maintains the power of the powerful and exploits the hopes of the less powerful. Cyprus's HE does not cater to members of the global elite since they have the privilege to choose—whether to pursue an English-medium HE at all and, if so, which university to enroll in. In these social groups, an EMI education does not have the same value as in other groups; members have to choose the right university, which is most likely in an Anglophone country. Furthermore, English is not primarily valued for its economic or communicative potential but for its native embeddedness and the power and superiority, which is associated with its homes, that is, with these Anglophone countries themselves or the quality of their education. While members of the global elite are unlikely to choose Cyprus for their HE, it represents an affordable alternative that still enables social upward mobility for students who, for various reasons, cannot or do not want to attend such a university.

Cyprus's HE landscape primarily caters to the needs of students who believe that they have to invest in the economic value of the English language when aiming at their social advancement. In so doing, universities in Cyprus follow varying strategies, depending on their target groups' needs and hopes. UCLan Cyprus, for example, is an affordable possibility for Ct- and nCt-students of higher social status to obtain a British education without moving to the UK. It combines a British degree, a location in the Global North, access to Europe, and comparably low living costs in Cyprus. For students from the Global South who can obtain the necessary visa and for Ct-students who do not want to or cannot go to the UK, UCLan Cyprus offers a well-regarded alternative to the education they desire in the first place (see Section 4.2.1; Excerpts 1b and 2g). However, not being in the UK leads to a limited interest in it by students from the Global North with a high-status background and the necessary financial possibilities to move to the UK. Consequently, UCLan Cyprus lacks the ideological value of a "proper" British university while offering a high economic value in the Global South and in local contexts. Like UCLan Cyprus, the universities in the TRNC represent a profitable compromise for most of their students. Although students in the TRNC appear to benefit less from their investment in the English language than their peers in the Republic of Cyprus (RoC), most students still perceive it as advantageous for their future goals (see Section 4.3.3). However, also in North Cyprus, the existing social stratification is reproduced through English-medium HE; while Turkish Cypriot students, due to their family ties to the UK, appear to pursue their HE in the UK whenever possible, a TRNC degree is expedient for nCt-students from Turkey and the Global South (see Sections 4.3.1 and 4.3.3). Turkish students, unlike other nCt-students, can rely on the validity of their TRNC degrees in Turkey and might even experience advantages when applying for a master's degree back home. For these students, like for students at UCLan Cyprus, an English-medium HE in Cyprus represents a stepping-stone to their desired social and financial positions. Outside Turkey, however, TRNC degrees are not as advantageous—especially in the Global North.

The reproduction of social structures through English includes the limitation of the powerless' access to power. This is most pronounced in the TRNC when nCt-students from the Global South are concerned. These students are, among other reasons, attracted to Cyprus due to its location at the crossroads of the Global North and the Global South, which promises proximity and access. For the more privileged of these students, Cyprus is, consequently, a rational investment in their future, which they potentially figure to take place in the Global North. However, while Cyprus is de jure part of the Global North, a TRNC degree does not offer students access to it due to its official status as "occupied territory." Nonetheless, a TRNC education enables the nCt-students' social and economic advancement in their home societies and ensures the preservation of their privileged status. Although these students are often unfamiliar with the TRNC and its geopolitical situation, they can persevere the temporary social othering they often experience as immigrants by the local population and overcome the potential disappointment of, de facto, not being in the Global North. Furthermore, their privileged background supports them and prevents them from being exploited, as it prepares them to interact with the chosen university directly and protects them from using middlemen or agencies during the admission process. While their investment in an EMI education in Cyprus turns out to be mostly profitable, less privileged students are more vulnerable. Less privileged nCt-students from the Global South form the group of students in the TRNC that is most often preyed upon since these students miss their privileged peers' social and financial support and feel more pressured to improve their future perspectives. These students are vulnerable to the predatory practices of middlemen and recruiting agencies, promising them access to Europe and the Global North. This group of students is willing to believe in the promise of English as an economic gatekeeper more intensely and risk more to gain access than any other group of students (see Sections 4.3.3 and 4.3.4). Hidden under a smokescreen of the positive connotations of education, the use of English in HE enables the exploitation of less privileged and less powerful students from the Global South, while maintaining and reproducing the prevailing ramifications of colonialism based on the increasing appreciation of the economic value of English. While the economic value of English used to be inseparable from its actual use, the objectification of English led to a detachment of its value from its use.

Following Laura's elaborations, it appears that the actual use of the English language is no longer automatically part of its usefulness in HE and occupational contexts. English is increasingly understood as a marketable attribute of its bearers who constitute human capital. Especially in local contexts, the language's actual use becomes secondary to its value as economic capital. Consequently, English in neoliberalism is no longer necessarily a skill; it might just be a name or a note on a person's CV or degree. Universities plan, offer, and attest degrees in EMI study programs that are not (only) taught in English—transferring the language from a communicative tool into an attachable attribute. Due to this ultimate commodification and unlike any other language, English is valuable as a theoretical concept, as the promise of possibilities, and as independent of the individual and his or her skills. This development has not yet been accessed and requires an epistemic realignment of research practices. The unmatched economic value of the English language enables the emergence of a market of HE that is no longer necessarily approachable based on an assessment of the use of English. Furthermore, this market is detached from the concept of education as empowering involved students and societies and creates an atmosphere of global competitiveness and exchange of commodities.

During the assessment of the value of English in Cyprus's HE landscape, its combination of commonly occurring practices and unique circumstances became obvious. Universities in Anglophone countries, primarily from the UK or the United States, distribute satellite campuses around the globe. However, they open these campuses predominantly in parts of the world where prospective students are otherwise unlikely to pursue an Anglophone education to enlarge the group of their prospective students. Consequently, UK universities tend to not open satellite campuses within the (Western) European Union, as they are already accessible for interested students. The unique geographical location of Cyprus at the edge of Europe, however, offers universities like UCLan access to a group of prospective students who might otherwise not consider a British university while building its local reputation on the preserved prestige of the UK. The exit of the UK from the European Union and the accompanied exacerbation of access to it will certainly increase the interest of local and international students in UCLan Cyprus. Like building satellite campuses, educational tourism in the TRNC is also fairly common. The increased geographical mobility of students resulted in an extension of the educational market; universities have to attract and convince students to enroll, while students are overwhelmed by the magnitude of their choice. Specific for the context of Cyprus, however, is the unmentioned interaction of the Global North and the Global South (see, e.g., Khattab and Mahmud 2018; Odeh 2010 for an overview). The complex geopolitical situation of Cyprus is altered to the needs of any involved party: for the universities in the North, the TRNC is an independent country and for recruiting agencies and middlemen, it is Europe and easily accessible. The negative results of these practices, however, are not openly discussed despite the increasing violence against Nigerian EMU students (e.g., the partaking Nigerian students did not mention any problems of this sort). While this might be because of social conventions and power relations among English speakers as well as between the

Global South and the Global North, the chosen silence of the students might also have been caused by the official approach taken, the assumed episteme, and the lack of a trusting relationship to the researcher.

In Cyprus, the cultural goods *education* reflects stakeholders of various sorts and is obedient to the rules of business, resulting in the radical reduction of the English language into an attribute. Although this is a development that can increasingly be found around the globe, research focuses on its institutional or linguistic aspects only while neglecting the centrality of the involved students and the effects of the global use of English on their life trajectories; the journeys, difficulties, and personal motivations of individual students remain mostly unseen. This book aimed at taking individual students' perspectives to assess their choosing to invest in the English language and found English to be the language of access for them; English promises access to communication, social and geographical mobility, and, hopefully, a better future. To be granted access, students invest in their HE and universities compete for their attention and tuition fees. Some students succeed, some strand, and some fall victim to the global economy. These students, who were promised access, remain unmentioned and disregarded whenever the success story of the English language is told. Quoting an Igbo proverb, "If the prey do not produce their version of the tale, the predators will always be the heroes in the stories of the hunt" (Obioma 2019a: para. 1). The global use of English enables a mass production of human capital that is composed in a way that reproduces colonial structures and assures that the social and economic power remains with the powerful. As learning English became accessible for all, speaking the language was no longer the ticket to social and financial upward mobility. The yardstick of social participation and power is constantly changing, keeping the less privileged from becoming equal. To reveal the social inequality reproduced by the value of English, linguistic researchers have to scrutinize their motives and epistemes; we have to look beyond the language itself and, in addition to attesting the level of proficiency of students and faculty, describing the difficulties of testing and standardization, ensuring educational quality, and interpreting sociolinguistic variables or the "nonconformity" of language use, we must explore the effects of language use on society and individual speakers. In doing so, we have to leave our neutral observer's position, create personal relationships, and participate in the social contexts we explore so that our interlocutors feel free to share their reality with us rather than hiding behind the veneer of their public personae.

# Appendix 1: Study Design

**Appendix 1.1** Background Questionnaire

| **Background Questionnaire** | | |
|---|---|---|
| Date of birth | | |
| Sex | Male | Female |
| Place of birth | | |
| Nationality | | |
| Occupation before coming to university X | | |
| Why did you come to (North) Cyprus? | | |
| Since when have you been in (North) Cyprus? | | |
| Since when have you been studying at X? | | |
| Native language(s) | | |
| What other languages do you speak? | | |

**Appendix 1.2** Interview Options

| | |
|---|---|
| **Interview Options** | |
| Can you tell me which languages you use on a usual day on-campus? | Introduction |
| And is it the same off-campus or on a weekend? Imagine your typical Saturday; can you describe which languages you use and how much you use them? | |
| Can you tell me your language biography? So, which languages did you learn during the course of your life? When did you learn them and how? You said your native language is X?! | |
| In your questionnaire, you said that your language repertoire is (not) typical for your family. Could you explain? Which languages are used in your family? | |
| Why did you come to university X? | All students |
| What do you like/dislike about Cyprus? In your questionnaire, you said X?! | |
| What do you like/dislike about your university? | |
| Have you been to the Turkish/Greek part? What is it like? Did you like it? | |
| What should I do while here on the island? Is there anything you can recommend or I should not miss? | |
| How do you pay the tuition fees? Do you have a scholarship? I have been told there are a lot of options for local/international students; could you explain them to me? | |
| What role does English play in your life? Do you think it is important at home/in Cyprus/in the nearest city? | |
| Did you have to do an English language test prior to starting at X? | |
| Is your English sufficient for your needs? | |
| How does it come you are in Cyprus? | NCt-students |
| How did you hear about Cyprus and its universities? Do you know many people who go abroad for their education? | |
| Can you tell me in which areas your life here differs from that in your home country? | |
| Did you know about Cyprus being divided when you came here? | |
| How often can you go home? | |
| To what extent did your language use change when moving to Cyprus? | |

**Appendix 1.3** Transcription Code

| | |
|---|---|
| & | phonological fragment |
| XXX | unintelligible speech |
| www | untranscribable material |
| [/] | retracing without correction, e.g., …: then [/] then |
| [//] | retracing with correction, e.g., …: then [//] but |
| [?] | best guess |
| mhm | utterance of agreement |
| ehm, eh, uh | utterance of reflection |
| **Additions** | |
| (X) | social interaction, e.g., (laughs) |
| … | interruption/continuation of an utterance, e.g., and then … (right) … I stopped |

# Appendix 2: Relevant Questionnaire Data

Interview transcripts and more detailed descriptive analyses can be made available from the author upon reasonable request.

**Appendix 2.1** Biographic Information

| Biographic Information (in Percentage, Rounded) | | | | |
|---|---|---|---|---|
| University | All Participants | UCLan Cyprus | UCy | EMU |
| Participants | 52.7 RoC 47.3 TRNC | 40 | 12.7 | 46.8 |
| Age | Mean 21.02; range: 1739, SD 3.59 | Mean 19.87; range: 1739, SD 2.88 | Mean 20.16; range: 1926, SD 1.63 | Mean 22.19; range: 1737, SD 3.98 |
| Sex | Male: 43.4 Female: 56.6 | Male: 63.4 Female: 36.6 | Male: 15.4 Female: 84.6 | Male: 34.4 Female: 65.6 |
| Cyprus-tied | nCt: 39 Ct: 61 | nCt: 9.8 Ct: 90.2 | nCt: 19.2 Ct: 80.8 | nCt: 68.8 Ct: 31.3 |
| Nationality | Cypriot: 57.1 English-speaking country: 33.7 | Cypriot: 79.3 English-speaking country: 3.7 | Cypriot: 80.8 English-speaking country: 15.4 | Cypriot: 32.3 English-speaking country: 63.5 |
| Place of birth | Cyprus: 50.1 English-speaking country: 10.7 | Cyprus: 78 English-speaking country: 6.1 | Cyprus: 84.6 English-speaking country: 0 | Cyprus: 18.8 English-speaking country: 16.7 |
| Native language(s) | Greek: 31.7 English (only or +X): 13.7 Turkish: 20.5 Other: 20.5 | Greek: 50 English+X: 9.8 Turkish: 3.7 Other: 9.8 | Greek: 92.3 English+X: 0 Turkish: 0 Other: 7.7 | Greek: 0 English (only or +X): 20.9 Turkish: 40.6 Other: 33.3 |
| Reason to be in Cyprus? | Born in Cyprus: 25.9 To study: 29.3 Missing: 33.7 | Born in Cyprus: 23.2 To study: 4.9 Missing: 58.5 | Born in Cyprus: 26.9 To study: 15.4 Missing: 57.7 | Born in Cyprus: 28.1 To study: 53.1 Missing: 6.3 |
| NCt-students who arrived in the TRNC the year they enrolled in a university | Overall: 87.5 In the TRNC: 70 | | | |

**Appendix 2.2** English Language Proficiency

| English Language Proficiency (in Percentage, Rounded) | | | | | |
|---|---|---|---|---|---|
| Please Rate Your Proficiency | No Knowledge | Beginner | Intermediate | Advanced | Near-native |
| Speaking skills |  | 3.9 | 34.1 | 45.4 | 16.6 |
| Listening skills | 0.5 | 2.9 | 32.2 | 46.3 | 18 |
| Reading skills | 0.5 | 2.9 | 25.4 | 50.7 | 20.5 |
| Writing skills | 0.5 | 3.9 | 35.1 | 47.8 | 12.2 |
| **UCLan Cyprus** | | Ct | nCt | Ct | nCt | Ct | nCt | Ct | nCt |
| Speaking skills |  | 2.7 | 25 | 40.5 | 62.5 | 44.6 | 12.5 | 12.2 |  |
| Listening skills |  | 1.4 | 25 | 37.8 | 37.5 | 44.6 | 37.5 | 16.2 |  |
| Reading skills |  | 2.7 | 50 | 35.1 | 37.5 | 45.9 | 12.5 | 16.2 |  |
| Writing skills |  | 4.1 | 50 | 48.6 | 37.5 | 41.9 | 12.5 | 5.4 |  |
| **UCy** | | Ct | nCt | Ct | nCt | Ct | nCt | Ct | nCt |
| Speaking skills |  |  |  | 38.1 |  | 38.1 | 80 | 23.8 | 20 |
| Listening skills |  |  |  | 14.3 | 20 | 52.4 | 60 | 33.3 | 20 |
| Reading skills |  |  |  | 4.8 | 20 | 66.7 | 40 | 28.6 | 40 |
| Writing skills |  |  |  | 19 | 20 | 66.7 | 60 | 14.3 | 20 |
| **EMU** | Ct | nCt | Ct | nCt | Ct | nCt | Ct | nCt | Ct | nCt |
| Speaking skills |  |  | 3.3 | 4.5 | 16.7 | 33.3 | 33.3 | 56.1 | 46.7 | 6.1 |
| Listening skills | 1.5 |  |  | 4.5 | 20 | 37.9 | 43.3 | 48.5 | 36.7 | 7.6 |
| Reading skills | 1.5 |  |  |  | 16.7 | 24.2 | 46.7 | 59.1 | 36.7 | 15.2 |
| Writing skills | 1.5 |  |  | 1.5 | 13.3 | 36.4 | 50 | 51.5 | 33.3 | 9.1 |

**Appendix 2.3** Language Attitudes and Use of All Participants

| | |
|---|---|
| The language of my education is/has been English | Never: 2.4<br>Sometimes: 10.2<br>Often: 20<br>Usually: 24.4<br>Always: 34.1<br>Missing: 8.8 |
| At university, I talk to my friends in English | Never: 2.4<br>Sometimes: 11.2<br>Often: 21.5<br>Usually: 29.8<br>Always: 32.7<br>Missing: 2.4 |
| What language do you use when talking to academic staff? | (Cypriot) Greek: 7.8<br>(Cypriot) Turkish: 3.9<br>English (only or +X): 79.6 |
| What language do you, in your opinion, use during the majority of your day? | (Cypriot) Greek: 30.2<br>(Cypriot) Turkish: 14.6<br>English (only or +X): 47.8 |
| In your private life, do you think English is important to know? | Yes: 72.2<br>No: 16.1<br>Don't know: 1<br>Missing: 10.7 |
| Do you like the English language? | Very much: 71.7<br>Much: 22.4<br>Indifferent: 5.9 |
| Why do you reside in Cyprus? | Born in Cyprus: 25.9<br>To study: 29.3<br>Missing: 33.7 |
| Are you planning to stay in Cyprus after finishing your studies? | Yes: 30.7<br>No: 38<br>Don't know: 23.4<br>Missing: 7.8 |
| Why did you pick X for your education? | English language: 6.8<br>Recommendation: 21.5<br>Reputation: 20.5<br>Location: 6.3<br>More than one: 15.6 |

**Appendix 2.4** Language Attitudes and Use at UCLan Cyprus

|  | **Ct-Students** | **NCt-Students** |
| --- | --- | --- |
| The language of my education is/has been English | Never: 1.4<br>Sometimes: 9.5<br>Often: 32.4<br>Usually: 25.7<br>Always: 17.6<br>Missing: 13.5 | Sometimes: 37.5<br>Often: 25<br>Usually: 12.5<br>Always: 25 |
| At university, I talk to my friends in English | Never: 5.4<br>Sometimes: 16.2<br>Often: 29.7<br>Usually: 24.3<br>Always: 21.6<br>Missing: 2.7 | Often: 12.5<br>Usually: 12.5<br>Always: 75 |
| What has been the language of your previous schooling? | English (only or +X): 25.7<br>(Cypriot) Greek: 59.5<br>(Cypriot) Turkish: 1.4<br>Missing: 12.2 | English (only or +X): 62.5<br>Other: 12.5<br>Missing: 25 |
| What language do you use when talking to academic staff? | English (only or +X): 78.4<br>Cypriot Greek: 13.5<br>Missing: 8.1 | English (only or +X): 100 |
| What language do you, in your opinion, use during the majority of your day? | English (only or +X): 35.1<br>(Cypriot) Greek: 56.8<br>(Cypriot) Turkish: 4.1 | English (only or +X): 50<br>Other: 50 |
| In your private life, do you think English is important to know? | Yes: 71.6<br>No: 12.2<br>Missing: 16.2 | Yes: 50<br>No: 12.5<br>Missing: 37.5 |
| Why do you reside in Cyprus? | To study: 4.9<br>Born in Cyprus: 23.2<br>Missing: 58.5 | To study: 37.5<br>Missing: 62.5 |
| Why did you pick UCLan for your education? | English language: 12.2<br>Location: 10.8<br>Recommendation: 16.2<br>Reputation: 23<br>Missing: 23 | English language: 12.5<br>Recommendation: 12.5<br>More than one: 50<br>Missing: 25 |
| Are you planning to stay in Cyprus? | Yes: 41.9 Not sure: 24.3<br>No: 20.3 Missing: 13.5 | Yes: 25 Not sure: 25<br>No: 25 Missing: 25 |

**Appendix 2.5** Language Attitudes and Use at EMU

|  | **Ct-Students** | **NCt-Students** |
|---|---|---|
| The language of my education is/has been English | Never: 3.3<br>Sometimes: 3.3<br>Often: 16.7<br>Usually: 20<br>Always: 53.3<br>Missing: 3.3 | Never: 4.5<br>Sometimes: 7.6<br>Often: 6.1<br>Usually: 27.3<br>Always: 43.9<br>Missing: 10.6 |
| At university, I talk to my friends in English | Never: 0<br>Sometimes: 0<br>Often: 20<br>Usually: 43.3<br>Always: 35.7<br>Missing: 0 | Never: 0<br>Sometimes: 4.5<br>Often: 10.6<br>Usually: 34.8<br>Always: 45.5<br>Missing: 4.5 |
| What has been the language of your previous schooling? | English (only or +X): 49.9<br>(Cypriot) Turkish: 40<br>Missing: 6.7 | English (only or +X): 42.4<br>Turkish: 22.7<br>Missing: 7.6 |
| What language do you use when talking to academic staff? | English (only or +X): 83.3<br>(Cypriot) Turkish: 16.7 | English (only or +X): 89.4<br>(Cypriot) Turkish: 4.5 |
| What language do you, in your opinion, use during the majority of your day? | English (only or +X): 56.7<br>(Cypriot) Turkish: 43.3 | English (only or +X): 69.7<br>(Cypriot) Turkish: 21.2 |
| In your private life, do you think English is important to know? | Yes: 76.7 Not sure: 3.3<br>No: 13.3 Missing: 6.7 | Yes: 71.2<br>No: 21.2 Missing: 7.6 |
| Why do you reside in North Cyprus? | To study: 6.7<br>Born in Cyprus: 63.3<br>Missing: 10 | To study: 74.2<br>Other: 9.1<br>Missing: 4.5 |
| Why did you pick EMU for your education? | Location: 16.7<br>Reputation: 33.3<br>Recommendation: 13.3<br>More than one: 10 | English language: 6.1<br>Reputation: 7.6<br>Recommendation: 34.8<br>More than one: 13.6<br>Missing: 19.7 |
| Are you planning to stay in Cyprus? | Yes: 53.3 Not sure: 3.3<br>No: 33.3 Missing: 3.3 | Yes: 12.1 Not sure: 30.3<br>No: 53 Missing: 4.5 |

**Appendix 2.6** Language Attitudes and Use at UCy

| | **Ct-Students** | **NCt-Students** |
|---|---|---|
| The language of my education is/has been English | Never: 0<br>Sometimes: 19<br>Often: 19<br>Usually: 23.8<br>Always: 38.1 | Never: 0<br>Sometimes: 20<br>Often: 40<br>Usually: 20<br>Always: 20 |
| At university, I talk to my friends in English | Never: 4.8<br>Sometimes: 38.1<br>Often: 19<br>Usually: 28.6<br>Always: 9.5 | Never:<br>Sometimes:<br>Often: 80<br>Usually:<br>Always: 20 |
| What has been the language of your previous schooling? | (Cypriot) Greek: 100 | English (only or +X): 20<br>Greek: 60<br>Other: 20 |
| What language do you use when talking to academic staff? | English (only or +X): 42.8<br>(Cypriot) Greek: 23.8<br>Missing: 33.3 | English (only or +X): 60<br>(Cypriot) Greek: 20<br>Missing: 20 |
| What language do you, in your opinion, use during the majority of your day? | English (only or +X): 14.3<br>(Cypriot) Greek: 85.7 | English (only or +X): 20<br>(Cypriot) Greek: 40<br>Other: 40 |
| In your private life, do you think English is important to know? | Yes: 81 Not sure: 4.8<br>No: 14.3 | Yes: 60<br>No: 40 |
| Why do you reside in Cyprus? | Born in Cyprus: 33.3<br>Missing: 66.7 | To study: 80<br>Missing: 20 |
| Why did you pick UCy for your education? | Reputation: 47.6<br>Recommendation: 4.8<br>More than one: 33.3 | Recommendation: 60<br>More than one: 40 |
| Are you planning to stay in Cyprus? | Yes: 19 Not sure: 9.5<br>No: 71.4 | Yes: 20 Not sure: 40<br>No: 20 Missing: 20 |

# References

Agaba, Vivian (2015), "Parents of student murdered in Cyprus demand justice." Available online: https://www.newvision.co.ug/new_vision/news/1330912/parents-student-murdered-cyprus-demand-justice (accessed August 1, 2020).

Agha, Asif (2011), "Commodity registers," *Journal of Linguistic Anthropology*, 21 (1): 22–53.

Agreement of Cooperation with Institutions Abroad (n.d.), Retrieved January 11, 2021, from http://www.ucy.ac.cy/ir/documents/Inter.Relations/AgreementsCooperation/AgreementsofCooperationwithInstitutionsoutsid_Cyprus_EN_06.06.2019.pdf.

Almeida, Joana (2020), *Understanding student mobility in Europe: An interdisciplinary approach*, Abingdon: Routledge.

*Annual Colonial Reports for the social and economic progress of the people of Cyprus 1909–1936* (1937), London: His Majesty's Stationary Office.

Aronin, Larissa (2016), "Dominant Language Constellations as a method of research," Paper presented to *10th International Conference on Multilingualism and Third Language Acquisition*, University of Vienna, Austria, September 1–3.

Aronin, Larissa, and Singleton, David (2012), "The Dominant Language Constellation (DLC)," in L. Aronin and D. Singleton (eds.), *Multilingualism*, 59–75, Amsterdam: John Benjamins.

Aygin, Esra (2019), "Sorry end for Africans on 'education island,'" *CyprusMail*, July 21. Accessible online: https://cyprus-mail.com/2019/07/21/sorry-end-for-africans-on-education-island/ (accessed January 22, 2021).

Baker, Will (2012), "English as a lingua franca in Thailand: Characteristics and implication," *English in Practice: Working Papers of the Centre for Global Englishes*, 1 (1): 18–27.

Baker, Will (2015), *Culture and identity through English as a lingua franca: Rethinking concepts and goals in intercultural communication*, Berlin: De Gruyter Mouton.

Bauer, Laurie (2002), *An introduction to international varieties of English*, Edinburgh: Edinburgh University Press.

Benzie, Helen J. (2010), "Graduating as a 'native speaker': International students and English language proficiency in higher education," *Higher Education Research and Development*, 29 (4): 447–59.

Bergin, Michael, Wells, John S. G., and Owen, Sara (2010), "Relating realist metatheory to issues of gender and mental health," *Journal of Psychiatric and Mental Health Nursing*, 17 (5): 442–51.

Bilge, Ömer (2018), "Nigerian students killed by locals in Turkish Cyprus," *Hürriyet Daily News*, February 1. Available online: http://www.hurriyetdailynews.com/

nigerian-student-killed-by-locals-in-turkish-cyprus-126612 (accessed January 20, 2021).

Bingham, Derek, ed. (2010), "Girne American University," in *The CIS Higher Education Directory 2010*, 89, Suffork: John Catt Educational.

Björkman, Beyza (2013), *English as an academic lingua franca: An investigation of form and communicative effectiveness*, Boston, MA: De Gruyter Mouton.

Blackledge, Adrian, and Creese, Angela (2010), *Multilingualism: A critical perspective*, London: Continuum.

Block, David (2015), "Social class in applied linguistics," *Annual Review of Applied Linguistics*, 35: 1–19.

Block, David (2018a), "Inequality and class in language policy and planning," in J. Tollefson and M. Pérez-Milans (eds.), *The Oxford handbook of language policy and planning*, 568–88, Oxford: Oxford University Press.

Block, David (2018b), "Some thoughts on education and the discourse of global neoliberalism," *Language and Intercultural Communication*, 18 (5): 576–84.

Block, David (2019), "What on earth is 'language commodification'?," in B. Schmenk, S. Breidbach, and L. Küster (eds.), *Sloganization in language education discourse*, 121–41, Bristol: Multilingual Matters.

Block, David, Gray, J., and Holborow, Marnie, eds. (2012), *Neoliberalism and applied linguistics*, London: Routledge.

Blommaert, Jan (2014), "Language: The great diversifier," in S. Vertovec (ed.), *Routledge international handbook of diversity studies*, 83–90, London: Routledge.

Bolton, Kingsley (2004), "World Englishes," in A. Davies and C. Elder (eds.), *The handbook of applied linguistics*, 369–96, Oxford: Blackwell.

Bonfiglio, Thomas P. (2013), "Inventing the Native Speaker," *Critical Multilingualism Studies*, 1 (2): 29–58.

Botsis, Hannah (2018), *Subjectivity, language and the postcolonial. Beyond Bourdieu in South Africa*, London: Routledge.

Bourdieu, Pierre (1977), "The economics of linguistic exchange," *Social Science Information*, 16 (6): 645–68.

Bourdieu, Pierre (1986), "The forms of capital," in J. G. Richardson (ed.), *Handbook of theory and research in the sociology of education*, 241–58, New York: Greenwood Press.

Bourdieu, Pierre (1990), *The logic of practice*, Stanford, CA: Stanford University Press.

Bourdieu, Pierre (1991), *Language and symbolic power*, Cambridge: Harvard University Press.

Brinck, Ingar (1997), *The indexical "I": The first person in thought and language*, Berlin: Springer Science and Business Media.

Brock-Utne, Birgit (2001), "The growth of English for academic communication in the Nordic countries," *International Review of Education*, 47 (3): 221–33.

Brock-Utne, Birgit (2007), "Language of instruction and research in higher education in Europe: Highlights from the current debate in Norway and Sweden," *International Review of Education*, 53: 367–88.

Brooks, Rachel, and Waters, Johanna (2009), "International higher education and the mobility of UK students," *Journal of Research in International Education*, 8 (2): 191–209.

Brooks, Rachel, and Waters, Johanna (2011), *Student mobilities, migration and the internationalization of higher education*, New York: Palgrave Macmillan.

Bruthiaux, Pierre (2003), "Squaring the circles: Issues in modeling English worldwide," *International Journal of Applied Linguistics*, 13: 159–78.

Brutt-Griffler, Janina (2002), *World English: A study of its development*, Clevedon: Multilingual Matters.

Bucholtz, Mary, and Hall, Kira (2005), "Identity and interaction: A sociocultural linguistic approach," *Discourse Studies*, 7 (4–5): 585–614.

Burgess, Robert G. (1984), *In the field: An introduction to field research*, London: Allen and Unwin.

Busch, Brigitta (2013). "Linguistic rights and language policy: A south-north dialogue," *Education as Change*, 17 (2): 209–18.

Busch, Brigitta (2017), "Expanding the notion of the linguistic repertoire: On the concept of Spracherleben—the lived experience of language," *Applied Linguistics*, 38 (3): 340–58.

Buschfeld, Sarah (2013), *English in Cyprus or Cyprus English: An empirical investigation of variety status*, Amsterdam: John Benjamins.

Buschfeld, Sarah (2020), *Children's English in Singapore: Acquisition, properties, and use*, London: Routledge.

Buschfeld, Sarah, and Kautzsch, Alexander (2017), "Towards an integrated approach to postcolonial and non-postcolonial Englishes," *World Englishes*, 36 (1): 104–26.

Buschfeld, Sarah, and Kautzsch, Alexander (2020), "Theoretical models of English as a world language," in D. Schreier, M. Hundt, and E. W. Schneider (eds.), *The Cambridge handbook of World Englishes*, 51–71, Cambridge: Cambridge University Press.

Canagarajah, Suresh (2007), "The ecology of global English," *International Multilingual Research Journal*, 1 (2): 89–100.

Canagarajah, Suresh (2013), *Translingual practice: Global Englishes and cosmopolitan relations*, London: Routledge.

Chen, Zan, and Goh, Christine (2011), "Teaching oral English in higher education: Challenges to EFL teachers," *Teaching in Higher Education*, 16 (3): 333–45.

Cogo, Alessia, and Dewey, Martin (2012), *Analysing English as a lingua franca: A corpus-based investigation*, London: Continuum.

Cook, Vivian (1999), "Going beyond the native speaker in language teaching," *TESOL Quarterly*, 33 (2): 185–209.

Coupland, Nikolas (2003), "Sociolinguistic authenticities", *Journal of Sociolinguistics*, 7 (3): 417–31.

Cox, Andrew (2005), "What are communities of practice? A comparative review of four seminal works," *Journal of Information Science*, 31 (6): 527–40.

Crotty, Michael (1998), *The foundation of social research: Meaning and perspective in the research process*, London: Sage.

Crystal, David (2003), *English as a global language*, 2nd ed., Cambridge: Cambridge University Press.

Curry, Mary J., and Lillis, Theresa (2018), "Problematizing English as the privileged language of global academic publishing," in M. J. Curry and T. Lillis (eds.), *Global academic publishing: Policies, perspectives and pedagogies*, 1–22, Bristol: Multilingual Matters.

"Cyprus: Students duped by 'good life' in the north," *Financial Mirror*, February 21, 2019. Available online: http://www.financialmirror.com/news-details.php?nid=36569 (accessed January 20, 2021).

CYSTAT (Statistical Service of the Republic of Cyprus) (2017a), *Cyprus in figures. 2017 edition*. Available online: https://www.mof.gov.cy/mof/cystat/statistics.nsf/All/9C0E2C4E8479795CC22583740037E1EA/$file/CYPRUS_IN_FIGURES-2017-EN-271217.pdf?OpenElement (accessed January 20, 2021).

CYSTAT (Statistical Service of the Republic of Cyprus) (2017b), *Demographic report 2016*. Available online: https://www.mof.gov.cy/mof/cystat/statistics.nsf/All/FB511581537B8938C225835500343940/$file/DEMOGRAPHIC_REPORT-2016-271117.pdf?OpenElement (accessed January 20, 2021).

CYSTAT (Statistical Service of the Republic of Cyprus) (2018), *Statistics of education 2015/2016*. Available online: https://www.mof.gov.cy/mof/cystat/statistics.nsf/All/0B2667C2FA10B3ACC22583CC0039FF78/$file/EDUCATION-15_16-EN-180618.pdf?OpenElement (accessed January 20, 2021).

CYSTAT (Statistical Service of the Republic of Cyprus) (2019), *Cyprus in figures. 2019 edition*. Available online: https://www.mof.gov.cy/mof/cystat/statistics.nsf/All/C91603BD82050327C22582030022C7F2/$file/CYPRUS_IN_FIGURES-2019-EN-201219.pdf?OpenElement (accessed January 20, 2021).

CYSTAT (Statistical Service of the Republic of Cyprus) (2020a), *Demographic statistics 2019*. Available online: https://www.mof.gov.cy/mof/cystat/statistics.nsf/All/6C25304C1E70C304C2257833003432B3/$file/Demographic_Statistics_Results-2019-EN-301120.pdf?OpenElement (accessed January 20, 2021).

CYSTAT (Statistical Service of the Republic of Cyprus) (2020b), *Statistics of education 2017/2018*. Available online: https://www.mof.gov.cy/mof/cystat/statistics.nsf/All/204AA86C4060D499C22577E4002CA3E3/$file/EDUCATION-17_18-EN-300330.pdf?OpenElement (accessed January 20, 2021).

Da Costa, Dinis F., Dyers, Charlyn, and Mheta, Gift (2014), "Language standardisation," in Z. Bock and G. Mheta (eds.), *Language, society and communication: An introduction*, 333–60, Pretoria: Van Schaik.

Davies, Alan (2003), *The native speaker: Myth and reality*, Clevedon: Multilingual Matters.

Davy, Jim, and Pavlou, Pavlos (2001), "Is Cyprus an ESL country?," in *Proceedings of the 12th International Conference of the Greek Applied Linguistics Association*, 209–15, Thessaloniki: Gramma.

de Swaan, Abram (2001), *The world of words: The global language system*, 1st ed., Malden, MA: Polity Press.

de Winter, Joost C., and Dodou, Dimitra (2010), "Five-point Likert items: t test versus Mann-Whitney-Wilcoxon," *Practical Assessment, Research and Evaluation*, 15 (11): 1–12.

Demir, Nurettin, and Johanson, Lars (2006), "Dialect contact in Northern Cyprus," *International Journal of the Sociology of Language*, 181: 1–9.

Dewey, Martin (2007), "English as a lingua franca and globalization: An interconnected perspective," *International Journal of Applied Linguistics*, 17 (3): 332–54.

Doiz, Aintzane, Lasagabaster, David, and Sierra, Juan M. (2014), "What does 'international university' mean at a European bilingual university? The role of language and culture," *Language Awareness*, 23: 172–86.

Dörnyei, Zoltán, Csiziér, Kata, and Németh, Nóra (2006), *Motivation, language attitudes and globalization: A Hungarian perspective*, Clevedon: Multilingual Matters.

Durant, Alan, and Shepherd, Ifan (2009), "'Culture' and 'communication' in intercultural communication," *European Journal of English Studies*, 13 (2): 147–62.

Eckert, Penelope (2000), *Language variation as social practice*, Oxford: Basil Blackwell.

Eckert, Penelope (2006), "Communities of practice," in K. Brown (ed.), *Encyclopedia of language and linguistics*, 2nd ed., 683–5, Amsterdam: Elsevier.

Eckert, Penelope (2008), "Variation in the indexical field," *Journal of Sociolinguistics*, 12 (4): 453–76.

Edley, Nigel, and Litosseliti, Lia (2010), "Contemplating interviews and focus groups," in L. Litosseliti (ed.), *Research methods in linguistics*, 155–79, London: Bloomsbury.

Elega, Adeola A., and Özad, Bahire E. (2017), "Technologies and second language: Nigerian students' adaptive strategies to cope with language barrier in Northern Cyprus," *Journal of International Students*, 7 (3): 486–98.

ELFA (2008), *The corpus of English as a lingua franca in academic settings*. Director: Anna Mauranen. Available online: https://www2.helsinki.fi/en/researchgroups/english-as-a-lingua-franca-in-academic-settings/research/elfa-corpus#section-67032 (accessed January 20, 2021).

EMU (n.d.-a), [Webpage] Admission requirements to graduate programs. Available online: https://grad.emu.edu.tr/en/admission/admission-requirements (accessed December 12, 2020).

EMU (n.d.-b), [Webpage] English language tests and the postgraduate English support program. Available online: https://grad.emu.edu.tr/en/admission/english-language-support (accessed January 22, 2021).

EMU (n.d.-c), [Webpage] Exemption criteria (English language requirements). Available online: https://fleps.emu.edu.tr/en/students/exemption-criteria (accessed January 22, 2021).

EMU (n.d.-d), [Webpage] Foreign languages and English preparatory school. Available online: https://fleps.emu.edu.tr/en (accessed January 22, 2021).

EMU I-REP (n.d.), Accessed February 10, 2019, from http://i-rep.emu.edu.tr:8080/xmlui/browse?order=DESC&rpp=20&sort_by=2&etal=-1&offset=80&type=dateissued.

EMU Web Office (n.d.-a), [Webpage] About EMU. Available online: https://www.emu.edu.tr/north-cyprus-universities (accessed January 22, 2021).

EMU Web Office (n.d.-b), [Webpage] Campus, Famagusta and Northern Cyprus. Available online: https://www.emu.edu.tr/en/campus/campus-famagusta-and-north-cyprus/666 (accessed January 22, 2021).

EMU Web Office (n.d.-c), [Webpage] EMU history. Available online: https://www.emu.edu.tr/en/about-emu/emu-history/593 (accessed January 22, 2021).

EMU Web Office (n.d.-d), [Webpage] Programs. Available online: https://www.emu.edu.tr/en/programs/695 (accessed January 22, 2021).

EMU Web Office (n.d.-e), [Webpage] Scholarships and support. Available online: https://www.emu.edu.tr/scholarships (accessed January 22, 2021).

EMU Web Office (n.d.-f), [Webpage] Undergraduate admission. Available online: https://www.emu.edu.tr/en/prospective-students/admission-requirements/undergraduate-programs/1292 (accessed January 22, 2021).

Eracleous, Natalya (2015), "Linguistic landscape in Limassol: Russian presence," MA thesis, University of Cyprus, Nicosia.

Evans, David (2014), *Language and identity: Discourse in the world*, London: Bloomsbury Academic.

Evripidou, Dimitris, and Çavuşoğlu, Çise (2015), "Turkish Cypriots' language attitudes: The case of Cypriot Turkish and Standard Turkish in Cyprus," *Mediterranean Language Review*, 22: 119–38.

Evripidou, Dimitris, and Karpava, Sviatlana (2016), "Attitudes of Russian L2 learners of Greek towards the Greek language varieties of Cyprus," in R. Muhr, K. E. Fonyuy, Z. Ibrahim, and C. Miller (eds.), *Pluricentric languages and non-dominant varieties worldwide*, vol. 1, 443–58, Frankfurt am Main: Peter Lang.

Ferguson, Gibson (2007), "The global spread of English, scientific communication and ESP: Questions of equity, access and domain loss," *Ibérica*, 13: 7–38.

Ferris, Fiona S., Peck, Amiena, and Banda, Felix (2014), "Language and identity," in Z. Bock and G. Mheta (eds.), *Language, society and communication: An introduction*, 409–31, Hatfield: Van Schaik.

Findlay, Allan M., King, Russell, Smith, Fiona M., Geddes, Alistair, and Skeldon, Ronald (2012), "World class? An investigation of globalization, difference and international student mobility," *Transactions of the Institute of British Geographers*, 31: 118–31.

Foskett, Nick (2012), "Global markets, national challenges, local strategies: The strategic challenge of internationalization," in F. Maringe and N. Foskett (eds.), *Globalization and internationalization in higher education: Theoretical, strategic and management perspectives*, 35–50, London: Continuum.

Foucault, Michel (2008), *The birth of biopolitics: Lectures at the Collège de France 1978–1979*, London: Palgrave Macmillan.

GAU (2019a), [Webpage] Faculties. Available online: http://www.gau.edu.tr/en/academic/faculties (accessed January 22, 2021).

GAU (2019b), [Webpage] Financial aid and scholarships. Available online: https://www.gau.edu.tr/en/prospective/page/financial-aid-and-scholarships (accessed January 22, 2021).

GAU (2019c), [Webpage] GAU in brief. Available online: http://www.gau.edu.tr/en/institutional/gau-in-brief (accessed January 22, 2021).

GAU (2019d), [Webpage] Girne. Available online: https://www.gau.edu.tr/en/prospective/page/girne-1 (accessed January 22, 2021).

GAU (2019e), [Webpage] History of GAU. Available online: http://www.gau.edu.tr/en/institutional/history-of-gau (accessed January 22, 2021).

GAU (2019f), [Webpage] International offices. Available online: https://www.gau.edu.tr/en/contact-us/international_offices (accessed January 22, 2021).

GAU (2019g), [Webpage] Language requirements. Available online: https://www.gau.edu.tr/en/prospective/page/foundation-english-school-exemption-criteria (accessed January 22, 2021).

GAU (2019h), [Webpage] Mission statement. Available online: http://www.gau.edu.tr/en/institutional/mission-statement (accessed January 22, 2021).

GAU (2019i), [Webpage] Postgraduate programs. Available online: http://prospective.gau.edu.tr/?page=pageandid=17 (accessed August 12, 2020).

GAU (2019j), [Webpage] Program design. Available online: http://foundation.gau.edu.tr/program_design.html (accessed August 12, 2020).

GAU (2019k), [Webpage] Regional offices. Available online: https://www.gau.edu.tr/en/prospective-page/regional-offices (accessed January 22, 2021).

GAU (2019l), [Webpage] Shuttle service. Available online: http://www.gau.edu.tr/en/services/bus_shuttle_service (accessed January 22, 2021).

GAU Foundation School (2019), [Webpage] Program design. Available online: https://www.gau.edu.tr/en/foundation-school/departments.html (accesses January 22, 2021).

Gerritsen, Marinel, and Nickerson, Catherine (2009), "BELF: Business English as a lingua franca," in F. Bargiela-Chiappini (ed.), *The handbook of business discourse*, 180–92, Edinburgh: Edinburgh University Press.

Goldenchips Educational Services International (2019), *Study in North Cyprus*. Available online: https://www.goldenchipseducation.com/north-cyprus.html (accessed January 22, 2021).

Görlach, Manfred (1990), "The development of standard English," in M. Görlach (ed.), *Studies in the history of the English language*, 9–64, Heidelberg: Carl Winter.

Goutsos, Dionysis, and Karyolemou, Marilena (2004), "Language, ethnicity and nationality in Cyprus," *International Journal of the Sociology of Language*, 168: 1–17.

Graddol, David (1997), *The future of English: A guide to forecasting the popularity of English in the 21st century*, London: British Council.

Graddol, David (2006), *English next: Why global English may mean the end of "English as a Foreign Language"*, London: British Council.

Graeber, David (2001), *Towards and anthropological theory of value: The false coin of our own dreams*, New York: Palgrave.

Gramling, David (2009), "The new cosmopolitan monolingualism: On linguistic citizenship in twenty-first century Germany," *Die Unterrichtspraxis/Teaching German*, 42: 130–40.

Gramling, David (2016), *The invention of monolingualism*, New York: Bloomsbury.

Gray, John, O'Regan, John P., and Wallace, Catherine (2018), "Education and the discourse of global neoliberalism," *Language and Intercultural Communication*, 18 (5): 471–7.

Grin, François (2002), *Using language economics and education economics in language education policy*. Reference Study for the Council of Europe. Available online: https://www.ecml.at/Portals/1/documents/CoE-documents/GrinEN.pdf (accessed January 22, 2021).

Grin, François (2014), "50 years of economics in language policy: Critical assessment and priorities," *ELF Working Paper 13*, University of Geneva. Available online: https://www.unige.ch/fti/elf/files/7614/5865/9203/elfwp13.pdf (accessed January 22, 2021).

Grin, François, and Vaillancourt, François (2012), "Multilingualism in economic activity," in C. Chapelle (ed.), *Encyclopedia of applied linguistics (online)*, Oxford: Blackwell. doi: 10.1002/9781405198431.wbeal0808.

Grosjean, François (2010), *Bilingual: Life and reality*, Cambridge, MA: Harvard University Press.

Gumperz, John J. (1964), "Linguistic and social interaction in two communities," *American Anthropologist*, 66 (6): 137–53.

Gunnarsson, Britt-Louise (2000), "Swedish tomorrow – a product of linguistic dominance of English?," *Current Issues in Language and Society*, 7: 51–69.

Gürüz, Kemal (2011), *Higher education and international student mobility in the global knowledge economy*, 2nd ed., Albany, NY: SUNY Press.

Haberland, Hartmut (2014), "English from above and below, and from outside," in A. K. Hultgren, F. Gregersen, and J. Thogersen (eds.), *English in Nordic universities: Ideologies and practices*, 251–63, Amsterdam: John Benjamins.

Hackert, Stephanie (2012), *The emergence of the English native speaker: A chapter in nineteenth-century linguistic thought*, Berlin: Mouton de Gruyter.

Hadjioannou, Xenia, Tsiplakou, Stavroula, and Kappler, Matthias (2011), "Language policy and language planning in Cyprus," *Current Issues in Language Planning*, 12 (4): 503–69.

Hall, Graham (2010), "International English language testing: A critical response," *ELT Journal*, 64 (3): 321–8.
Hall, Joan K. (2012), "Language and identity," in J. K. Hall (ed.), *Teaching and researching language and culture*, 2nd ed., 30–46, London: Routledge.
Hanks, William F. (1999), "Indexicality," *Journal of Linguistic Anthropology*, 9: 124–6.
Harvey, David (2005), *A brief history of neoliberalism*, Oxford: Oxford University Press.
Heller, Monica (1994), *Crosswords: Language, education and ethnicity in French Ontario*, Berlin: Mouton de Gruyter.
Heller, Monica (2010), "The commodification of language," *Annual Review of Anthropology*, 39: 101–14.
Heller, Monica, and Duchêne, Alexandre (2013), "Pride and profit: Changing discourses of language, capital and nation-state," in A. Duchêne and M. Heller (eds.), *Language in late capitalism: Pride and profit*, 1–21, London: Routledge.
Heller, Monica, and Duchêne, Alexandre (2016), "Treating language as an economic resource: Discourse, data and debate," in N. Coupland (ed.), *Sociolinguistics: Theoretical debates*, 139–56, Cambridge: Cambridge University Press.
Hertz, Tom, Jayasundera, Tamara, Piraino, Patrizio, Selcuk, Sibel, Smith, Nicole, and Verashchagina, Alina (2007), "The inheritance of educational inequality: International comparisons and fifty-year trends," *B.E. Journal of Economic Analysis and Policy*, 7 (2). doi: https://doi.org/10.2202/1935-1682.1775.
Hofstede, Geert (1991), *Cultures and organizations: Software of the mind*, London: Harper Collins Business.
Holborow, Marnie (2012), "What is neoliberalism? Discourse, ideology and the real world," in D. Block, J. Gray, and M. Holborow (eds.), *Neoliberalism and applied linguistics*, 33–55, London: Routledge.
Holborow, Marnie (2013), "Applied linguistics in the neoliberal university: Ideological keywords and social agency," *Applied Linguistics Review*, 4 (2): 229–57.
Holborow, Marnie (2015), "Neoliberalism," in C. A. Chapelle (ed.), *The encyclopedia of applied linguistics (online)*, Oxford: Blackwell. doi:10.1002/9781405198431.wbeal1475.
Holliday, Adrian (1994), *Appropriate methodology and social context*, Cambridge: Cambridge University Press.
Holliday, Adrian (2005), *The struggle to teach English as an international language*, Oxford: Oxford University Press.
Holliday, Adrian (2006), "Native-speakerism," *ELT Journal*, 60 (4): 385–7.
Holloway, Sarah L., O'Hara, Sarah L., and Pimott-Wilson, Helena (2012), "Educational mobility and the gendered geography of cultural capital: The case of international student flows between Central Asia and the UK," *Environment and Planning A*, 44 (9), 2278–94.
Holstein, James A., and Gubrium, Jaber F. (1995), *The active interview*, London: Sage.

House, Juliane (2003), "English as a lingua franca: A threat to multilingualism?," *Journal of Sociolinguistics*, 7 (4): 556–78.
House, Juliane (2010), "The pragmatics of English as a lingua franca," in A. Trosborg (ed.), *Handbook of pragmatics*, vol. 7, 363–87, Berlin: De Gruyter Mouton.
House, Juliane (2011), "Global and intercultural communication," in K. Aijmer and G. Andersen (eds.), *Handbook of pragmatics*, vol. 5, 363–90, Berlin: De Gruyter Mouton.
House, Juliane (2012), "English as a lingua franca and linguistic diversity," *Journal of English as a Lingua Franca*, 1 (1): 173–5.
Hülmbauer, Cornelia (2009), "'We don't take the right way. We just take the way that we think you will understand' – the shifting relationship between correctness and effectiveness in ELF," in A. Mauranen and E. Ranta (eds.), *English as a lingua franca: Studies and findings*, 323–47, Newcastle upon Tyne: Cambridge Scholars.
Hyland, Ken (2009), *Academic discourse: English in a global context*, London: Continuum.
Hymes, Dell (1968), "Linguistic problems in defining the concept of tribe," in J. Helm (ed.), *Essays on the problem of tribe*, 23–48, Seattle, DC: Washington Press for the American Ethnological Society.
Hynninen, Nina (2016), *Language regulation in English as a lingua franca: Focus on academic spoken discourse*, Berlin: De Gruyter Mouton.
Irvine, Judith T. (2018), "Divided values, shadow languages: Positioning and perspective in linguistic ideologies," *Signs and Society*, 6 (1): 25–44.
Irvine, Judith T., and Gal, Susan (2000), "Language ideology and linguistic differentiation," in P. V. Kroskrity (ed.), *Regimes of language: Ideologies, polities, and identities*, 35–84, Santa Fe: School of American Research Press.
Iversen, Vegard, Krishna, Anirudh, and Sen, Kunal (2017), "Beyond poverty escapes–social mobility in the Global South: A survey article," *Global Development Institute Working Paper Series*, 2017-017, 1–29.
Jalan, Jyotsna, and Murgai, Rinku (2008), "Intergenerational mobility in education in India," Paper presented at the Indian Statistical Institute, Delhi. doi:10.13140/RG.2.1.4160.9124.
Jarvis, Scott, and Pavlenko, Aneta (2007), *Crosslinguistic influence in language and cognition*, London: Routledge.
Jenkins, Jennifer (2000), *The phonology of English as an international language: New models, new norms, new goals*, Oxford: Oxford University Press.
Jenkins, Jennifer (2006), "Current perspectives on teaching World Englishes and English as a lingua franca," *TESOL Quarterly*, 40 (1): 157–81.
Jenkins, Jennifer (2007), *English as a lingua franca: Attitudes and identity*, Oxford: Oxford University Press.
Jenkins, Jennifer (2009), *World Englishes: A resource book for students*, 2nd ed., London: Routledge.

Jenkins, Jennifer (2014), "English, the lingua franca of the global academy," in J. Jenkins (ed.), *English as a lingua franca in the international university: The politics of academic English language policy*, 1–21, Abingdon: Routledge.

Jenkins, Jennifer, and Leung, Constant (2014), "English as a lingua franca," in A. Kunnan (ed.), *The companion to language assessment*, 1607–16, Malden, MA: John Wiley.

Jöns, Heike, Heffernan, Michael, and Meusburger, Peter (2017), "Mobilities of knowledge: An introduction," in H. Jöns, M. Heffernan, and P. Meusburger (eds.), *Mobilities of knowledge*, 1–19, Dordrecht: Springer International. doi: 10.1007/978-3-319-44654-7_1.

Joseph, John E. (2004), *Language and identity: National, ethnic, religious*, Basingstoke and New York: Palgrave Macmillan.

Kachru, Braj B. (1985), "Standards, codification and sociolinguistic realism: The English language in the outer circle," in R. Quirk and H. G. Widdowson (eds.), *English in the world: Teaching and learning the language and literatures*, 11–30, Cambridge: Cambridge University Press for the British Council.

Kachru, Braj B. (1988), "The sacred cows of English," *English Today*, 16: 3–8.

Kachru, Braj B. (1990), *The alchemy of English: The spread, functions, and models of non-native Englishes*, Champaign: University of Illinois Press.

Kachru, Braj B. (1992), *The other tongue: English across cultures*, 2nd ed., Urbana: University of Illinois Press.

Kanelakis, Nico (2006), *Die Wiedervereinigung Zyperns—Eine Illusion der internationalen Politikdiskussion?*, Norderstedt: GRIN Verlag.

Kappler, Matthias (2008), "Contact-induced effects in the syntax of Cypriot Turkish," *Turkic Languages*, 12: 196–213.

Kappler, Matthias, and Tsiplakou, Stavroula (2018), "Two Cypriot koinai? Structural and sociolinguistic considerations," *Mediterranean Language Review*, 25: 75–96.

Karatsareas, Petros (2018), "The fragile future of the Cypriot Greek language in the UK," *British Academy Review*, 33: 42–4.

Karoulla-Vrikki, Dimitra (2004), "Language and ethnicity in Cyprus under the British: A linkage of heightened salience," *International Journal of the Sociology of Language*, 168: 19–36.

Karpava, Sviatlana (2015), *Vulnerable domains for cross-linguistic influence in L2 acquisition of Greek*, Frankfurt am Main: Peter Lang.

Karpava, Sviatlana (2017), "Object clitic production by simultaneous Russian-Cypriot Greek bilinguals," *Selected papers of ISTAL*, 22, 235–50.

Karpava, Sviatlana, Ringblom, Natalia, and Zabrodskaja, Anastassia (2018), "Language ecology in Cyprus, Sweden and Estonia: Bilingual Russian-speaking families in multicultural settings," *Journal of the European Second Language Association*, 2 (1): 107–17. doi: https://doi.org/10.22599/jesla.41

Karyolemou, Marilena (2001), "From linguistic liberalism to legal regulation: The Greek language in Cyprus," *Language Problems and Language Planning*, 25 (1): 25–50.

Kastamonu (2014), [Forum] *Reasons not to go to North Cyprus to study and work*. Available online: https://www.nairaland.com/1902723/reasons-not-go-north-cyprus (accessed January 22, 2021).

Kelly-Holmes, Helen (2016), "Theorising the market in sociolinguistics," in N. Coupland (ed.), *Sociolinguistics: Theoretical debates*, 157–72, Cambridge: Cambridge University Press.

Kergoat, Danièle (2010), "Le rapport social de sexe de la reproduction des rapports sociaux à leur subversion," *Les Rapports Sociaux de Sexe*, 60–75, Paris: Presses Universitaires de France.

Ker-Lindsay, James (2011), *The Cyprus problem: What everyone needs to know*, Oxford: Oxford University Press.

Khattab, Nabil, and Mahmud, Hasan (2018), "Migration in a turbulent time: Perspectives from the global South," *Migration and Development*, 8 (1): 1–6.

Kirkpatrick, Andy (2007), *World Englishes*, Cambridge: Cambridge University Press.

Kirkpatrick, Andy (2010), *English as a lingua franca in ASEAN: A multilingual model*, Hong Kong: Hong Kong University Press.

Kızılyürek, Niyazi, and Gautier-Kızılyürek, Sylvaine (2004), "The politics of identity in the Turkish Cypriot community and the language question," *International Journal of the Sociology of Language*, 168: 37–54.

Knight, Jane (2012), *Internationalization: Three generations of crossborder higher education*, New Delhi: India International Centre. Available online: http://www.iicdelhi.nic.in/ContentAttachments/Publications/DiaryFiles/53511July92012_IIC%20Occasional%20Publication%2038.pdf (accessed January 5, 2021).

Kortmann, Bernd, Burridge, Kate, Mesthrie, Rajend, Schneider, Edgar W., and Upton, Clive (2004), *A handbook of varieties of English*, Berlin: De Gruyter Mouton.

Künstler, Viktoria, Mendis, Dushyanthi, and Mukherjee, Joybrato (2009), "English in Sri Lanka: Language functions and speaker attitudes," *Anglistik—International Journal of English Studies*, 20 (2): 57–74.

Labov, William (1966), *The social stratification of English in New York City*, Washington, DC: Center for Applied Linguistics.

Labov, William (1982), "Building on empirical foundations," in W. Lehmann and Y. Malkiel (eds.), *Perspectives on historical linguistics*, 17–92, Amsterdam: John Benjamins.

Labov, William (1984), "Field methods of the project on linguistic change and variation," in J. Baugh and J. Sherzer (eds.), *Language in use: Readings in sociolinguistics*, 28–54, Englewood Cliffs, NJ: Prentice-Hall.

Labov, William (2006), *The social stratification of English in New York City*, 2nd ed., Cambridge: Cambridge University Press.

LaDousa, Chaise (2014), *Hindi is our ground, English is our sky: Education, language, and social class in contemporary India*, New York: Berghahn Books.

Lasagabaster, David (2015), "Language policy and language choice at European Universities: Is there really a 'choice'?," *International Journal of Applied Linguistics*, 3 (2): 255–76.

Lave, Jean, and Wenger, Etienne (1991), *Situated learning: Legitimate peripheral participation*, Cambridge: Cambridge University Press.

Leeman, Jennifer (2018), "It's all about English: The interplay of monolingual ideologies, language policies and the U.S. Census Bureau's statistics on multilingualism," *International Journal of the Sociology of Language*, 252: 21–43.

Legewie, Nicolas, and Bohmann, Sandra (2018), "Upward and downward social mobility probabilities have converged for men and women," *DIW Weekly Report*, 8 (20): 169–78.

Leung, Maggi W. H. (2017), "Social mobility via academic mobility: Reconfigurations in class and gender identities among Asian scholars in the global north," *Journal of Ethic and Migration Studies*, 43 (16): 2704–19.

Levers, Merry-Jo D. (2013), "Philosophical paradigms, grounded theory, and perspectives on emergence," *SAGE Open*, 3 (4): 1–6. doi:10.1177/2158244013517243.

Li, Wei (2018), "Translanguaging as a practical theory of language," *Applied Linguistics*, 39 (1): 9–30.

Lüpke, Friederike, and Storch, Anne (2013), *Repertoires and choices in African Languages*, Berlin: De Gruyter Mouton.

MacWhinney, Brian (2000), *The CHILDES project: Tools for analyzing talk*, 3rd ed., Mahwah: Lawrence Erlbaum Associates.

Maley, Alan (2010), "The reality of EIL and the myth of ELF," in C. Gagliardi and A. Maley (eds.), *EIL, ELF, global English: Teaching and learning issues*, 25–44, Bern: Peter Lang.

Marginson, Simon (2018), "Higher education, economic inequality and social mobility: Implications for emerging East Asia," *International Journal of Educational Development*, 63: 4–11.

Maringe, Felix (2012), "The meanings of globalization and internationalization in HE: Findings from a World Survey," in F. Maringe and N. Foskett (eds.), *Globalization and internationalization in higher education: Theoretical, strategic and management perspectives*, 17–34, London: Continuum.

Mashininga, Kudzai (2018), "Universities in Northern Cyprus 'illegal' – ambassador," *University World News*, June 20. Available online: https://www.universityworldnews.com/post.php?story=20180620153414903 (accessed January 22, 2021).

Mason, Jennifer (2002), "Qualitative interviewing," in J. Mason (ed.), *Qualitative researching*, 2nd ed., 62–83, London: Sage.

Mauranen, Anna (2012), *Exploring ELF: Academic English shaped by non-native speakers*, Cambridge: Cambridge University Press.

Mauranen, Anna, Pérez-Llantada, Carmen, and Swales, John M. (2010), "Academic Englishes: A standardized knowledge?," in A. Kirkpatrick (ed.), *The Routledge handbook of World Englishes*, 634–52, London: Routledge.

Mauranen, Anna, and Ranta, Elina, eds. (2009), *English as a lingua franca: Studies and findings*, Newcastle upon Tyne: Cambridge Scholars.

May, Stephen (2001), *Language and minority rights: Ethnicity, nationalism, and the politics of language*, Harlow: Pearson Education.

Mazlish, Bruce, and Morss, Elliott R. (2005), "A global elite?," in A. Chandler and B. Mazlish (eds.), *Leviathans: Multinational corporations and the new global history*, 167–86, Cambridge: Cambridge University Press.

McArthur, Tom (1987), "The English languages?," *English Today*, 11 (3): 9–11.

McArthur, Tom (1998), *The English languages*, Cambridge: Cambridge University Press.

McArthur, Tom (2003), "World English, Euro English, Nordic English?," *English Today*, 19 (1): 54–8.

McEntee-Atalianis, Lisa J., and Pouloukas, Stavros (2001), "Issues of identity and power in a Greek-Cypriot community," *Journal of Multilingual and Multicultural Development*, 22: 19–38.

McEntee-Atalianis, Lisa J., and Pouloukas, Stavros (2005), "Issues of identity and power in a Greek-Cypriot community," in A. Papapavlou (ed.), *Contemporary sociolinguistic issues in Cyprus*, 213–36, Thessaloniki: University Studio Press.

McGill, Kenneth (2013), "Political economy and language: A review of some recent literature," *Journal of Linguistic Anthropology*, 23 (2): E84–E101.

McNamara, Tim (2014), "30 years on—evolution or revolution?," *Language Assessment Quarterly*, 11 (2): 226–32.

Meierkord, Christiane (2004), "Syntactic variation in interactions across international Englishes," *English World-Wide*, 25 (1): 109–32.

Meierkord, Christiane (2012), *Interactions across Englishes: Linguistic choices in local and international contact situations*, Cambridge: Cambridge University Press.

Menteşoğlu, İdil (2009), "Intergenerational phonological change in the Famagusta dialect of Turkish Cypriots," *International Journal of the Sociology of Language*, 200: 75–82.

Merriam-Webster (2018), *Higher education*. Available online: https://www.merriam-webster.com/dictionary/higher%20education (accessed January 22, 2021).

Mesthrie, Rajend, and Bhatt, Rakesh M. (2008), *World Englishes*, Cambridge: Cambridge University Press.

Milroy, Leslie (1980), *Language and social networks*, Baltimore, MD: University Perk Press.

Milroy, Leslie (1987), *Observing and analysing natural language: A critical account of sociolinguistic method*, Oxford: Blackwell.

Milroy, Lesley (2002), "Social networks," in J. K. Chambers, P. Trudgill, and N. Schilling-Estes (eds.), *The handbook of language variation and change*, 549–72, Cambridge: Cambridge University Press.

Mohanty, Ajit K. (2006), "Multilingualism of the unequals and predicaments of education in India: Mother tongue or other tongue?," in O. García, T. Skutnabb-Kangas, and M. E. Torres-Guzmán (eds.), *Imagining multilingual* schools: Languages in education and glocalization, 262–83, Clevedon: Multilingual Matters.

Mortensen, Janus (2013), "Notes on English used as a lingua franca as an object of study," *Journal of English as a Lingua Franca*, 2 (1): 25–46.

Murata, Kumiko (2015), *Exploring ELF in Japanese academic and business contexts: Conceptualization, research and pedagogic implications (online)*, London: Routledge. https://doi.org/10.4324/9781315732480.

Murray, Neil (2016), *Standards of English in higher education: Issues, challenges and strategies*, Cambridge: Cambridge University Press. doi:10.1017/CBO9781139507189.001.

Newton, Brian (1972), *Cypriot Greek: Its phonology and inflections*, The Hague: Mouton.

Norton, Bonny (2000), *Identity and language learning: Gender, ethnicity and educational change*, Harlow: Longman.

Norton, Bonny (2010), "Language and identity," in N. H. Hornberger and S. L. McKay (eds.), *Sociolinguistics and language education*, 349–69, Bristol: Multilingual Matters.

Obioma, Chigozie (2019a), *An orchestra of minorities*, London: Little, Brown.

Obioma, Chigozie (2019b), "At Europe's edge, unwanted migrants are stranded in an unrecognized country," *Feature*, June 23. Available online: https://foreignpolicy.com/2019/06/23/at-europes-edge-unwanted-migrants-are-stranded-in-an-unrecognized-country-nigeria-african-migrants-trnc-turkey-northern-cyprus-ciu-chigozie-obioma/ (accessed January 22, 2021).

Odeh, Lemuel E. (2010), "A comparative analysis of Global North and Global South economies," *Journal of Sustainable Development in Africa*, 12 (3): 338–48.

Oliver, Rhonda, Vanderford, Samantha, and Grote, Ellen (2012), "Evidence of English language proficiency and academic achievement of non-English-speaking background students," *Higher Education Research and Development*, 31 (4): 541–55. doi:10.1080/07294360.2011.653958.

Omoniyi, Tope (2006), "Hierarchy of identity," in T. Omoniyi and G. White (eds.), *The sociolinguistics of identity*, 11–33, London: Bloomsbury.

Onysko, Alexander (2016), "Modeling world Englishes from the perspective of language contact," *World Englishes*, 35 (2): 196–220. doi:10.111 lfweng.12191.

O'Regan, John P. (2014). English as a lingua franca: An immanent critique. *Applied Linguistics*, 35 (5): 533–52.

O'Regan, J. P. (2016), "Intercultural communication and the possibility of English as a lingua franca," in P. Holmes and F. Dervin (eds.), *The cultural and intercultural dimensions of English as a lingua franca*, 203–17, Clevedon: Channel View.

Osam, Necdet, and Kelepir, Meltem (2004), "Bibliography of the studies carried out on Turkish Cypriot dialect," *International Journal of the Sociology of Language*, 181: 107–17.

Papapavlou, Andreas N. (1994), *Language contact and lexical borrowing in the Greek Cypriot dialect*, Athens, GA: N.C. Grivas.

Papapavlou, Andreas N. (2005), "Attitudes towards the Greek Cypriot dialect: Sociocultural implications," in A. Papapavlou (ed.), *Contemporary sociolinguistic issues in Cyprus*, 53–64, Thessaloniki: University Studio Press.

Park, Joseph S., and Wee, Lionel (2009), "The Three Circles redux: A market-theoretic perspective on World English," *Applied Linguistics*, 30 (3): 389–406.

Park, Joseph S., and Wee, Lionel (2012), *Markets of English: Linguistic capital and language policy in a globalizing world*, New York: Routledge.

Parreñas, Rhacel S. (2001), *Servants of globalization*, Chicago: University of Chicago Press.

Pavlenko, Aneta. (2002), "'We have room but for one language here': Language and national identity at the turn of the twentieth century," *Multilingua*, 21: 163–96.

Pavlenko, Aneta, and Blackledge, Adrian (2004), *Negotiation of identities in multilingual contexts*, Clevedon: Multilingual Matters.

Paxton, Moragh, and Tyam, Nolubabalo (2010), "Xhosalising English? Negotiating meaning and identity in Economics," *Southern African Linguistics and Applied Language Studies*, 28 (3): 247–57.

Pehlivan, Ahmet, and Osam, Necdet (2010), "Vehicle-related expressions in Turkish Cypriot dialect," *Bilig*, 54: 231–42.

Pennycook, Alastair (2010), "One, many or none?," in A. Kirkpatrick (ed.), *The Routledge handbook of World Englishes*, 673–87, London: Routledge.

Pennycook, Alastair (2012), *Language and mobility: Unexpected places*, Bristol: Multilingual Matters.

Philips, Susan U. (1998), "Language ideologies in institutions of power," in B. B. Schieffelin, K. A. Woolard, and P. V. Kroskrity (eds.), *Language ideologies: Practice and theory*, 211–25, New York: Oxford University Press.

Phillipson, Robert (1992), *Linguistic imperialism*, Oxford: Oxford University Press.

Phillipson, Robert (2009), *Linguistic imperialism continued*, New York: Routledge.

Piller, Ingrid (2015), "Language ideologies," in K. Tracy, C. Ilie, and T. Sandel (eds.), *The international encyclopedia of language and social interaction*, vol. 1, 1–10, West Sussex: John Wiley.

Piller, Ingrid (2016), *Linguistic diversity and social justice*, Oxford: Oxford University Press.

Piller, Ingrid, and Cho, Jinhyun (2013), "Neoliberalism as language policy," *Language in Society*, 42 (1): 23–44. doi:10.1017/S0047404512000887.

Poew, René (2007), *Der Beitritt Zyperns zur EU—Probleme des Völkerrechts, des Europarechts und des zypriotischen Rechts. Leitideen für die Entwicklung eines zukünftigen reorganisierten gesamtzypriotischen Staates*, Hamburg: Lit Verlag.

Ponzo, Irene (2018), "Modes of migrant incorporation in contexts of socio-economic downward mobility," *Journal of Ethnic and Migration Studies*, 44 (14): 2435–52.

Prodromou, Luke (2008), *English as a lingua franca: A corpus-based analysis*, London: Continuum.

Quirk, Randolph (1985), "The English language in a global context," in R. Quirk and H. G. Widdowson (eds.), *English in the world: Teaching and learning the language and literatures*, 1–6, Cambridge: Cambridge University Press for the British Council.

Quirk, Randolph (1990), "Language varieties and standard language," *English Today*, 21: 3–10.

Rakoczy, Agnieszka (2017), "Badly treated with nowhere to turn," *Cyprus Mail*, December 24. Available online: https://cyprus-mail.com/2017/12/24/badly-treated-nowhere-turn/ (accessed January 22, 2021).

Rassool, Naz (2007), *Global issues in language, education and development: Perspectives from postcolonial countries*, Clevedon: Multilingual Matters.

Research Centre on Multilingualism (2004), *Euromosaic III—Cyprus*. Available online: https://publications.europa.eu/en/publication-detail/-/publication/4dc487cf-3c39-40ac-9b97-c55110263a56 (accessed January 22, 2021).

Richter, Heinz A. (1997), "Historische Hintergründe des Zypernkonflikts," in R. Stupperich and H. A. Richter (eds.), *THETIS—Mannheimer Beiträge zur klassischen Archäologie und Geschichte Griechenlands und Zyperns*, vol. 4, Mannheim: Rutzen Verlag.

Robson, Mark (2013), *The English effect—the impact of English, what it's worth to the UK and why it matters to the world*. Available online: https://www.britishcouncil.org/sites/default/files/english-effect-report-v2.pdf (accessed January 22, 2021).

Romaine, Suzanne (1999), *Communicating gender*, Mahwah, NJ: Lawrence Erlbaum.

Rowe, Charley, and Grohmann, Kleanthes K. (2013), "Discrete bilectalism: Towards co-overt prestige and diglossic shift in Cyprus," *International Journal of the Sociology of Language*, 224: 119–42.

Saraceni, Mario (2015), *World Englishes: A critical analysis*, London: Bloomsbury Academic.

Savage, Mike, Devine, Fiona, Cunningham, Niall, Taylor, Mark, Li, Yaojun, Hjellbrekke, Johs, Le Roux, Brigette, Friedman, Sam, and Miles, Andrew (2013), "A new model of social class? Findings from the BBC's Great British Class Survey experiment," *Sociology*, 47: 219–50.

Schmitz, John R. (2014), "Looking under Kachru's (1982, 1985) Three Circles model of World Englishes: The hidden reality and current challenges," *Revista Brasileira de Linguística Aplicada*, 14 (2): 373–411.

Schneider, Edgar W. (2007), *Postcolonial English: Varieties around the world*, Cambridge: Cambridge University Press.

Schneider, Edgar W. (2011), *English around the world: An introduction*, Cambridge: Cambridge University Press.

Sciriha, Lydia (1996), *A question of identity: Language use in Cyprus*, Nicosia: Intercollege Press.

Seidlhofer, Barbara (2004), "Research perspectives on teaching English as a lingua franca," *Annual Review of Applied Linguistics*, 24: 209–39.

Seidlhofer, Barbara (2005), "English as a lingua franca," *ELT Journal*, 59 (4): 339–41.

Seidlhofer, Barbara (2009), "Common ground and different realities: World Englishes and English as a lingua franca," *World Englishes*, 28 (2): 236–45.

Seidlhofer, Barbara (2011), *Understanding English as a lingua franca*, Oxford: Oxford University Press.

Seidlhofer, Barbara, Breiteneder, Angelika, and Pitzl, Marie-Luise (2006), "English as a lingua franca in Europe: Challenges for applied linguistics," *Annual Review of Applied Linguistics*, 26: 1–34.

Selinker, Larry (1972), "Interlanguage," *IRAL—International Review of Applied Linguistics in Language Teaching*, 10: 209–31.

Shin, Hyunjung, and Park, Joseph S. (2016), "Researching language and neoliberalism," *Journal of Multilingual and Multicultural Development*, 37 (5): 443–52.

Shkoler, Or, and Rabenu, Edna (2020), "Defining international student mobility and higher education," in O. Shkoler, E. Rabenu, P. M. W. Hackett, and P. M. Capobianco (eds.), *International students mobility and access to higher education*, 1–28, New York: Palgrave Macmillan. doi:10.1007/978-3-030-44139-5.

Silverstein, Michael (1976), "Shifters, linguistic categories and cultural description," in K. H. Basso and H. A. Selby (eds.), *Meaning in anthropology*, 11–55, Albuquerque: University of New Mexico Press.

Sklair, Leslie (2001), *The transnational capitalist class*, Oxford: Blackwell.

Smit, Ute (2010), *English as a lingua franca in higher education*, Berlin: De Gruyter Mouton.

Spencer-Oatey, Helen (2012), "'What is culture? A compilation of quotations.'" *GlobalPAD*, University of Warwick. Available online: https://warwick.ac.uk/fac/soc/al/globalpad/openhouse/interculturalskills/global_pad_-what_is_culture.pdf (accessed October 22, 2020).

Spradley, James ([1979] 2002), "Asking descriptive questions," in M. Pogrebin (ed.), *Qualitative approaches to criminal justice: Perspectives from the field*, 44–61, Thousand Oaks, CA: Sage.

State Planning Organization, Prime Ministry TRNC (2017), *Economic and social indicators 2016*. Available online: http://www.devplan.org/Eco-sos/Book/SEG-2016.pdf (accessed January 22, 2021).

State Planning Organization, Prime Ministry TRNC (2018), *Statistical yearbook 2017*. Available online: http://www.devplan.org/Ist_yillik/IST-YILLIK-2017.pdf (accessed August 2, 2020).

State Planning Organization, Prime Ministry TRNC (2020), *Economic and social indicators 2018*. Available online: http://www.devplan.org/Eco-sos/Book/SEG-2018.pdf (accessed January 22, 2021).

Strang, Barbara M. H. (1970), *A history of English*, London: Methuen.

"Student murder was drug related," *LGC News*, n.d. Available online: https://www.lgcnews.com/student-murder-drug-related/ (accessed January 22, 2021).

Study in North Cyprus (2017), *The advantages of studying in North Cyprus*. Available online: http://www.studyinnorthcyprus.com.ng/study-in-north-cyprus/why-north-cyprus.html (accessed July 10, 2020).

Study in North Cyprus (n.d.), [Webpage] Girne American University. Available online: https://studyinnorthcyprus.org/universities/girne-american-university/ (accessed January 22, 2021).

Studyportal B.V. (2019), Study in Cyprus. Available online: https://www.bachelorsportal.com/countries/5/cyprus.html (accessed January 22, 2021).

Sultanzade, Vügar (2013), "Phonetic adaption of loanwords in Cypriot Turkish," *Dialectologia et Geolinguistica*, 21 (1): 70–81. doi:10.1515/dialect-2013-0004.

Sung, Chit C. M. (2015), "Exploring second language speakers' linguistic identities in ELF communication: A Hong Kong study," *Journal of English as a Lingua Franca*, 4 (2): 309–32.

Tagliamonte, Sali A. (2006), "The sociolinguistic interview," in S. Tagliamonte (ed.), *Analysing sociolinguistic variation*, 37–49, Cambridge: Cambridge University Press.

The Public Relations Department TRNC, Ministry of Foreign Affairs (2014), *The TRNC factbook*. Available online: http://mfa.gov.ct.tr/wp-content/uploads/extras/facts-about-trnc-2014-kitapcik/pdf/facts_about_TRNC_2014.pdf (accessed January 22, 2021).

Thompson, John B. (1984), *Studies in the theory of ideology*, Cambridge: Polity Press.

Tollefson, James W., and Tsui, Amy B. (2014), "Language diversity and language policy in educational access and equity," *Review of Research in Education*, 38: 189–214.

Treaty concerning the establishment of the Republic of Cyprus. Signed at Nicosia, on August 16, 1960. United Nations, New York. Retrieved January 10, 2021, from https://peacemaker.un.org/sites/peacemaker.un.org/files/CY_600816_TreatyNicosia.pdf.

Treaty of Alliance (with additional protocols). Signed at Nicosia, on August 16, 1960. United Nations, New York. Retrieved January 10, 2021, from https://peacemaker.un.org/sites/peacemaker.un.org/files/CY%20GR%20TR_600816_Treaty%20of%20Alliance%20%28with%20additionnal%20protocols%29.pdf .

Treaty of Guarantee. Signed at Nicosia, on August 16, 1960. United Nations, New York. Retrieved January 10, 2021, from https://peacemaker.un.org/sites/peacemaker.un.org/files/CY%20GR%20TR_600816_Treaty%20of%20Guarantee.pdf.

TRNC Ministry of National Education and Culture (2005), *The Cyprus Turkish education system*. Available online: http://talimterbiye.mebnet.net/CypTurEduSys.pdf (accessed January 22, 2021).

TRNC Public Information Office (2018), [Webpage] Turkish Cyprus has its delights. Available online: https://pio.mfa.gov.ct.tr/en/turkish-cyprus-has-its-delights/ (accessed January 22, 2021).

Trudgill, Peter (1986), *Dialects in contact*, Oxford: Blackwell.

Tsiplakou, Stavroula (2006), "Cyprus: Language situation," in K. Brown (ed.), *Encyclopedia of language and linguistics*, 337–9, Amsterdam: Elsevier.

Tsiplakou, Stavroula (2009), "English in Cyprus: Outer or expanding circle?," *Anglistik*, 20 (2): 75–87.

Tsiplakou, Stavroula (2011), "Linguistic attitudes and emerging hyperdialectism in a diglossic setting: Young Cypriot Greeks on their language," in C. Yoquelet (ed.), *Proceedings of the 29th annual meeting of the Berkeley Linguistics Society—Special Session on Minority and Diasporic Languages of Europe*, 120–32, Berkeley: Sheriadan Books.

Tsiplakou, Stavroula, Armosti, Spyros, and Evripidou, Dimitris (2016), "Coherence 'in the mix'? Coherence in the face of language shift in Cypriot Greek," *Lingua*, 172–3: 10–25.

Tsiplakou, Stavroula, and Georgi, Fani (2008), "Aspects of language alternation in a trilingual classroom setting," *Scientia Paedagogica Experimentalis—International Journal of Experimental Research in Education XLV*, 1: 195–220.

*Tuition fees for newly registered students* (n.d.), [EMU Portal]. Available online: https://portal.emu.edu.tr/YeniOgrenciOgrenimUcreti.aspx?lang=en (accessed January 6, 2021).

Tum, Danyal O., Kunt, Naciye, and Kunt, Mehmet (2016), "Language learning in conflictual contexts: A study of Turkish Cypriot adolescents learning Greek in Cyprus," *Language, Culture and Curriculum*, 29 (2): 207–24.

UCLan Cyprus (2017a), [Webpage] Entry requirements. Available online: https://www.uclancyprus.ac.cy/study/admissions/entry-requirements/ (accessed January 22, 2021).

UCLan Cyprus (2017b), [Webpage] Erasmus+. Available online: https://www.uclancyprus.ac.cy/life/study-abroad/erasmus/ (accessed January 22, 2021).

UCLan Cyprus (2017c), [Webpage] Fees and scholarships. Available online: https://www.uclancyprus.ac.cy/study/international-students/fees-scholarships/ (accessed May 1, 2019).

UCLan Cyprus (2017d), [Webpage] Fees and scholarships (local students). Available online: https://www.uclancyprus.ac.cy/study/admissions/fees-scholarships/ (accessed May 1, 2019).

UCLan Cyprus (2017e), [Webpage] Life in Larnaka. Available online: https://www.uclancyprus.ac.cy/life/university-life/life-in-larnaka/ (accessed January 22, 2021).

UCLan Cyprus (2017f), [Webpage] Research projects. Available online: https://www.uclancyprus.ac.cy/research/research-centres/research-centres-ciel/ (accessed January 22, 2021).

UCLan Cyprus (2017g), [Webpage] UCLan Cyprus. Available online: https://www.uclancyprus.ac.cy/discover/the-university/uclan-cyprus/ (accessed January 22, 2021).

UCLan Cyprus (2017h), [Webpage] Welcome to UCLan Cyprus. Available online: https://www.uclancyprus.ac.cy/discover/the-university/welcome-message/ (accessed January 22, 2021).

UCLan Cyprus (2017i), [Webpage] 10 reasons to choose UCLan Cyprus. Available online: https://www.uclancyprus.ac.cy/discover/the-university/10-great-reasons-to-choose-uclan-cyprus/ (accessed January 22, 2021).

UCLan Cyprus (2019), [Webpage] Undergraduate and postgraduate prospectus 2019/20. Available online: https://www.uclancyprus.ac.cy/wp-content/uploads/2019/03/Prospectus2019-20_March19.pdf (accessed January 22, 2021).

UCy (University of Cyprus) (2017), [Webpage] 2017–2019 postgraduate prospectus. Available online: http://www.mba.ucy.ac.cy/images/media/file/Postgraduate%20Prospectus%202017-2019.pdf (accessed January 22, 2021).

UCy (University of Cyprus) (2018), [Webpage] Undergraduate prospectus 2018–2020. Available online: http://www.ucy.ac.cy/publications/documents/Ekdoseispdf/Prospectuses/Undergr.Prosp.En18-20.pdf (accessed May 1, 2019).

UCy (University of Cyprus) (n.d.-a), [Webpage] Academic staff. Available online: http://ucy.ac.cy/dir/en/academicstaff (accessed January 22, 2021).

UCy (University of Cyprus) (n.d.-b), [Webpage] Administrative staff. Available online: http://ucy.ac.cy/dir/en/administrative-staff (accessed January 22, 2021).

UCy (University of Cyprus) (n.d.-c), [Webpage] Admission requirements. Available online: http://www.ucy.ac.cy/graduateschool/en/admissions/admission-requirements (accessed January 22, 2021).

UCy (University of Cyprus) (n.d.-d), [Webpage] Fees. Available online: http://ucy.ac.cy/graduateschool/en/postgraduate-studies/fees (accessed May 1, 2019).

UCy (University of Cyprus) (n.d.-e), [Webpage] General information (Department of English Studies). Available online: http://ucy.ac.cy/eng/en/generalnformation (accessed January 22, 2021).

UCy (University of Cyprus) (n.d.-f), [Webpage] General information (International Relations). Available online: http://www.ucy.ac.cy/ir/en/general-information (accessed January 22, 2021).

UCy (University of Cyprus) (n.d.-g), [Webpage] Postgraduate. Available online: http://www.ucy.ac.cy/eng/en/academicprogramms/postgraduate#B (accessed January 22, 2021).

UCy (University of Cyprus) (n.d.-h), [Webpage] Postgraduate programmes of study. Available online: http://ucy.ac.cy/graduateschool/en/postgraduate-studies/postgraduate-programmes-of-study (accessed January 22, 2021).

UCy (University of Cyprus) (n.d.-i), [Webpage] Undergraduate studies office. Available online: http://ucy.ac.cy/fmweb/en/studies-sector/undergraduate-office (accessed January 22, 2021).

United Nations Peacemaker (2004), "The comprehensive settlement of the Cyprus problem." Retrieved January 10, 2021, from https://peacemaker.un.org/sites/peacemaker.un.org/files/Annan_Plan_MARCH_30_2004.pdf.

Urciuoli, Bonnie (2008), "Skills and selves in the new workplace," *American Ethnologist*, 35 (2): 211–28.

Van der Walt, Christa (2013), *Multilingual higher education: Beyond English medium orientations*, Bristol: Multilingual Matters.

Vandrick, Stephanie (2014), "The role of social class in English language education," *Journal of Language, Identity, and Education*, 13 (2): 85–91.

Vetter, Eva (2012), "Multilingualism pedagogy: Building bridges between languages," in J. I. Hüttner (ed.), *Theory and practice in EFL teacher education: Bridging the gap*, 228–46, Bristol: Multilingual Matters.

Vichiensing, Matava (2018), "Investigating 'Othering' in Sandra Cisneros's *The House on Mango Street*," *International Journal of Applied Linguistics and English Literature*, 7 (2): 52–7.

Vogel, Sara, and García, Ofelia (2017), "Translanguaging," *Oxford Research Encyclopedia of Education*, 1–21. doi:10.1093/acrefore/9780190264093.013.181.

Ward, Steven C. (2012), "Introduction: The contemporary politics of knowing and learning," in S. C. Ward (ed.), *Neoliberalism and the global restructuring of knowledge and education*, 1–14, New York: Routledge.

Waters, Johanna (2006a), "Emergent geographies of international education and social exclusion," *Antipode*, 38 (5): 1046–68.

Waters, Johanna (2006b), "Geographies of cultural capital: Education, international migration and family strategies between Hong Kong and Canada," *Transactions of the Institute of British Geographers*, 31 (2): 179–92.

Waters, Johanna (2012), "Geographies of international education: Mobilities and the reproduction of social (dis)advantage," *Geography Compass*, 6 (3): 123–36.

Waters, Johanna, and Brooks, Rachel (2010), "Accidental achievers? International higher education, class reproduction and privilege in the experiences of UK students overseas," *British Journal of Sociology of Education*, 31 (2): 217–28.

Widdowson, Henry G. (1994), "The ownership of English," *TESOL Quarterly*, 28: 377–89.

Widdowson, Henry G. (2012), "Closing the gap, changing the subject," in J. I. Hüttner (ed.), *Theory and practice in EFL teacher education: Bridging the gap*, 3–15, Bristol: Multilingual Matters.

Wiley, Terrence G. (2014), "Diversity, super-diversity, and monolingual language ideology in the United States: Tolerance or intolerance?," *Review of Research in Education*, 38: 1–32.

Wilkinson, Robert (2013), "English-medium instruction at a Dutch university: Challenges and pitfalls," in A. Doiz, D. Lasagabaster, and J. M. Sierra (eds.), *English-medium instruction at universities: Global challenges*, 3–24, Bristol: Multilingual Matters.

Woolard, Kathryn A. (1998), "Introduction—language ideology as a field of inquiry," in B. B. Schieffelin, K. A. Woolard, and P. V. Kroskrity (eds.), *Language ideologies: Practice and theory*, 3–47, New York: Oxford University Press.

Wortham, Stanton (2001), "Language ideology and educational research," *Linguistics and Education*, 12 (3): 253–9.

Wright, Erik O. (2015), *Understanding class*, London: Verso.

Yazgin, Nagme (2007), *The role of the English language in Cyprus and its effects on the ELT classroom*, Cyprus: n.p. Available online from ERIC database: https://files.eric.ed.gov/fulltext/ED496971.pdf (accessed January 22, 2021).

# Index

advancement
  economic 6, 35, 61–4, 137, 145–7, 190, 198–200
  social 7, 39, 54–7, 61 (*see also* social mobility)
  via education 54–7, 64, 185–90
  of students in Cyprus 138–41, 174–5, 199
agencies, *see under* recruiting agencies
attracting students 31–2, 57–8, 84–7, 133–7, 143–7, 174, 181–6
authentic users 17, 29, 36–9, 60, 182

biographical questionnaire 90, 101, 203, 207

capital 80, 138, 143–6, 181–2, 184–7
  cultural 3, 52, 54, 128, 178, 182–3, 185
  economic 3, 52–4, 133, 182–5 (*see also* English-as-a-marketable-attribute)
  social 52, 80, 178, 183–5
commodification of English 12–13, 29–31, 36–9, 60–2, 142–5, 180–3, 190
commodification of HE 32–4, 57, 120, 135, 147, 193–4 (*see also* higher education markets)
communicative potential 20–2, 47–9, 58, 127–32, 173–80, 190
communicative value 20–6, 45–50, 57–64, 127–132, 140–1, 174–81, 187
communities of practice 21–2, 24, 176
criminality 3, 6, 79, 176, 184–90
Ct-students, *see* Cyprus-tied students
cultural embeddedness 5, 118, 127–32, 186–90, 195–6
Cypriot Greek 68, 73–6, 82, 99, 108, 112, 125
Cypriot Turkish 68, 73–5, 82, 141, 178
Cyprus, *see also* Republic of Cyprus; Turkish Republic of Norther Cyprus
  colonial history of 68–70, 80–3
  division 69–73, 197
  independence 68–73, 75
  as a stepping stone 1–2, 120, 139, 142, 189, 199
Cyprus-tied students 83, 89–90, 124–32, 136–7, 139–41, 174

data collection 101–3
devaluation
  of language 16, 53, 132, 179
  of speakers 15, 132, 141
DLC, *see* Dominant Language Constellation
Dominant Language Constellation (Aronin and Singleton) 45–6, 146, 184
Dynamic Model (Schneider) 10, 16, 18–19

Eastern Mediterranean University 100, 122–6, 133–5, 141–4
  language requirements 87
  language use and attitudes data 110–11, 208, 211
  staff 126
  students 87, 110–11, 125, 131, 134–9
  study programs 87, 134
  tuition fees 87, 125, 134–5, 142
  webpages 102–3
economic value 26–40, 45–51, 56–65, 133–7, 140–7, 174–6, 180–90 (*see also* English-as-a-marketable-attribute)
economies of English 80–3, 174–5
EFL, *see* English as a Foreign Language
ELF, *see* English as a Lingua Franca
ELT, *see* English Language Teaching
EMI, *see* English as the medium of instruction
employability 31–5, 42, 53–8, 140, 145, 184–6
EMU, *see* Eastern Mediterranean University
English as a Foreign Language 35, 62–3

English as a global language  9, 13–5, 21–8, 44–5, 128, 140, 184–91
English as a Lingua Franca  15, 20, 23–6, 81, 179–82, 197
English-as-a-marketable-attribute  36–40, 132, 137, 142–7, 174–6, 180–90, 193
English as a Native Language  15, 19, 34–5, 61–2, 124, 132
English as a Second Language  19, 35, 62–3
English as a skill  36–9, 60, 143, 181–3
English as capital  51–4, 80, 146, 178, 181, 185–6 (*see also* capital)
English as gatekeeper  53, 64, 118, 137–8, 145, 200
English as the Medium of Instruction  31–8, 58–9
  in Cyprus  77–88, 133–43, 174, 181–2, 194–200
English in Cyprus  50–1, 75, 79–81, 176
English in higher education  30–9, 53–4, 67, 126, 131–2, 174–81, 184–6 (*see also* English as the Medium of Instruction in Cyprus)
English in the RoC  76–7, 127–32
English in the TRNC  77, 121–3, 127–32, 140–1, 172–4
English Language Teaching  100, 123, 125
ENL, *see*  English as a Native Language
ESL, *see*  English as a Second Language
Extra- and Intra-Territorial Forces model (Buschfeld and Kautzsch)  16, 18–19

functions of English, *see under*  roles of English

GAU, *see*  Girne American University
Girne American University  88–9, 100, 121–2, 133–5, 143
  language use and attitudes data  113–14
  regional offices  89, 133
  staff  88
  students  88–9
  study programs  88
  tuition fees  89, 114, 134–5, 142
  webpages  102–3
Global English, *see under*  English as a global language

Global North  62, 64, 185, 188, 199 (*see also* Global South)
  Cyprus as part of  68, 83, 131, 139, 189, 194, 197–8 (*see also* Cyprus as stepping-stone)
Global South, *see also*  Global North
  Global South-Global North trajectory  14, 55, 59, 64–8, 80, 139, 188
  students from  1–2, 59, 197–9
globalization  14, 19–20, 34–5, 55–60, 192
Greek Cypriots  69, 70–2, 73–5

hegemony of English  11, 27, 56, 139
higher education  1–5, 48, 55, 59 (*see also* English in higher education)
  landscape  3, 6, 67, 84, 145, 201
  markets  31–9, 77–80, 83, 121–6, 143–4, 175, 192–3
  marketplace, *see under* higher education markets
  in the RoC  77–8, 84–6, 131, 137
  in the TRNC  78–9, 86–9, 139, 199

identification with English  37, 41–6, 65, 127–31, 140–1, 144–6, 190
  as clever investors  177–84
  as willing users  177–8
ideological value  10–19, 35–9, 46–50, 58–65, 127–32, 174–6, 182
ideology of monolingualism  10, 11–16, 20
illegal activities  6, 176, 184, 187–8 (*see also* criminality)
indexicality  4, 29–30, 45, 56, 139
instrumentalization  5–6, 145–6, 176, 185–7, 189–90 (*see also* language utilization)
international students  31–3, 58–9, 133–7, 181–2, 190, 194
  in the RoC  78, 119–21
  in the TRNC  1–2, 79, 121–4
internationalization of universities (Foskett)  33–4, 133, 136–7, 186

job market, *see under*  employability

language and identity  42–5, 70, 177–8 (*see also* identification with English)

language and power 4, 9–13, 44, 52–6, 60–61, 185–9, 198–9
language as a system 5, 21, 26, 175–7, 180–1, 197
language as commodity 12–13, 28–31, 36–9, 62, 182–3 (*see also* commodification of English)
language as social practice 5–6, 20, 22, 26, 39, 176
language attitudes 44, 74, 101–2, 107–13, 178
  toward English 75–6, 81, 107–13, 140, 209–12
language hierarchies 7, 14–18, 45, 47, 65, 130
  global 7, 47–9
  local 7, 50–1
language ideologies 17, 21–22, 37–8, 56, 60, 177–8, 190
languages in Cyprus 73–6, 82
language objectification 28–9, 36, 40, 132, 143–5, 176, 180–7
language ownership 12–13, 16, 23–5, 61–4, 124, 131, 176
language utilization 26, 42, 55, 59, 81, 142, 174–5, 189, 193 (*see also* instrumentalization)
layers of value 4–6, 26, 39, 58, 132, 176, 190
levels of value 6–7, 41
  global level 56–65, 130–2, 135, 192
  personal level 41–7, 61–5, 130–2, 192
  societal level 45–56, 62–5, 130–2, 192
linguistic repertoire 22, 45–6, 49, 126, 144, 179, 192
local students, *see under* Cyprus-tied students
L1 English, *see under* native English

Marxism 5, 29–30, 54, 191
mobility 32–5, 57–60, 85–8, 136–40, 174–5, 186–90, 201–2 (*see also* social mobility)
  ideology of monolingualism 10–12, 16

native English 11–14, 17–19, 24–5, 35–8, 174–7, 180 (*see also* nativeness)
native speaker authority 13, 64, 124
native speaker ideology 10, 124, 131–2
native speaker standards 35, 118, 127, 180, 195
nativeness 13–14, 16–17, 20, 37, 131–2, 182 (*see also* native English)
neoliberal ideology 27–9, 144, 191
neoliberalism 26–9, 40, 59, 180–19, 190–1, 198
neoliberalization 181, 183
  of English 143, 146, 181–3, 185, 193, 200
  of higher education 28, 31–4, 57, 127, 175, 193–4
neutrality of English 25, 123–4, 185
non-native English 15, 24, 38, 44, 50

one nation–one language ideology 11

plurality of English 15–16, 123
political economy 4
prestige of language 13–15, 32–4, 73–6, 81–2, 128–9, 177–8
privilege of language users 25–6, 38–9, 55–6, 59–61, 64, 131, 191–3

qualitative interview 101, 104–7, 117
  questions 204
  techniques 104–6
  transcription 107, 205
questionnaire 101–3 (*see also* biographical questionnaire; sociolinguistic questionnaire)
  analysis 107, 207–12
  coding 103
  questions 203

recruiting agencies 2–3, 89, 122, 133, 145–6, 189, 200–1
regional offices, *see under* Girne American University
Republic of Cyprus 51, 68, 70–2, 74–9, 81–2 (*see also* Cyprus; Turkish Republic of Northern Cyprus)
reunification 125–6, 129, 196
RoC, *see* Republic of Cyprus
roles of English 73, 80–3, 124–30, 138–9, 172–5, 191

social class 52–61, 73, 141, 185, 188, 191–2 (*see also* social hierarchy)

social hierarchy  25, 54–6, 65, 140, 177, 188, 193
social inequality  61, 173, 191, 202 (*see also* social injustice; social othering)
social injustice  57, 60–4, 176, 184, 187–93 (*see also* social inequality)
social justice, *see under*  social injustice
social mobility 54–6, 174 (*see also* social advancement)
  downward 136–42, 174, 186–90, 192
  upward 118–21, 137–44, 174, 178–9, 186–90, 196
social othering  15, 124, 132, 138, 141, 178, 187–8
social status, *see under*  social class
social stratification  60, 126, 131, 139, 188–93, 198–9 (*see also* social hierarchy)
social structures  20, 39, 54–6, 138–41, 144, 174, 185–6 (*see also* social stratification)
sociolinguistic questionnaire 101–2
standard variety 13–17, 22, 24, 29, 74–5, 176–7
standardization 13–14, 17, 19–21, 25, 36–8, 59–61, 176–7 (*see also* standard variety)
symbolic economy (Bourdieu)  7, 51–4, 185

Three Circles model (Kachru)  10, 16–17, 37, 176, 182
TRNC, *see*  Turkish Republic of Northern Cyprus
Turkey in the TRNC  51, 72, 122, 126, 132, 139–42, 187

Turkish Cypriots 69–75, 129, 140–1, 199
Turkish Republic of Northern Cyprus  51, 68, 72–82, 139–42, 188–9, 196, 200 (*see also* Cyprus; Republic of Cyprus)

UCLan Cyprus, *see*  University of Central Lancashire Cyprus
UCy, *see*  University of Cyprus
universities in Cyprus  77, 84–9
University of Central Lancashire Cyprus  33, 77–8, 99, 119–21, 127–8, 143–6, 186
  language requirements 84–5
  language use and attitudes data 109–10, 208, 210
  students 84–5, 131, 139–40
  study programs 84–5
  tuition fees  85, 136
  webpages 102–3
University of Cyprus  77, 99, 136–7, 143, 151
  language use and attitudes data 112–13, 208, 212
  staff  86
  students 85–6, 131
  study programs 85–6
  tuition fees  86
  webpages 102–3

valorization by English  30, 36–9, 60, 135–7, 142–6, 181–5, 197
value of language varieties 13–14, 17, 124, 176

www.ingramcontent.com/pod-product-compliance
Lightning Source LLC
Chambersburg PA
CBHW062143300426
44115CB00012BA/2015